This book is one I wish were available about eight years ago when taking my first CAE position. Lynn's writing style, similar to her speaking style, uses real-life examples and brings the reader into easily understanding the concept she conveys. The reader may use the concepts in this book in any industry, an environment, whether public or closely held; manufacturing or service; for profit or nonprofit. I highly recommend it to new CAEs as well as a reality check for current CAEs who wish to improve the position of internal audit in their organizations.

Renee Wessel Jaenicke
Audit Director
CHM2M Hill

Ms. Fountain succinctly captures the challenges chief audit executives (CAEs) face in their roles today. She provides a roadmap that will enable those servicing in this critical role to execute their responsibilities in alignment to the published Institute of Internal Audit Standards and within the company culture that they operate in on a daily basis. As a former CAE, her lessons and wisdom provide a foundation for this outstanding book of advice.

Tom Andreesen
Managing Director
Protiviti, Chicago

Lynn is one of the highest rated and most popular instructors on our learning platform. That would be good if the platform were limited to internal audit content and users. What is amazing is that the platform covers the entire office of the CFO, and here she is, leading the way for all of these functions. Bravo Lynn and keep the great learning coming.

John Kogan
Past five-time CFO
Current Founder of Proformative Academy

Leading the Internal Audit Function

Internal Audit and IT Audit

Series Editor: Dan Swanson

A Guide to the National Initiative for Cybersecurity Education (NICE) Cybersecurity Workforce Framework (2.0)
Dan Shoemaker, Anne Kohnke, and Ken Sigler
ISBN 978-1-4987-3996-2

A Practical Guide to Performing Fraud Risk Assessments
Mary Breslin
ISBN 978-1-4987-4251-1

Corporate Defense and the Value Preservation Imperative: Bulletproof Your Corporate Defense Program
Sean Lyons
ISBN 978-1-4987-4228-3

Data Analytics for Internal Auditors
Richard E. Cascarino
ISBN 978-1-4987-3714-2

Fighting Corruption in a Global Marketplace: How Culture, Geography, Language and Economics Impact Audit and Fraud Investigations around the World
Mary Breslin
ISBN 978-1-4987-3733-3

Investigations and the CAE: The Design and Maintenance of an Investigative Function within Internal Audit
Kevin L. Sisemore
ISBN 978-1-4987-4411-9

Internal Audit Practice from A to Z
Patrick Onwura Nzechukwu
ISBN 978-1-4987-4205-4

Leading the Internal Audit Function
Lynn Fountain
ISBN 978-1-4987-3042-6

Mastering the Five Tiers of Audit Competency: The Essence of Effective Auditing
Ann Butera
ISBN 978-1-4987-3849-1

Operational Assessment of IT
Steve Katzman
ISBN 978-1-4987-3768-5

Operational Auditing: Principles and Techniques for a Changing World
Hernan Murdock
ISBN 978-1-4987-4639-7

Securing an IT Organization through Governance, Risk Management, and Audit
Ken E. Sigler and James L. Rainey, III
ISBN 978-1-4987-3731-9

Security and Auditing of Smart Devices: Managing Proliferation of Confidential Data on Corporate and BYOD Devices
Sajay Rai and Philip Chuckwuma
ISBN 9781498738835

Software Quality Assurance: Integrating Testing, Security, and Audit
Abu Sayed Mahfuz
ISBN 978-1-4987-3553-7

The Complete Guide to Cybersecurity Risks and Controls
Anne Kohnke, Dan Shoemaker, and Ken E. Sigler
ISBN 978-1-4987-4054-8

Tracking the Digital Footprint of Breaches
James Bone
ISBN 978-1-4987-4981-7

Leading the Internal Audit Function

Lynn Fountain, CRMA, CGMA

CRC Press
Taylor & Francis Group
Boca Raton London New York

CRC Press is an imprint of the
Taylor & Francis Group, an **informa** business
AN AUERBACH BOOK

CRC Press
Taylor & Francis Group
6000 Broken Sound Parkway NW, Suite 300
Boca Raton, FL 33487-2742

Printed on acid-free paper
Version Date: 20160223

International Standard Book Number-13: 978-1-4987-3042-6 (Hardback)

Library of Congress Cataloging-in-Publication Data

Fountain, Lynn.
Leading the internal audit function / Lynn Fountain.
pages cm. -- (Internal audit and IT audit)
Includes bibliographical references and index.
ISBN 978-1-4987-3042-6
1. Auditing, Internal. I. Title.

HF5668.25.F68 2016
657'.458--dc23 2015013764

Visit the Taylor & Francis Web site at
http://www.taylorandfrancis.com

and the CRC Press Web site at
http://www.crcpress.com

Contents

Forewords

I've known Lynn for close to 20 years, having had the opportunity to work with her in Kansas City and share a neighborly back fence with her as well. From the beginning, it was clear to me that she was serious about her career and profession. It was also apparent that she was a good auditor and had very high principles, two pretty important attributes for someone who's dabbled in both internal and external auditing as well as being a consultant and trainer. But I could probably say that about a lot of people I've worked with.

What makes Lynn really unique are the life experiences she's had. She's had some trials and tribulations in life that have hardened her convictions and commitment to integrity. I believe these have helped shape her into the professional she's become; one who has pushed herself to continue growing in her career and who willingly shares her knowledge to help others. That is what I think will make this book worth reading for so many people.

In addition to the content of the book, she shares many of the lessons she's learned from her professional journey. Many of those lessons will resonate with readers, whether they are an experienced audit professional or someone early in their career. In the last chapter (The Final Word) she offers her Ten "Potential" Commandments for

Auditors. I believe these commandments provide advice and important reminders to all of us as we move forward both in our careers and in our lives.

I congratulate Lynn on the completion of her book and hope all readers will find their own ways to leverage the messages and advance their own career.

Paul Sobel
Vice-President/Chief Audit Executive Georgia Pacific LLC
Chairman of the Board — Institute of Internal Auditors
July 2013–July 2014

I met Lynn Fountain more than 15 years ago through our mutual activities with the IIA. In fact, I think the first time I met her was at a dinner hosted by the storied Arthur Andersen firm at one of the IIA conferences — probably the International or the GAM conference. That is when Lynn was working at Aquila.

Over the years, I have gotten to know Lynn and I like to describe her as a real professional, honest, and inquisitive, always improving herself and her knowledge base, contributing to her chosen profession, being a good listener, and then responding to what she has heard. She has good self-discipline and she follows up and follows through. All of us should hope we are as good at following up on things as Lynn is.

The book that follows is excellent and critical reading for all — not just CAEs — but for all internal auditors and even all internal audit stakeholders. The book is very appropriately about leading and moving, influencing and guiding people, making easy and tough decisions and in fact making the wrong decision sometimes. It is also about helping people and organizations to be and become better and move forward, not backward.

The lessons in here are simple and powerful. I'd refer you to the Ten Commandments in The Final Word section. Read them carefully and completely. You can't go wrong if you follow them.

Robert Hirth
Chairman COSO Fountain
Past Senior Managing Director, Protiviti

Preface

Lessons learned during our working years can be very different from those gained during our educational years. There are no happy faces or gold stars affixed to lessons by teachers, mentors, or supervisors. We don't have the opportunity to earn a letter grade like we did in our educational years. There are even no considerations for plus or minus grades when supervisors evaluate our work. And worse yet, many times in the working world, there is no room for "do-overs." By the time we reach this stage of our lives, lessons learned result from everyday actions and interactions. Those lessons might be good or bad. They can be difficult or easy, or they can even be those lessons that we wish we never had to face or speak about again. As adults and professionals, we all handle lessons learned in very different ways. In some cases, we internalize them and try to block them out of our memory. In other cases, they are so defining to our character that they seem to form components of our individual DNA.

As you read through this book, the information you will find is a culmination of lessons learned as a CAE as well as lessons learned from instructing hundreds of auditors and listening and discussing their stories and challenges. No two lessons are the same, and everyone will interpret things differently and find varying alternatives to solutions. The concepts presented are intended to provide ideas and recommendations that may be applicable in your own day-to-day responsibilities.

Introduction

My career path started in public accounting. Graduating in the early 1980s, I evaluated what path to follow for my first “real” job. I considered internal auditing but observed that many of these functions maintained a low profile within their companies. As I was interviewing with external audit firms, I came to understand that at that time those firms did not place the internal auditor’s skill level very high on their list of professions to consider. Like most professionals who graduated in that time period and wished to attain the certified public accountancy license, I chose to enter public accounting. Twelve years into my career, I began looking at internal audit positions.

Times have changed, and with the impetus of increased stakeholder and shareholder interest, regulatory scrutiny, and stringent legislation, internal audit has become a critical function for many companies. In addition, the individual leading the internal audit function often has gained the coveted “seat at the table” and “attention of the board.”

In the eyes of the internal audit profession, the term “chief audit executive” (CAE) has become synonymous with the person serving the lead role for an internal audit department. The actual organizational positioning, job title, and perceived stature can vary significantly based on the organization and its internal culture. In many organizations, management does not recognize the term “CAE” as one that represents an individual who should be part of the senior leadership team. This is often the case when the positioning of the internal audit function is buried deeply within organizational structures.

Even in today's world of increased visibility and governance, the CAE role and the internal auditor role can be difficult jobs to effectively execute. The internal audit function continues to face many challenges including

- Gaining a seat at the table
- Executing complete independence and professional skepticism
- Maintaining an open and transparent relationship with the audit committee and board
- Obtaining the respect and trust of management
- Establishing an independent and trusting relationship with the external auditors
- Determining the organization's risk tolerance
- Preparing and issuing independent internal audit reports

The Institute of Internal Auditors (IIA) is recognized as the authority that establishes the guidelines and standards for the internal audit profession. The organization has made significant advancements over the past decade with development of the International Professional Practices Framework. The framework guides auditors in utilizing a structured methodology when performing internal audit evaluations. The framework can provide greater assurances to management on internal audit projects and identified issues. However, when all is said and done, internal auditors may sometimes find it difficult to fully execute in accordance with the *Standards*. Many times, this difficulty ties back to the lack of understanding and or acceptance by management that the *Standards* exist.

Although theoretically the internal audit function is independent from management, in reality, it is a part of the organization and may report in some manner to management. In addition, internal audit reports are often subject to significant process owner and management scrutiny prior to release. These dynamics make it inherently difficult to fully execute the requirements of objectivity and true independence.

The true challenge for any CAE or internal auditor is learning to appropriately apply the *Standards*, exert adequate independence and objectivity, and appropriately balance management expectations.

Many individuals who have held the CAE role can attest to the difficulties and realities of attempting to uphold the *Standards* while balancing the political position of the CAE role. It can be a significant challenge and not one that should be entered into lightly.

Throughout this book, we will evaluate and outline various perspectives and realities faced when performing the CAE role. Comparison will be drawn between *Standards* and the challenges and realities CAEs and internal auditors face when executing their fiduciary duty. In addition, we will explore alternative scenarios for gaining the coveted seat at the table for the CAE.

1

LESSONS OF AN AUDITOR

Introduction

Individuals who have performed the chief audit executive (CAE) role can most likely compile a never-ending list of lessons learned from the experience. It can be beneficial to reevaluate those lessons at various crossroads in an individual career and share the experiences with others who may be considering a similar role. Through the act of sharing and identifying lessons learned, individuals who continue to pursue internal audit as a profession can assist in the advancement of the role of the internal auditor in today's business.

I have held the CAE role for two separate international companies. One company was a publically traded utility, whereas the other was a privately held engineering and construction company. The lessons learned from each experience were different, but in many ways, the challenges were similar. Lessons learned came from a variety of incidents and experiences faced while attempting to execute the responsibilities of the role. Post my role as CAE, I have worked with and trained thousands of auditors. In many ways, my own personal lessons are very similar to issues faced by other internal auditors and CAEs. The difference is the manner in which the individual involved chose to utilize the lesson or allow the challenge to define how he or she executes the role.

When speaking to auditors about the CAE role, I often relay,

> "If you can't stand the heat then stay out of the kitchen!"

This phrase is insightful when attempting to fulfill the CAE role. The phrase was one of my mother's favorite sayings when I was young. I was raised in an era prior to central air-conditioning, so my siblings and I would often complain about how hot the kitchen would get when mom cooked. My mother would get tired of our complaints, and ultimately, the dreaded phrase of "staying out of the kitchen" would be relayed.

There are CAEs who have been fortunate and had the full support of management and the board while maneuvering through challenges faced while executing their role. Other CAEs have struggled with aspects of the role, whereas others have had both challenges and successes.

Management's View

Management typically understands the basics of internal control and the role internal audit should play when validating control processes. The catchphrases of Sarbanes–Oxley, Foreign Corrupt Practices Act, Dodd Frank, whistle-blower, and internal control over financial reporting are all well understood. But in reality, management's focus is on the day-to-day operations and growth of the business. With this in mind, management periodically perceives the responsibility for internal control as one that internal audit should manage. Sarbanes–Oxley made it clear that internal control is the responsibility of management, not internal or external auditors. Confusion over the ownership of internal controls may come from how management and employees view the difference between job tasks and control points.

Consider the following scenario that involves an internal auditor interviewing an accounts receivable clerk.

Internal auditor: "Talk me through your job responsibilities and the process you follow when receiving payments in the mail."

Clerk: "I open the mail. If there is a check from a customer, I log relevant information related to the payment in a manual journal. I then take the check to the controller for deposit."

Internal auditor: "What would you describe as 'relevant information'?"

Clerk: "I have been informed that I am to log the check amount, check number, payee, customer number (if available), and the receipt date."

Internal auditor: "What controls are in place for ensuring that the check is deposited into the customer's account?"

Clerk: "That is the controller's responsibility; I just open the mail."
Internal auditor: "What happens if the controller is not at his desk when you go to deliver the check?"
Clerk: "I put the check in his top-right hand drawer."
Internal auditor: "Do you lock the drawer after placing the check in it?"
Clerk: "No."
Internal auditor: "How do you know that the controller actually found the check?"
Clerk: "Well, no one else sits at his desk."
Internal auditor: "Does anyone ever reconcile your log to deposits that are made to customer accounts?"
Clerk: "I'm not sure what you mean. I give the controller the log at the end of the month."

You should be able to identify where this conversation is leading. In essence, the purpose for the clerk opening the mail, logging the check, and taking it to the controller represents a control that auditors refer to as segregation of duties. From the conversation above, it is evident that the clerk does not understand they play a crucial link in the control system.

If you were to ask management or process owners to list specific control points within their functional area, you may find that they recite job tasks without realizing that some of the tasks are actually control points. When was the last time you evaluated if management understands that the responsibility for compliance and internal control rests in their hands and not the internal auditors? If management and the audit committee are of the opinion that internal audit and the external auditors will verify that everything is in full compliance, then the CAE role and the internal audit function may be in for more challenges than expected.

As I have revisited my own lessons learned, I have developed a Top 10 list that reflects many of the challenges of the CAE position as well as that of being an internal auditor. Individuals who consider entering a CAE role should be aware of these issues and prepared to address them head on. Undoubtedly, others will have similar or additional lessons that can be added to the list. But for purposes of this discussion, we will review the lessons and utilize them in later chapters to further develop concepts important for the CAE to address.

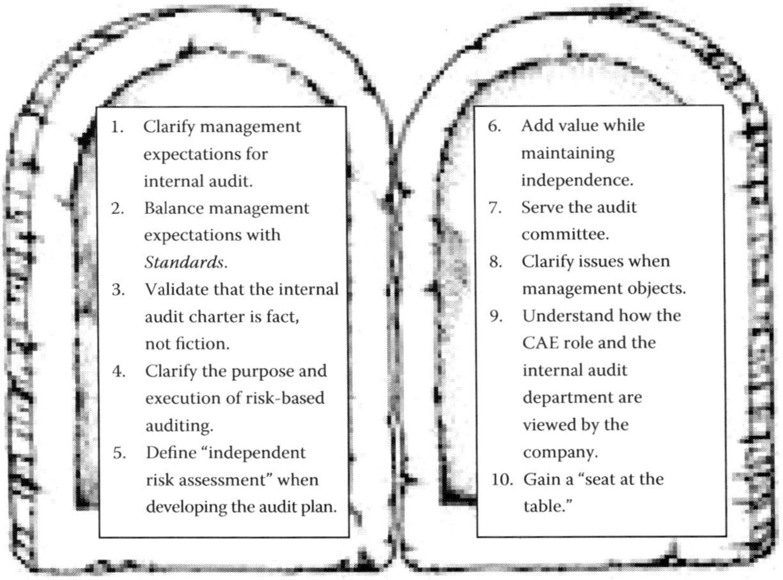

Exhibit 1.1 Lessons learned of a CAE.

The graphic in Exhibit 1.1 is a summary of the lessons learned outlined in the remainder of this chapter.

Section 1: Lessons Learned

Introduction

The poem by Robert Fulghum titled "All I Really Need to Know I Learned in Kindergarten" provides an analogy of how the simplistic concepts learned in kindergarten can be applied within everyday life. These concepts extend past personal lives into business and government. The poem recites simple learnings such as "share everything," "play fair," "clean up your own mess," and many other factors of leading a balanced life. The poem even speaks to the need to "hold hands when you go out in the world, watch out for traffic, and stick together."

As you review the lessons learned outlined in this chapter, consider the kindergarten rules and whether any particular phrase resonates with regards to the particular lesson identified. Consider the rule interpreted in each lesson. It some cases, the same or similar rule applies—the interpretation may vary. Consider whether the identified lesson and interpretation provide any insight to the particular challenges your function faces.

Lesson 1: Clarify/Define Management Expectations for Internal Audit

Kindergarten rule: *When you go out into the world, watch out for traffic, hold hands, and stick together.*

Interpretation: Not everyone sees things in the same light or recognizes concepts that may seem clearly outlined. It is important to make sure management and the internal audit team work together and are on the same page of the handbook when working through departmental responsibilities and expectations.

Companies utilize the internal audit function in very different manners. The profession has standards of practice; however, internal audit is not regulated by a law-making body. This allows organizations to determine how they believe internal audit should operate in their own individual environment.

When the Sarbanes–Oxley legislation was released in 2002, the role of internal audit became more standardized for publically traded companies. However, there are still a myriad of ways the function is viewed and utilized when it comes to assurance or consulting activities. The disparity can be witnessed by the many ways internal audit takes part in compliance services such as Sarbanes–Oxley versus consulting activities. The role may depend on the company's industry, culture, history, management, and a multitude of other variables.

CAEs and internal auditors strive to provide value to their organizations through a multitude of activities outlined in the *Standards*. In an attempt to provide proactive and progressive services, many CAEs evaluate how their audit groups can be involved in activities that allow for a visible profile for the department as well as initiatives that provide long-term value for the company. These may include

- Strategy and merger activities
- Operational, compliance, and financial reviews
- New system initiatives

- Consulting projects
- Continuous auditing
- Fraud and ethics reviews
- Enterprise risk management activities

Although the profession defines the internal audit activity as one that can incorporate all of the listed activities, the CAE may experience challenges from management when attempting to execute work on these various initiatives. If the internal audit function has previously been narrowly defined in scope and responsibility, the probability that the organization will embrace these additional services may be very low. An example is the experience many CAEs have when attempting to provide assistance toward enterprise risk management procedures. In some cases, the internal audit function is the actual facilitator and administrator of the process, whereas in other situations, management does not believe that internal audit should be involved with the process.

It is critical that CAEs enter their role with a full understanding of how the company has traditionally defined the responsibilities of the function along with their longer-term view for services. The inability to ensure that the CAE's expectations are in line with management and the board will result in ongoing challenges and potential stalemates on various initiatives and efforts. In the long run, this is not effective for the company.

Lesson 2: Balance Management Expectations with the International Institute of Auditors Standards

Kindergarten rule: *Play fair.*

Interpretation: Internal auditors understand the purpose and intent of the *Standards*. However, it is not unusual for management to have varying views that may conflict with the internal auditor's professional obligation to the *Standards*. The concept of playing fair correlates to ensuring that the *Standards* are not used as a bat or whipping stick when working to get management on the same page as the auditors. Keep in mind that the *Standards* are not laws; they are professional guidelines. The entire organization must understand the importance of playing fair and according to the guidelines of the profession.

Internal audit is a profession that is guided by *Standards*. Individuals entering the CAE role must be prepared to personally and professionally uphold the *International Professional Practices Framework* and *Standards* and execute the role with professionalism and independence. If there are gaps in management's awareness and acceptance of the existence of the *Standards*, the CAE will face pressures when attempting to execute their fiduciary duty.

Auditors play a role in validation and assurance. When under the scrutiny of an audit, process owners may not always be receptive to hearing that something in their area is not being properly executed. But inherently, the auditor's responsibility is to evaluate if the process was performed in accordance with controls in place. If a gap exists, the auditor may help to identify the potential exposure to risk and the related mitigating action needed to close the gap.

The internal audit profession has placed a significant focus on raising the profile of the internal audit function. As internal audit professionals, we strive to abide by the *Standards* and guidelines. With this in mind, consider a few questions:

- Have you asked management if they are aware that *Standards* for the internal audit profession exist?
- Does management understand the internal auditor's professional obligations to the *Standards*?
- Does management truly understand the concepts of risk-based auditing, independence, obligations to the board, and charter requirements?
- Have you discussed the concepts of a quality assurance review with management and the board, and do they understand the potential implications?

More often than we would like to admit, these basic concepts are not fully understood by management. Leading practice would suggest that the CAE provide periodic updates to management and the board regarding the status of the *Internal Audit Professional Practices Framework* and *Standards*. In addition, the CAE should ensure that any deviations from *Standards* is fully communicated to management and the board. The board and audit committee should understand the potential risks and exposures that exist when the internal audit group does not perform their responsibility in line with the *Standards*.

Lesson 3: Validate the Internal Audit Charter as Fact and Not Fiction

Kindergarten rule: *Remember the Dick-and-Jane books and the first word you learned—the biggest word of all—LOOK. Everything you need to know is in there somewhere.*

Interpretation: Internal auditors are accustomed to clarifying and documenting. We look to leading practice to guide us on the procedures most relevant to apply. We often utilize leading practice documents when developing departmental protocols and documents like charters. However, it is important to *look* at departmental charters periodically to ensure that the elements listed are executable and true in fact. Elements that appear in a charter that are not relevant to the organization or that could never be executed given the current structure may actually put the organization at greater risk.

An important attribute for an effective internal audit function is the existence of a well-defined and documented department charter. CAEs typically will ensure their department charter incorporates aspects considered appropriate by the IIA. CAEs must be cautious when adopting a generally phrased charter. Management and the audit committee must comprehend the words behind the document. The information may appear adequate on paper and may truly reflect internal audit *Standards*, but if the organization does not understand and accept the various aspects of the charter, the internal audit function will face many difficulties.

As an example, assume that the charter states, "The CAE has full access to the audit committee." *Standards* suggest this as a leading practice. Full access to the audit committee allows the internal audit department to maintain a level of independence and transparency. Although the concept may be included within a department charter, CAEs must evaluate whether the concept is embraced in practice by the organization. Consider the following:

- When was the last time the CAE had a one-on-one conversation with the audit committee chairman outside of private session?
- Does the audit committee have input to the CAE's annual review, compensation, or staffing requests?

- Is the audit committee involved in the placement or removal of the CAE?
- Can the CAE have conversations with the audit committee that remain confidential?
- Is the CAE comfortable talking to management and the audit committee about controversial issues?
- How is the CAE perceived by management and the audit committee when standing their ground on issues where facts support their position?
- Does the audit committee have sufficient input into the development of the annual audit plan?

A formal written document may exist, if the intent and purpose are not being executed, then the document is not worth the paper it is written on. The CAE must have the fortitude and conviction to surface concerns when actions are not being executed in line with the internal audit charter. If management and the audit committee do not accept the concept of free and open access, then the CAE must be able to address the fact that this is a guideline within the *Standards*. Absent this access, internal audit is not in compliance with the *Standards*. Then the question should be asked, is internal audit truly independent or performing a quality improvement function? There is a distinct difference between the objectives of a quality improvement group such as six sigma or total quality management and those of internal audit. The CAE and management must recognize this.

Lesson 4: Clarify the Purpose and Execution of Risk-Based Auditing

Kindergarten rule: *When you go out into the world, watch out for traffic, hold hands, and stick together.*

Interpretation: Make sure that management and internal audit are on the same page concerning concepts and the need for a true risk-based audit approach.

Management may communicate their expectations that the internal audit function operates utilizing a risk-based audit process. This may seem to be a clear directive. However, is it clear how management views the concept of risk-based auditing? Management may have a different interpretation than outlined in the *Standards*. Internal auditors view the concept of risk-based auditing as described by the *Standards* as well as other documents like Auditing Standard 5 and the Public Companies and Accounting Oversight Board interpretations. The CAE must gain an understanding of how management defines and views risk-based auditing.

Risk-based auditing obviously begins with identification of those risks that may prevent the organization from achieving strategic objectives. But holistic risk-based auditing can extend further than simple identification of risks to be covered within an audit plan. Auditors who execute risk-based auditing may extend the concept beyond audit plan development. Risk-based auditing can be used to determine the specific risks to test within an individual audit as well as the manner in which overall findings are reported. It can also incorporate the concepts of risk appetite and risk tolerance.

If the audit team extends their execution of risk-based auditing to include risks to be tested and the level of testing and reporting techniques, management should be in full agreement regarding the application of this process. Management must understand how the application of a complete risk-based approach will manifest in the full audit process.

If management and internal audit are not on the same page regarding how risk-based auditing will be applied, more confusion than clarity will be created. It may be important to ask a few questions to evaluate variations between management's understanding and internal audit application.

- Does management understand and embrace the term "inherent risk impact"?
- Has management and the audit committee agreed to an acceptable tolerance rate or risk appetite?
- How does management view the concept of control effectiveness rankings like strong, moderate, weak, effective, or ineffective?
- Does the internal audit function have a definitive outline of how they rank their findings (e.g., high, moderate, weak, acceptable, or unacceptable)?

- Can management and internal audit come to a consensus on the intent and meaning behind the rankings?

These questions may sound simple, but it is critical that management and the auditors sing from the same hymnal as well as from the same page. If not, the CAE should be prepared for disagreements.

Lesson 5: Define "Independent Risk Assessment" in Relation to the Audit Plan

Kindergarten rule: *Be aware of wonder. Remember the little seed in the Styrofoam cup: The roots go down and the plant goes up, and nobody really knows how or why, but we are all like that.*

Interpretation: Everyone sees things in a distinct and separate manner. Similarly, the concept of independent risk assessment may be viewed differently by each company, management, and internal audit function. It is important to clarify the concept of independent risk assessment to ensure a consistent organizational understanding and application.

The concept of independence and development of the annual audit plan can be viewed from various perspectives. Frequently, management will take the position that the internal audit group should "independently" determine areas to include on the audit plan. Auditors may understand how to structure a risk assessment and develop an audit plan; however, without management input on the related processes and embedded risks, the plan could be subject to questions when executed. In this respect, management must understand that the most effective plans are a combination of management input and assessment, auditor evaluation, and senior executive and board input. If those inputs cannot be tied together, the audit team can expect difficulties.

Lesson 6: Add Value While Maintaining Independence

Kindergarten rule: *Play fair. Put things back where you found them. Clean up your own mess. Don't take things that aren't yours.*

Interpretation: The concepts of independence are complicated, and it is important to remember to play fair when executing responsibilities.

Adding value may mean giving credit where credit is due or "putting things back where you found them." It may also mean cleaning up your own mess.

Independence and objectivity are critical attributes for internal audit, yet they are also very difficult to effectively execute. As employees of the company, an inherent conflict is created when applying independence. This is one of the reasons many CAEs struggle with exerting their independent authority.

CAEs who are unable to fully exert independence and objectivity in their job roles are not in compliance with professional *Standards*. This doesn't mean that the CAE must continually buck the system or prove their opinion is the right one. However, it does mean that the CAE should be able to openly express and relay their opinion to management and the audit committee. In the end, it is not the CAE's responsibility to make sure that management follows every recommendation that internal audit suggests. Management is responsible for internal controls, and they have the responsibility for ensuring that procedures implemented are relevant and workable in the business. It is possible that internal audit will provide a recommendation that is not in line with management's overall directions and purpose. Management ultimately must determine whether they will accept the control recommendation. However, the CAE and internal audit must execute their fiduciary role of communication of observations to the proper governance authority. Consider the following scenario.

Scenario: When the CAE Is Expected to Be a Yes Person Management may disagree with internal audit's recommendations and there can be strategic business reasons why the recommendation may not be relevant for the business at any particular point in time. However, the CAE has a responsibility to explain to management and the audit committee how the decision not to implement a recommendation will impact the company. There have been instances where CAEs have been told by their superiors that "It is not proper to disagree with management." This is a classic example of where the internal audit group may not be able to execute full independence. If the CAE sees things differently from management, they should have the ability to openly disagree and explain their opinion. Ultimately, it is management's choice as to what will occur, but for the CAE to be told that "You cannot disagree with management" is an attempt to influence or undermine the CAEs authority and position.

Lesson 7: Serve the Audit Committee

Kindergarten rule: *The complete poem*

Interpretation: In this instance, the responsibility of serving the audit committee can be correlated to almost every lesson outlined in Robert Fulghum's poem. When serving the audit committee, auditors should employ all aspects of playing fair, sticking together, taking responsibility for their own actions, and learning when and how to appropriately communicate the aspect of cleaning up messes. As a challenge, internal auditors should revisit the poem and link individual responsibilities and challenge areas to components outlined in the kindergarten rules. Think simplistically. Everything can be translated into everyday life.

The audit committee is tasked with oversight for financial reporting and oversight of internal audit. Serving the audit committee is one of the top priorities for any CAE or internal audit function. With the impetus of Sarbanes–Oxley, the audit committee's responsibilities and obligations have dramatically expanded. The time requirements to fulfill the role have become greater over the years. In addition, audit committee members are held more accountable for their increased responsibilities. This increased time commitment and responsibility can impact the ability of the internal audit group to obtain the required attention of the audit committee implied by the *Standards*. Yet, it is the responsibility of the CAE to ensure effective use of the audit committee's time through appropriate and timely reporting and communication. This can be easier said than done. Difficulties can be encountered from many angles.

One dilemma faced by internal audit is the limited time allocated to deliver reports during the quarterly audit committee meetings. Internal audit *Standards* suggest that the CAE work with the audit committee chairman to establish the quarterly agenda. However, the reality is that in many organizations, the agenda is controlled by the chief financial officer (CFO) or chief executive officer (CEO). The allocation of time is often concentrated on financial reporting procedures or legal issues. This limits the time available for internal audit reporting. In addition, often, the materials or board book provided to the committee is organized by the CFO or CEO. Internal audit may be allocated a minimal number of slides or pages to communicate their message. All of these challenges contribute to how well the audit group can truly serve the audit committee.

The manner in which internal audit groups report information to their audit committees is as varied as the manner in which administrative reporting lines are handled. Some organizations provide the audit committee with the entire audit report, whereas other companies provide the committee with an executive summary. In instances where the company has defined a risk tolerance threshold, internal audit may only communicate issues to the committee that breaches that tolerance level. In addition, the timing of delivery of the reports may be varied. In some circumstances, reports are delivered at the quarterly audit committee meetings, whereas in other instances, reports are sent to the committee at the same time they are issued to the process owners and management. All of these factors may impact the time and attention that the committee has to allocate to issues identified within the reports.

A critical concept is for CAEs to work with audit committees to ensure there is an agreed to process for the type and method for communicating audit issues. The prevalence of increased audit committee responsibilities has facilitated the utilization of risk tolerance and risk threshold when determining issues communicated to the committee. This process may assist committees in sorting through issues of significance. Auditors have been trained to document all testing exceptions or potential control gaps. This can result in lengthy detailed reports on issues that may be classified as low risk or simple policy concerns that do not have a significant impact to the organization. For internal audit groups who provide their entire detailed report to the audit committee, they may find that it becomes difficult for committee members to identify the most significant issues that were uncovered during the audit.

To most effectively utilize the limited time of the audit committee, CAEs should work closely with the committee members to understand the type and significance of issues that reach the tolerance threshold for communication.

Verbal Communication You may have heard the phrase that "A CEO's relationship with the board and audit committee is sacred." CAEs who are informed of this relationship are being softly advised to use caution in their communications outside of management purview. This advice from management can make establishment of a close and trusting relationship with the audit committee difficult.

In theory, the CAE should be able to contact the audit committee when deemed necessary. Leading practice states that the CAE should meet with the audit committee, or at a minimum the audit committee chair, privately and more frequently than a quarterly basis. This again can be a difficult task to execute. Often, members of the audit committee reside in geographical locations other than the company they serve. This makes it difficult for the CAE to have casual meetings, lunches, or information sessions with the audit committee chair. However, there are many ways frequent and timely communication can be managed. In today's world of advanced technology, CAEs have the ability to utilize teleconferencing, web-based meetings, or even conference calls to stay in touch with the audit committee. Communication methods and frequency should be agreed to with the audit committee and fully understood by management. In addition, the CAE should have assurances that information relayed to the audit committee will be kept confidential. Many CAEs experience challenges in this area. If management's relationship with the audit committee is closer or more trusting than the relationship that the CAE holds with the committee, it is not unusual for information to inadvertently circle back to management. This creates the increased dynamics of third-hand communication, which can result in the message being altered in its delivery. Ultimately, if the CAE and the audit committee are unable to establish mutual trust and respect, the best interest of the company is not being served.

Lesson 8: Communication of Issues When Management Objects

Kindergarten rule: *Don't hit people, and when you go out into the world, watch out for traffic, hold hands, and stick together.*

Interpretation: Communication is an art. Be cognizant of how communication is perceived especially when others are not in full agreement. Gaining agreement and acceptance or sticking together will take you much further than fighting over irrelevant issues.

Auditors may be taught that overcommunication is a virtue when it comes to identified issues and communicating with the management. "No surprises" can be the mantra. There are opposing sides to this issue. Communication of findings prior to ensuring all items are validated can result in many difficulties. Auditors should ensure they have a strong protocol established within their audit methodology for how and when issues will be communicated not only to the process owner but also to management and the audit committee. Considerations include the following:

- *Ensure the observations and facts are correct and that the timing of the communication is proper.* Otherwise, management may view actions as jumping to conclusions.
- *Be cognizant of e-mail communications.* With today's technology, it is easy to default to sending a question via e-mail. However, think about the volume of e-mails received daily. What may be viewed as an efficient way of obtaining information from an audit perspective may be seen as time consuming and bothersome by the process owner. In addition, there is always the potential that the written request will be misunderstood or misinterpreted.
- *Understand the company culture and how report communications are expected and accepted.* If the company exists in a culture that operates on the principle that all T's should be crossed and I's dotted before an issue is relayed, the CAE should understand when it is acceptable to step on either side of the communication line. Some may view this as a potential independence question, but this is not the issue at hand. Lack of independence is related to the inability to report a validated finding to the respective party because of management pressure. Timing and form of communication will be variable in all companies. The bottom line is to ensure that issues are validated and communicated in the most efficient and effective manner to ensure proper risk mitigation.

Lesson 9: Understand How the CAE Role and Audit Department Are Viewed

Kindergarten rule: *Live a balanced life—learn some and drink some and draw some and paint some and sing and dance and play and work every day some.*

Interpretation: Internal auditors understand the role of the CAE as defined by professional *Standards*. However, it is important to "balance" our perceptions and how we execute the role with the manner in which management and the audit committee view the role. In essence, ensure that you are "living a balanced role."

When entering a new company or simply accepting the CAE role within your existing company, understanding the perception of the role and the function can be critical to how job tasks will be approached and executed. Think of the concept of the internal audit process from the eyes of auditees. An audit, no matter how well planned and announced, interrupts the normal flow of daily work. It is unusual when auditors are welcomed with open arms to conduct an unplanned audit. When evaluating the organization's view of internal audit and how the CAE role is viewed, consider how your organization would respond to the following questions:

- What is the CAE's organizational positioning?
- Is the CAE or the internal audit group included in strategic business initiatives?
- Is the internal audit group considered the go-to group for fraud evaluations?
- When was the last time the CAE was involved in a strategy discussion?
- How often does the CAE have an independent discussion with the CEO?
- Does the CAE have open access to all process areas, the management, and the board?

When considering a CAE role, work to obtain complete insight to the expectations of the internal audit function. Interviewers like to represent the position as one that is an important contribution to the company. The phrase "We are working to upgrade our function and obtain increased value from internal audit" may be utilized during the recruiting cycle. This is a great concept and definitely an attractive challenge for any professional. However, if the history of the organization has been one where the internal audit function has experienced significant flux or difficulty, it is important that the CAE be aware of the political challenges that may be faced. Some of the important aspects to be aware of in order to be properly prepared to execute the role include the following:

- *What is the organizational positioning of the internal audit function?* Is it buried deep within organizational ranks, or does the CAE have a direct reporting role to the CEO? The answer to these questions can provide important insight into the status of the function.
- *Has the internal audit function and CAE position experienced frequent turnover?* If so, why has this occurred? Has the CAE moved on to different areas within the company, or have they left the company? Inability to maintain some continuity within the audit department and the CAE role can be a leading indicator of how the function is viewed or valued.
- *Does the CAE have authority and responsibility for independently issuing audit reports?* What influence does executive management have on how issues are stated or outlined within reports? If the internal audit group experiences significant challenges in issuing reports due to management resistance or pushback, the CAE should evaluate whether the current reporting process is effective for the organization.
- *How does process area management respond to identified issues?* When an issue is identified, management's basic instinct may be to justify and explain why something may have not been done in the manner expected. This is a natural reaction and a challenge faced in most audits. If management refuses to accept responsibility for validated and identified issues and places blame on the auditors, the CAE must be able to address this with senior management and the audit committee.
- *Are there political sensitivities when the CAE speaks to the audit committee outside of board meetings or without preinforming management?* If the CAE feels they do not have open access to the audit committee, independence, trust, and respect are in question.

- *Does the CAE maintain responsibility for their departmental budget?* When the internal audit function is buried deep within organizational ranks, periodically, the CAE may not have responsibility for control of their own budget. When this occurs, it is difficult for the CAE to properly manage their resources and execute their responsibilities.
- *What is the method for determining staffing for the internal audit function?* Companies utilize many methods to determine necessary staffing for internal audit. Staffing may be tied to the perceived role of internal audit. If an organization views internal audit as an asset assurance area, the function may be staffed utilizing benchmarking of company physical assets. Other companies may view auditors as responsible for revenue assurance. In this instance, the function may be staffed based on the scale of revenue generated by the company. Still, other functions may see internal audit as a compliance function and staff with resources based on needs for Sarbanes–Oxley compliance or other regulatory and legislative compliances. However, if staffing is sparse or limited when comparing to benchmarks, the CAE has the responsibility to alert the audit committee regarding the ability for the department to meet expectations.

  As a CAE, understanding the charge and obligations of the function and how the organization views staffing needs will assist in appropriately managing resources. If the organization is typically staffed based on a revenue scale, and expectations are changed to include asset verification or Sarbanes–Oxley compliance, it is important that the CAE be able to explain to management and the audit committee the ramifications or needs for changes to the internal audit staffing levels. Today's business world is one in which professionals are often expected to do more work with less resources. Internal audit is not immune to that theory. Even though there are many ways internal audit can gain and achieve efficiency in their work, it is still critical that the appropriate resources exist to meet expectations.
- *How does the company view the need to utilize internal audit as a training ground for professionals?* Some companies view the need to rotate professionals through the internal audit

function to provide them with a more holistic view of organizational processes. The exposure an auditor may be able to obtain through various audits can be invaluable to the company. But there are a few things to remember and consider.

- *How large is the audit group?* Large audit groups may be able to more efficiently absorb the need for ongoing retraining and organization flux resulting from a rotation program.
- *Does the organization view internal audit as a profession?* Just like any strong profession, the desire to be a career auditor should not be viewed negatively by an organization.
- *Does internal audit staffing maintain some semblance of stability?* This is critical to provide overall value to the organization. Continual rotation or turnover within the function exacerbates the concern that many process owners will often express that "the auditors don't understand our processes."

These may be a few red flags that the CAE may have a tough road to climb in transforming the function to one that abides by the *Standards* and is accepted and embraced by the organization. Understanding the challenges faced and the road that must be traveled will assist in mapping out the right path.

We will discuss the concepts of internal audit staffing and auditor rotation within Chapter 3 of this book. For our initial purposes, the important lesson learned is to understand the various implications of staffing scenarios that may be presented.

Lesson 10: Gaining a "Seat at the Table"

Kindergarten rule: *When you go out into the world, watch out for traffic, hold hands, and stick together.*

Interpretation: To gain the perennial seat at the table, the CAE must build strong relationships with management that include developing trust and respect. It is important that internal auditors stick together and understand the professional *Standards* to enable proper communication of requirements and expectations to management. Through holistic application of the *Standards* by all CAEs, internal auditors will be able to more readily gain the coveted seat at the table. However, absent CAEs sticking together and abiding by the *Standards*, management will continue to view the profession as one in which they can dictate the acceptance of guidelines.

The term "seat at the table" is in reference to having the ability to provide direct input or influence to the company's strategy and leadership processes. The internal audit profession refers to the need for the CAE to gain a seat at the table. If management would fully embrace the *Standards*, this concept would be much easier to facilitate.

Statistics continue to show the majority of CAE's report to someone other than the CEO. This is one factor that makes the ability to gain a seat at the table very difficult. Even when the CAE has open access to the CEO, the ability to understand the direction, strategy, and risks of the company is difficult unless they are part of the table where those decisions are openly discussed and vetted.

As a CAE, I have been in the position where I had a true seat at the table and in other positions where I did not. The advantage and knowledge gained by being part of a formal leadership team afforded me as well as the audit department invaluable information. In my case, prior to having the perennial seat at the table, I had been employed by the company for over six years. The CAE position had reported to a variety of functional areas including a chief risk officer, corporate compliance officer, and corporate financial officer (CFO). In the later years of the company's history, the CFO resigned, and the company chose not to replace the position. A decision had to be made on how to realign the CFO's direct reports.

This was an instance where, as a CAE, I faced a very difficult and political challenge. When the CFO resigned, the company immediately realigned three of his direct reports to the CEO. However, my position and another direct report were left in limbo for a period of time. I was not consulted regarding my opinion for alternative reporting lines for internal audit.

As time passed, I felt that the company was considering realigning the internal audit function under the legal department. Although that is a possible alternative, I did not believe that it was the proper alignment for our company at the time in our evolution. I made a personal decision to voice my opinion. I contacted the CEO to set up a meeting to provide him information about recommendations from the *Standards* and potential alternatives for reporting lines. Unfortunately, he was not available and would be out of contact for several weeks. This resulted in having to break one of the golden rules of strong communication. I had to carefully script my message and relay it via voice mail. My next step was to reach out to the audit committee. I was fortunate that I had gained the trust and respect of the committee members. I had been placed in the CAE position for the company after an exhaustive search performed by a retained search firm. After my promotion, the committee often expressed their appreciation regarding my openness and transparency of communication. In this instance, I made the decision that the proper and ethical thing to do was to inform the committee about the alternative reporting line options and to also further educate them on the *Standards*. Ultimately, the committee agreed with my recommendation. The audit committee chairman informed the CEO that my reporting line should be moved directly to him.

This action and decision came with many political and social ramifications that lasted for almost a full year. Obviously, several leadership team members were not happy with the fact that I brought the issue to the audit committee. However, as outlined in the *Standards*, part of the committee's responsibility was oversight of the CAE and input into the authority, reporting responsibility, and compensation. Since my company was a publically traded entity, I felt responsible to ensure that the committee knew the various options as well as the pros and cons of the alternatives. Although there were many challenges ahead, the issue worked out positively. It was a difficult time but one that I accepted. Two years later, my company entered into a strategic sale process. My ability to have a true seat at the table allowed our internal audit group to continue to effectively function during the sales process and transaction close.

I am often asked, "How does the CAE gain a seat at the table?" In my opinion, there is not one universally correct answer. Many variables must be considered. Those include the following:

- *Trust and respect for the internal audit function and the CAE position*. If the internal audit function is not viewed as a respected area of the company, it is doubtful that a seat at the table is in the CAE's near future.

- *An open and transparent relationship with the audit committee.* When the CAE has a close and trusting relationship with the audit committee, their voice and opinion are more likely to be solicited.
- *The company's industry and status as either a publicalty traded organization or a privately held entity.* A CAE in a publically traded company is in a stronger position to work their way to the table. In a privately held company, the internal audit function is not necessarily a requirement, and as such, the CAE position is seen in many different lights. The ability to gain the seat at the table may be more difficult in those situations.
- *The company's overall structure and geographic disparity.* In complex organizational structures, the positioning of internal audit can be very different than it may be within a more simplistic organizational structure. This dynamic may contribute to where the CAE role resides in the organization.
- *Internal audit's relationship with the external auditors.* Often, the opinion and relationship with the external auditors can impact how management views the organizational positioning of the CAE. Management typically sees the external auditors as independent. If the external audit firm supports the need for the CAE to have a seat at the table and can assist management in understanding the strategic value that could be provided, the organization is more likely to consider such a move.

Regardless of the variables involved, an important element of gaining a seat at the table is ensuring that management understands the internal audit *Standards*, the reasons behind the *Standards*, and the suggested reporting lines. Also, the ability to have the respect and trust of the audit committee is a critical hinge pin in the decision.

Section 2: Is It Legal or Is It Ethical?—The CAE's Dilemma

Introduction

The phrase "Is it legal or is it ethical?" can be a mini mantra of the internal audit function. Auditors will sometimes describe the dilemma when identifying a control gap that legally may be acceptable but morally may not. Many professions have their own code of conduct. The code is established to ensure that professionals follow proper morals and behavior as expected in their roles. Lawyers, doctors, certified public accountants, as well as other professional roles have detailed codes of conduct. The IIA has defined a code of ethics for the profession. The code states the principles and expectations governing the behavior of individuals in the conduct of internal auditing. It also describes the minimum requirements for conduct and behavioral expectations. But the ethical line is not always a black-and-white demarcation. In addition, legal implications can impact how gray the line may appear.

The business world has become very complicated. Business ethics can be difficult to instill in everyday business practices. The concept in a vacuum seems obvious, but in application, actions and consequences can become blurred. The development of voluntary, written codes of conduct has been a practice for many years. The American Medical Association established its first code of conduct in 1847. The concept of business ethics didn't become common in the United States until the early 1970s. The idea of a socially responsible company or one that is motivated to behave morally or ethically arose following public outrage over various business scandals. Scandals led to increased regulatory scrutiny, which led to companies developing their own business ethics policies.

Outsiders have questioned the motivation of the trend for businesses to put in writing a business ethics policy. In spite of increased regulatory attention and companies' self-promotion of ethical conduct, years after the Enron scandal, incidents of questionable business conduct continue. The actions of the financial industry in the fall of 2008, which nearly brought down the national economy, is a case in point. "What went wrong?" or "What wasn't clear?" Let's dissect the term ethics and discuss components that contribute to the concept.

Everyone is responsible.
Tone at the top is essential.
Honesty is still the best policy.
Integrity can be a measure of ethics.
Corporate responsibility and communication must be prevalent.
Silence is not acceptable.

Everyone Is Responsible

When the word ethics is surfaced, individuals tend to promulgate that its primary responsibility lies with the leaders of the organization. Although it is true that ethical behavior must be demonstrated at the top, it is an imperative for everyone in the organization to display similar behavior. Think back to the first real ethical dilemma you encountered. It may have occurred long before you entered into the business world, whether it was an incident you faced with some decision as a child or later into your teenage years. Often, those experiences and how they evolved impacted your moral sense of ethical responsibility. If professionals view that certain individuals are not held accountable for their actions, they may question the concept that everyone is responsible. Ethics can be an unquestionable choice for some, whereas others may find that certain elements can be rationalized. This is why organizations find it important to standardize their view of conduct and ethics into a written, well-communicated, and well-trained code that is made an integral part of the organization. However, the code must be more than a written document; it must be practiced and evident in the behavior of the organization. Professionals must be able to clearly see that all employees are held equally accountable for their actions and behavior. If questions exist, some will debate the concept of whether ethics is truly valued by the organization or whether the organization places more value on protecting certain individuals through legalities.

Tone at the Top Is Essential

Many experts will claim that ethical behavior and conduct must start with tone at the top. Although it is a critical attribute, we must accept that not all individuals will have the same morality and opinion as ours. In other words, simply addressing tone will not ensure that the organization appropriately acts when faced with an ethical dilemma. If there is any question as to the path that is most appropriate, individuals may find it easier to rationalize alternatives that may not be in line with the company's overall code. This is exactly why organizations must not only rely on what they deem as tone at the top but also ensure that that tone is actually exemplified in day-to-day practices.

Tone at the top must be communicated frequently, openly, and honestly and put into practice by every individual within the organization. Individuals will follow their leaders and learn from their actions. These actions should be undeniable if questioned.

Honesty Is Still the Best Policy

All too often, ethics and corporate responsibility don't equate to honesty in the workplace. Honesty may mean admission of wrongdoing, poor judgment, or even an honest mistake. If employees are conditioned to act with caution when discussing actions in the workplace that may have negative implications, the concept of open and transparent communication is not being upheld. Organizations must ensure that all professionals can openly discuss concerns with the appropriate level of management. This doesn't mean that everyone's word or opinion is taken at face value, but if employees do not feel that they can freely express their thoughts, ideas, and observations, the culture may be sending the wrong message. Ethics deals with morality issues. Most people's level of morality reaches varying tolerances. When you are personally faced with an ethical dilemma, ask yourself whether you are looking at the situation as honestly and transparently as possible. If questions still arise, it is your obligation to raise those questions to individuals in positions of responsibility. The legality of the issue may not be the right answer when looking at the moral side of the issue. That is when the assistance of others must be enlisted to ensure that the organization's needs are being met.

Integrity Can Be a Measure of Ethics

Can you identify three individuals who you feel display unquestionable integrity? Do those same individuals measure high on the ethics scale? Most likely, they would. Integrity is adherence to a moral code reflected in honesty and harmony in what a person thinks, says, and does. Those regarded with high integrity normally possess a strong set of morale ethics. From a corporate viewpoint, are the members of your leadership team individuals whom the employee population will view as having strong integrity and moral ethics? These are the professionals employees will attempt to emulate. This can be the mirror into your organization. If the concept of integrity is masked through legalities, employees may question adequate tone at the top.

Corporate Responsibility and Communications Must Be Prevalent

Since the early 1960s when business ethics came in vogue, the topic of corporate responsibility, ethical behavior, and compliance has been on the radar for the Securities and Exchange Commission and other federal and state regulatory agencies. Yet, corporate responsibility goes far beyond environmental initiatives, community support, and being a good neighbor. Corporate responsibility is owned by each and every employee. Whether it is a dedication to recycling efforts, contributing to community causes, or providing appropriate feedback to your staff and supervisors regarding how to make the business better, this is the true intent of corporate responsibility. Organizations must learn to embrace the concept that individuals who work in the organization have daily observations that can improve operations and business processes. The inability to encourage feedback from employees and to find an outlet to use these creative ideas is a failure of corporate responsibility.

Silence Is Not Acceptable

Silence can occur due to the fear of retribution. The only way to advance the elimination of business scandals that have pervaded our everyday life is to erase the concern that silence is golden. Many employees see things in their day-to-day job that may be questionable. However, they turn the other eye due to fear of retribution or potential legal threats. Ensure that your employees know the appropriate outlet for surfacing concerns or questions. Consider the following questions:

- Do you have an independent hotline? If so, how many calls does the hotline receive?
- Do those numbers appear to be realistic given your employee base and business?
- How well is your hotline publicized?
- What comprises the issues reported to the hotline?
- Do vendors know about your hotline and understand that they can register a complaint?

- How is your hotline managed?
- Have you ever attempted to call the hotline yourself? You may be surprised at the level of questions/comments you do or don't receive.

Ethics and corporate responsibility will continue to be hot topics in corporate America for years to come. As the economy continues to struggle, or rebound, the ethical behavior of those within business will dramatically impact the success of that recovery. It is no longer acceptable to be the Enrons of the world where a best-practice code of conduct sits on the shelf but is not embraced or actually displayed in practice. Organizations must focus on all aspects of their ethics program and look further than the policy itself. They should ensure that the policy is practiced, enforced, and updated, and compliance is adequately measured and reported. Those are the true signs of a policy in action.

Internal audit may face specific challenges if the administrative reporting line runs through the corporate legal department. There can be an inherent conflict when determining which side of the gray line is best for the organization. Lawyers have a duty to legally protect the company. Although internal auditors also have a strategic interest in protecting the company, when sensitive issues are identified, the manner in which they must be communicated and relayed may create legal exposure to the company. As they say, a picture is worth a thousand words. So let's paint a picture.

Scenario: Legality versus Ethics Assume a scenario where internal audit has completed a review of executive expenditures. During the review, abnormalities are identified in a senior leader's business expense reports. The auditors find that not only were expenditures artificially inflated, but also there were numerous instances where proper documentation was not maintained. Assume that the internal audit group also found discrepancies with issues that may have Internal Revenue Service income-reporting issues.

Now, view the issue from both the legal side and the internal audit side. The legal side would definitely have an interest in rectifying the issue; however, they are also obligated to legally protect the company and its employees and executives. They may prefer that the issue be reported quietly and discretely to eliminate the exposure to public criticism. The legal department is interested in protecting reputational or customer perceptions. From an internal audit viewpoint, regardless of the level of dollar impact, this instance could be viewed an intentional misappropriation that the auditors feel obligated to communicate to the audit committee. So, the question becomes, "Is it legal or is it ethical?" From a legal perspective, it may be sufficient to resolve the issue and ensure that the proper reporting occurs. From an ethical perspective, the issue reflects the tone of the company and the overall control environment, thus the dilemma and predicament.

Ethics is often tied to individual or organizational morality. Legal issues are a matter of stated law or legislation. As evidenced by the many opinions and challenges that exist on various legal standards, the ethical question can be just as debatable. The answer to "Is it legal or is it ethical?" can be very different. Ultimately, how an organization addresses this question contributes to how the organization tone and culture are maintained.

As auditors, we must expect resistance and skepticism when it comes to certain issues, especially those involving senior leaders. However, the internal auditor must acknowledge that the profession maintains a code of conduct. If the auditor feels that the issue is one that should be reported to the audit committee, they have an obligation to follow through on that action.

Summary

These are a few lessons learned. These concepts will be used in later chapters to further analyze their connection to the *Standards* and their challenges to internal auditors.

2

Defining the Purpose of the Internal Audit Function

Introduction

Chapter 1 reviewed lessons learned from performing the internal audit role. Individuals considering a role in the profession will typically turn to leading practice sources that describe how internal audit should be structured and managed along with studies about the potential value that the function can provide to an organization. These sources deal with the theory. If theory were always reality, the world might be a better place. But often, theory is not fully understood, and the reality can take on different perspectives.

Professionals entering the role of internal audit, or specifically the role of internal audit management, should be prepared to understand the challenges that may be presented when working to execute their role as outlined by professional *Standards*. Understanding the challenges and addressing them in a proactive manner will assist audit management and the CAE in meeting the organization objectives while balancing those objectives with professional *Standards*.

This chapter is dedicated to examining the challenges auditors face when attempting to comply with the holistic definition of internal audit as outlined in the *Standards*. In addition, we will evaluate scenarios for various challenges and discuss potential actions that could be considered to address the challenges. The following challenges are covered within this chapter:

- Challenge 1: Independence and Objectivity
- Challenge 2: Assurance and Consulting Activity

- Challenge 3: Add Value and Improve an Organization's Operation
- Challenge 4: Disciplined Approach to Evaluate and Improve the Effectiveness of Risk Management, Control, and Governance Processes
- Challenge 5: Internal Audit Charter
- Challenge 6: Positioning and Authority
- Challenge 7: Internal Audit versus Quality Assurance
- Challenge 8: *Attribute Standards* Integrity and Ethical Values
- Challenge 9: *Attribute Standards* Proficiency and Due Care
- Challenge 10: *Attribute Standards* Quality Assurance and Improvement
- Challenge 11: *Performance Standard 2000*
- Challenge 12: *Performance Standard 2400* Communicating Results
- Challenge 13: Risk-Based Auditing
- Challenge 14: Internal Audit's Role in Governance

Section 1: Understanding the Definition and Purpose of Internal Audit

Internal auditing, as defined by the Institute of Internal Auditors (IIA), outlines the fundamental purpose, nature, and scope of the function.

> Internal auditing is an independent, objective assurance and consulting activity designed to add value and improve an organization's operations. It helps an organization accomplish its objectives by bringing a systematic, disciplined approach to evaluate and improve the effectiveness of risk management, control, and governance processes.
>
> **The Institute of Internal Auditors**

Internal auditors understand the definition of the profession. The concepts outlined in the definition are undeniably sound. When attempting to apply the concepts in practice, internal auditors may find elements that are difficult to facilitate within their organizations. Since we are discussing the realities of executing responsibilities in line with expectations of the profession, it is important to understand what aspects may create challenges for any internal auditor. These include the following portions of the definition:

- Independent, objective
- Assurance and consulting activity
- Add value and improve organization's operations
- Disciplined approach to evaluate and improve the effectiveness of risk management, control, and governance processes

The definition of internal audit has evolved over the years along with the capabilities and aspirations of the individuals employed in the profession. The Sarbanes–Oxley legislation assisted in raising the profile of the profession and attracting a new generation of internal auditors. In the years after Sarbanes–Oxley implementation, internal auditors have gained skills in a variety of areas that extend beyond typical assurance processes. Yet, with the positive advancements made by professionals who have dedicated their careers to internal audit, there remain challenges and obstacles to overcome when ensuring the ability to adequately execute the role in line with the *Standards* outlined by the profession. These challenges can be linked to how organizations interpret or understand the *Standards*.

As mentioned, the IIA is a standard-setting body and does not have authority over laws or regulations that could govern requirements to abide by the recommended *Standards*. In some respects, management views the *Standards* as guidelines rather than requirements. This contributes to the challenges that auditors face when attempting to execute their fiduciary duty. When organized, staffed, and positioned properly, internal audit can serve as a catalyst for improving an organization's governance, risk management, and controls process. However, without a clear understanding of the professional guidelines and appropriate buy-in from the organization, internal auditors can face a multitude of challenges. Let's dissect portions of the definition of the profession and discuss potential challenges.

Challenge 1: Independence and Objectivity

Independence and objectivity are critical attributes within the definition of internal auditing. Yet, they remain two of the most debated principles when it comes to application. Let's start by evaluating a formal definition of independence as provided by the Webster dictionary:

- The professional can be independent without bias or influence.
- The professional is uninfluenced by emotions or personal prejudices.

Webster's definition of the term independence specifically indicates "independence without bias or influence." Individuals who have worked within an internal audit role may experience some semblance of management influence toward day-to-day job responsibilities. With this in mind, the *Standards* acknowledge that internal auditors must have the ability to execute their job without undue pressure from outside parties, including management. The concept is recognized within *Standard 1100* related to Independence and Objectivity:

> The internal audit activity must be independent, and internal auditors must be objective in performing their work.
>
> **Institute of Internal Auditor Standards 1100—Independence and Objectivity**

Further clarification is provided through the following interpretation for *Standard 1100*: Independence and Objectivity:

> Independence is the freedom from conditions that threaten the ability of the internal audit activity or the chief audit executive to carry out internal audit responsibilities in an unbiased manner. To achieve the degree of independence necessary to effectively carry out the responsibilities of the internal audit activity, the chief audit executive has direct and unrestricted access to senior management and the board.
>
> **Institute of Internal Auditor Standards 1100—Interpretation**

The standards are clear, yet the challenge internal auditors face is the ability to completely and efficiently execute the traits of independence and objectivity within their organization. Many professionals confuse the organizational attribute of objectivity with the concept of independence. Some assert that in order to be objective in mindset, the internal auditor must be fully independent in the manner in which they perform their assessments. However, as we all recognize, the internal audit function is a part of the company in which it operates. This inherently establishes barriers to the concept of full organizational independence. The IIA recognized this inherent conflict when defining the *Standards*. However, the IIA expressed the opinion that regardless of organizational positioning, the internal auditor must be able to display objectivity in mindset and approach.

The *International Professional Practices Framework* (*IPPF*) provides guidance on the topic of objectivity and independence. When defining the expectations for internal auditor objectivity, the standards are very clear. The interpretation of *Standard 1100* on Independence and Objectivity states:

> Objectivity is an unbiased mental attitude that allows internal auditors to perform engagements in such a manner that they believe in their work product and that no quality compromises are made. Objectivity requires that internal auditors do not subordinate their judgment on audit matters.
>
> **Institute of Internal Auditor Standards 1100—Interpretation**

A key phrase embedded in the interpretation of objectivity provides an additional challenge for internal auditors. The phrase "internal auditors do not subordinate their judgment on audit matters" can be subjective. Most internal auditors understand the protocol of gaining management agreement on issues and working toward agreed upon solutions. Internal auditors are not infallible, and sometimes, conclusions reached or observations made are not relevant. This could occur due to business situations that the auditor was not aware of or a misinterpretation of information evaluated. With this in mind, the auditor understands there are instances where their observations and conclusions are not accurate. Does this mean they are subordinating their judgment on audit matters? In reality, it should not be interpreted in this manner. However, sometimes, auditors feel responsible to defend their findings and conclusions at all costs.

Challenge 1 Potential Actions: Independence and Objectivity The ability to execute objectivity and assert independence is not solely dependent on organizational status or reporting line. It can relate to the individual personality traits of the internal auditor. The *IPPF* practice guide on objectivity and independence recognizes several factors that can influence these traits. Aspects that influence independence include:

- Reporting structure of the function
- The governing body's involvement with the internal audit function
- The CAE's ability to access information required to conduct audits

Factors that influence objectivity include:

- Cognitive bias (unconscious and unintentional personal bias)
- Self-review (situations where the auditor is reviewing their own work from a previous engagement)
- Familiarity (long-term relationship with client)
- Social pressures (from external parties)
- Economic interest (when the auditor has a stake in the outcome)
- Personal relationship (close friendships or relationships with auditees)
- Intimidation threats (coercion by audit clients)

Each professional will possess and display unique traits and characteristics that manifest in each of the incidents noted as impacting objectivity and independence. How the traits are displayed can also be impacted by the specific situation at hand as well as the professional's personal status within the organization. Because so many variables are at play, internal audit management must work to establish a strong control environment and culture within the internal audit function that encourages auditors to exhibit these traits in the manner expected by professional *Standards*. These may include the following:

- *Evaluate the structure of your internal audit department and the formal reporting line of the function within the organization.* A great deal of emphasis is often placed on the specific reporting line of the CAE, but do not underestimate the need to have the appropriate internal structure that allows adequate supervision and mentoring for auditors.
- *In relationship to the CAE reporting line, the IIA provides guidance on the leading practice structures.* Recognizing this guidance, the reality is that all organizations have their view on where the function should administratively report. It is incumbent upon the CAE or internal audit management to proactively address concerns about the structure or reporting line with management and the audit committee. If this action is deemed "off-limits" by the organization, the CAE must be prepared to respond with the relevant guidance provided by the profession. If that guidance is not accepted by management and the audit committee, then the CAE must clearly articulate how the function's objectivity will be impacted.
- *Regardless of official organizational charts, the internal audit function must have open access to the audit committee.* Without this access, independence and objectivity will inevitably be difficult to execute.
- *Openly discuss with management the concept of subordination of judgment.* Auditors must be willing to be open to management's opinion and perceptions and utilize that information when arriving at their overall observations. However, they must understand when this process crosses into the gray area and becomes "subordination" of judgment.
- *Ensure internal auditors as well as management have a clear understanding of the Standards.* Without a clear and definitive understanding, the internal audit function will face many challenges in exerting independence and objectivity.
- *Consider employing a process within the internal audit department that allows auditors to disclose any potential conflicts of interest or close relationships that may impair their ability to execute independence and objectivity.* If internal audit management is aware of these situations upfront, they can consider these factors when assigning workload.

- *Consider including information about the Standards within preaudit meetings with process owners.* Setting the stage upfront with auditees regarding the expected professional behavior of auditors may assist in establishing the proper foundation for an audit.
- *Maintain an open atmosphere within the internal audit function, and encourage auditors to speak directly to the CAE or internal audit management when they experience issues with objectivity or independence.* Encouraging direct communication between auditors and internal audit management may minimize the perceived need for auditors to try to handle the situation themselves.
- *If issues are surfaced with objectivity or independence, address them proactively.* Don't wait until the end of an audit to discuss the issue with the internal auditor or with process area management. Proactive communication will assist in clearing the air before issues rise to a level that becomes problematic.
- *Consider the "profile" of the audit project when assigning resources.* To facilitate effective execution of independence, auditors must have appropriate organizational positioning as well as a relevant skill level related to the audit area. This will assist in gaining the respect and trust of the auditee. Also, consider the technical aspects of the audit area as well as the profile of the process area management. Situations that assign young, inexperienced auditors to technical process areas or areas where there are known management issues may be ineffective. Don't set your auditors up for failure! There are always projects where management wishes to allow the auditor to obtain on-the-job training by gaining exposure to a new area. In these instances, consider matching the auditor with an experienced member of the team to facilitate strong learning while establishing the appropriate level of respect and trust with management.

Independence and objectivity are critical attributes to the effective execution of the internal audit function. Auditors must have a holistic understanding of these concepts and be properly positioned to execute on these traits. Chapter 4 will further evaluate the concept of independence and objectivity, and utilize scenarios to help examine the difficulties faced by auditors along with potential alternative solutions.

Challenge 2: Assurance and Consulting Activity

Many factors are considered when determining whether internal audit groups can or will be used for consulting activities. When the internal audit profession was originally initiated, the primary purpose was to provide assurance on a process or activity to third parties. As the role and definition of the profession has evolved, internal auditors have extended their services to other processes that may provide value to the organization including consulting engagements. In order to effectively execute on this concept, it is important to delineate between the concepts of assurance and consulting activities.

Assurance services involve the internal auditor's objective assessment of evidence to provide an independent opinion or conclusion regarding a process. The nature and scope of the assurance engagement are determined by the internal auditor. There are generally three parties involved in assurance services:

- Person or group directly involved with the process (the process owner)
- Person or group making the assessment (the internal auditor)
- Person or group using the assessment (the user)

Consulting services are advisory in nature and are performed at the specific request of an engagement client. The nature and scope of the consulting engagement are subject to agreement with the client. Consulting services generally involve two parties:

- Person or group offering the advice (the internal auditor)
- Person or group seeking and receiving the advice (the engagement client)

In essence, there are two primary differences between assurance and consulting services:

- Assurance services rely on the internal auditor to determine the nature and scope of the assessment. Consulting services include an agreement with the client on the scope of services.
- Assurance services involve providing some level of acknowledgment or assurance to a third party. Consulting services do not involve the assurance of procedures to a third party.

The inherent difficulty an auditor may face when engaging in consulting activities relates to the organization's historical perception of the role of internal audit. If the organization perceives internal audit as a sole assurance function, their role may be primarily relegated to compliance activities like Sarbanes–Oxley. Organizations may perceive the inclusion of internal audit professionals on consulting engagements as impairing the ability to be independent in the event that a future review of the activity is warranted. This perception will minimize the ability of internal audit to act as a proactive function. It will prevent internal audit from providing upfront analysis and mitigation of potential control gaps.

Challenge 2 Potential Actions: Assurance and Consulting Activity If internal audit is viewed as a pure assurance function, there is a strong probability that the organization does not fully understand the guidelines and *Standards* of the profession. The organization may not recognize the considerations provided in the *Standards* for consulting versus assurance engagements. In these instances, the action may depend upon the charter of the department along with allocated resourcing and staffing availability. CAEs may want to consider the following:

- *Clarify with management the aspects of the Standards for consulting activities performed by internal auditors.* Outline the variances between assurance activities and consulting activities as provided in the *Standards*. Prior to engaging in consulting activities, ensure that there is a clear understanding of the role of the internal auditor.
- *Evaluate whether aspects such as geographical location, company size, industry type, or other factors may impact whether the internal audit function would have the ability (time or expertise) to engage in consulting engagements.* Just because the current definition of internal audit includes consulting activities does not mean that this role is one that is relevant to your organization. The CAE must utilize their understanding of the organization risks and culture to evaluate whether these assignments are something that should be within the purview of their department.

We will further discuss the concept of executing upon consulting engagements in Chapter 5.

Challenge 3: Add Value and Improve an Organization's Operation

The term adding value infers a great deal of subjective judgment. Professionals have varying views of what they consider to add value. Those views may depend on the particular situation and individuals involved along with whether the value is considered long term or short term. The value term has many definitions, but in general, it can be thought of as "the worth in usefulness or importance to the possessor." Since the determination of value is often the judgment of the possessor, the internal auditor may face inherent difficulty in fulfilling the objective. This is due to the inability to predict the judgment of the person receiving the service. As an example, consider the challenge faced for internal auditors when executing formal post-audit survey evaluations. Your internal audit group may have a satisfaction survey process utilized at the end of each audit to gauge the value of services provided. Assume that the rating scale is based on a 1–5 prioritization defined as follows:

- 1—Not satisfied
- 2—Somewhat satisfied
- 3—Satisfied
- 4—Very satisfied
- 5—Extremely satisfied

If the scale provided to the auditee does not provide definitive guidance about the expected meaning of the term satisfied, it is left up to the person completing the survey to use their personal judgment and expectations when assigning a score. Some individuals have an inherent resistance to ranking any evaluation at the uppermost ranking. An operations supervisor of the company I worked for at one time informed me during an audit evaluation process that he never gives a rating of "5." In his mind, to reach a "5" rating, the services would need to be perfect in all aspects of initiation, execution, and communication. His exact comment was "I don't believe anyone except the heavenly authorities deserves a five rating." If this was indeed his perception, it would be near impossible to meet.

The other dynamic is that each person has a different process when interpreting the meaning of satisfied. One person's rating of satisfied could be equivalent to another person's rating of extremely satisfied. This makes it difficult when an internal audit department has metrics that strive to maintain an average ranking greater than "4." As a trainer and speaker, I often find the post-session evaluations interesting. It is an amazing dynamic to review survey responses from 50 individuals who attend the same session. Some individuals provide rankings of "5" (extremely satisfied) while others give rankings that are much lower. Even more perplexing are those individuals who may assess a moderate ranking of "3" and then provide lavish comments on how much value they received from the session. It is obvious that individuals have various methods of assigning their assessments to rankings.

If assessments are completed solely through survey, the audit team must question whether assignment of a numeric ranking is a good indicator of how well the audit was performed or the level of value truly provided.

Challenge 3 Potential Actions: Add Value and Improve an Organization's Operation When assessing ultimate value, there is an inherent challenge in meeting the expectations of another individual. Internal auditors have little to no control over how others interpret actions or how their own personal rating system is calibrated. Professionals must be conscious of this challenge and be prepared to address any rating questions with relevant facts and observations. As CAE or internal audit management, when your department is faced with the question of adding value and improving the organization's operations, consider the following:

- *Evaluate the process your department utilizes to measure organizational value.* If that process includes an end-of-engagement survey, take a fresh look at the questions and scale outlined on your survey. A question that states "the audit provided value to my department" may be interpreted in various ways by your auditees. Consider whether your survey rating process is providing the information that allows the department to actively address its effectiveness or need for improvement actions.

- *Examine how postaudit surveys are executed.* Are they completed via e-mail, in person by the auditor-in-charge, or through a separate interview process executed by the CAE? All of these variables could impact the outcome of the survey. There may not be one universally correct answer for all organizations. The CAE should be knowledgeable enough of the organization to determine the value of the survey process to the organization.
- *Revisit your current internal audit metrics.* Does your department have guidelines or metrics for the percent or amount of time spent in each stage of an audit (planning, fieldwork, reporting)? How effective are these metrics given the dynamics of your organization? In today's world, standard metrics may not always be applicable to each audit. Companies that deal in new and emerging markets or technologies where processes are continually evolving may spend a significant amount of time on the audit planning stage and find that the amount of time is more than typical audit metrics cite as relevant. In addition, some departments may measure budgeted hours to actual audit hours and hold auditors accountable to those metrics. In some cases, this can be a relevant metric, whereas in other cases, circumstances that evolved during the audit may cause a significant expansion or contraction of the audit scope. If this is the case, how have your procedures allowed for the adjustment to projected actual audit hours? If there is not this consideration, the metric may not provide the audit group with a true picture of the effectiveness of an audit.
- *Consider the relevance of audit metrics that may dictate performance based on the number of findings or potential recovery of funds.* This protocol is similar to one used in sales organizations or even customer service organizations that measure their personnel based on how quickly an issue is resolved or how many sales are closed. If auditors feel that they are judged based on the number of findings, they may focus on quantity over quality. In addition, if metrics are set that encourage

auditors to identify a dollar savings or to "find the money," the CAE should have specific guidelines for how savings will be measured. Otherwise, the metrics may provide incentives that result in nonproductive output.

- *Take a fresh look at your post-audit staff feedback process.* Is there a process in place that provides for debriefing of lessons learned by both the auditors and internal audit management? Some organizations have supervisors or managers provide individual performance evaluations to audit staff post-individual engagements. Have you considered the possibility of developing a 360° feedback process for all personnel? This may not work in all circumstances, but it may be a consideration that could help with the overall efficiency of the department.
- *Consider whether your annual review process allows for input on auditor performance from key stakeholders.* Some organizations have a process in place that allows for written feedback from process owners during annual review time. In these instances, the auditor is asked to provide management with the names of audit clients they have worked with during the past year. The audit clients are asked for a short written summary of observations of the performance of the auditor during their interactions. The feedback is provided to the direct supervisor and is used as an ancillary measurement or consideration within the individual's personnel evaluation.

Each of these considerations is meant to be thought provoking. What works for one organization may not work for another. Remember that the term value can be viewed in many ways. Internal audit management must be cognizant of identifying multiple avenues to measure the value that they may be providing to the organization.

Challenge 4: Disciplined Approach to Evaluate and Improve the Effectiveness of Risk Management, Control, and Governance Processes

This portion of the formal definition of internal audit presents a host of challenges. First is the concept of a disciplined approach. Disciplined approached can be defined as

> Behavior in accordance with rules of conduct or behavior and order maintained by training and control.

Internal audit groups who strive to abide by the *Standards* will work to instill a disciplined and strong audit methodology or framework for executing individual engagements. In the event that an external quality assessment is performed, the assessors will evaluate the approach and methodology to ensure adequacy of its application as well as appropriateness of execution.

Internal audit methodologies can be compared to policies and procedures established by other process areas. Procedures are established to ensure that work is executed to meet departmental and organizational goals. Internal audit departments often incorporate guidelines outlined in the *Standards* within their methodology. However, as previously discussed, many companies don't understand the full extent and purpose of the professional *Standards*. They are unable to see the benefit that guidelines provide to the internal audit group. This may be due to the inability to align the concepts of the *Standards* with contribution to the overall organizational value. Management may challenge the procedures or *Standards* of internal audit functions when those procedures don't align with management's expectations.

When attempting to determine the reason management may not fully embrace the *Standards* and the importance of a disciplined approach, think about the concept of how risk-based auditing is viewed. If you recall, this was one of the lessons learned outlined in Chapter 1. Assume that the internal audit methodology incorporates all aspects of risk-based analysis. This methodology includes the process from initial identification of audit risks to utilization of a risk-based approach to define audit tests and report results. If the organization has a different view of risk-based auditing, the ability to apply a disciplined approach may be challenged. Assume that management's definition of risk-based auditing lies solely in how the annual audit plan is determined and developed. If the internal audit group executes their methodology as a holistic process that extends from audit area identification to audit planning, audit testing, and audit reporting, the organization may not view this approach as value added. They may not understand the aspects of risk reporting and risk language and may view the utilization of these methods as one not relevant to their organization. Ultimately, the challenge is the ability to understand and reconcile management's definition of value-add versus internal audit's definition.

Another area to examine that is related to the definition of internal audit is the utilization of the words "improve effectiveness of risk management control and governance processes." The ability to meet this requirement hinges on the organization's willingness to embrace the full scope of the definition of internal auditing. Historically, internal auditors have been viewed as an assurance function for the evaluation of internal control processes. Involvement in risk management activities and governance processes may be a concept that the organization has not yet embraced. The challenge of meeting the requirement to improve effectiveness of risk management control and governance processes should be addressed when outlining the scope of the internal audit function and the related charter responsibilities.

Challenge 4 Potential Actions: Disciplined Approach to Evaluate and Improve the Effectiveness of Risk Management, Control, and Governance Processes Actions to meet the challenge of employing a disciplined approach and improve effectiveness of risk management, control, and governance processes may include the following:

- *Evaluate your current audit methodology or framework for conducting audits.* Consider the following questions:
  - Does the methodology provide auditors a clear guide of expectations for each phase of the audit?
  - Do auditors understand the timing expectations for each audit phase?
  - Is automated software utilized to assist in audit documentation efforts? If not, how does your department ensure that the proper procedures and protocols are followed for each stage of an audit?
  - Are quality checkpoints established within the engagement to ensure the audit is addressing the objectives and scopes outlined?
  - Does an efficient process exist for final review of work papers and audit reports prior to closing out the project?

- Are protocols in place for managing documentation and data gathered during the audit?

The reality is many internal audit groups do not have fully documented audit methodologies that outline expectations for work, documentation, and reports. This is a very fundamental responsibility of internal audit. Help your auditors succeed. If you enter a new internal audit function that has not addressed the procedures needed to adequately plan, conduct, and report on an audit, the CAE must take action. Procedures, protocols, templates, documentation expectations, timing requirements, and testing expectations are all fundamental components of completing a comprehensive audit. Take time to revisit your current audit methodology to ensure you are providing an effective and appropriately disciplined approach to conducting work.

- *Establish an internal quality assurance program within your function.* Executing periodic internal quality assurance reviews to evaluate the sufficiency of audit documentation, reporting, and the review process will assist in maintaining a disciplined approach. This process will also prove to be value added if the function undergoes an external quality assessment review.
- *Evaluate the department's ability to add value within the risk management and governance arena.* Similar to processes discussed for consulting engagements, not all internal audit groups have the capability to provide effective risk management or governance guidance. However, there are specific concepts that internal audit should clarify regarding work that would be considered within their sphere of influence.
  - *Determine the department's role in risk management.* If a separate risk management function exists within the organization that focuses on enterprise-wide risk management, identify the role that internal audit will have within that process. The act of assessing risk is an activity that internal auditors are familiar with and regularly engage in. Risk management, on the other hand, infers a process whereby management takes action to mitigate risk. Auditors should have sufficient exposure and insight into

risk management functions throughout the organization. This insight will provide a broader view of the organization's risks. As internal audit management, you must pave the way to identify methods to allow internal auditors to be incorporated within risk discussions throughout the company. These discussions can extend from business strategy planning to specific risk evaluation processes undertaken within various business areas. The ability for auditors to have a seat at the table during these evaluations will enhance your department's capabilities within the risk management and risk assessment arenas.

- *Determine the department's goal in governance.* This concept is more difficult and may involve political or organizational issues. Governance issues are often represented as being owned at the board and senior management levels. The ability for internal audit to take part in governance reviews can hinge on the organizational positioning of the function. Governance procedures and activities may require the specific attention of the CAE and involve relevant discussions with the audit committee and executive management to determine the most relevant role. Although in theory, internal audit should have access to perform governance reviews of board and committee charters, this may be deemed a responsibility of the legal or compliance function within the organization. If internal audit is to provide value in the area of governance, they must have the proper stature and knowledge within the organization to ensure their observations are deemed relevant. Review of board processes or senior strategy-setting processes may be those that are best managed directly by the CAE with support from the audit committee.

Summary: Internal Audit Definition Challenges

Internal auditors face many challenges when attempting to meet the expectations of the professional definition of their roles. These challenges can be addressed through transparent and open discussion of the issues with management and the audit committee. The challenges are not always easily resolved. The CAE must be persistent and diligent in efforts to assist management in recognizing the value internal audit can provide. This is best executed when the internal audit function is initially developed, but it is also a process that deserves ongoing attention. These concepts must be periodically reviewed and discussed with management and the audit committee to ensure that the function can continue to evolve and mature.

Scope of Internal Audit

The breadth and scope for an internal audit function will take on many variations. These variations can involve some of the following concepts:

- The company's industry and type of entity (e.g., publicly traded, privately held, etc.)
- Expectations of management and the board on value-added services for the organization
- Company expectations for ownership of governance activities
- Existence of a separate enterprise risk management (ERM) function within the organization
- Management of compliance issues such as Sarbanes–Oxley or regulatory compliance
- Existence of process improvement areas within the company such as six sigma or total quality management
- Requirements imposed by regulatory or governmental authorities
- Existence of specific mini-audit areas such as environmental, health and safety, security processes, customer interaction quality assurance, and operational quality management
- Focus on the reliability of financial and management reporting
- Procedures employed by the company for fraud evaluation and investigative protocols

The ability for internal audit to effectively meet the full definition of internal audit will be impacted by the factors listed as well as cultural, political, geographical, and organizational issues. The diversity and variance in how internal audit functions are scoped in today's business world support the need for a strong and consistent understanding of *Standards* and the *IPPF*.

Professional *Standards*—Principles for Internal Auditor Effectiveness

In 2014, the IIA announced proposed changes to the *IPPF*. The changes include a proposed new mission statement that recognizes for each organization, internal audit strives "to enhance and protect organization value by providing stakeholders with risk-based, objective and reliable assurance, advice and insight." In addition, 12 principles were proposed to articulate internal audit effectiveness. The proposal suggests that for internal audit to be considered effective, all 12 principles must be present and operating effectively. As of the date of this publication, the proposal is still under review. The principles listed are sound and can be linked to the topics that will be covered within this publication. As we evaluate various criteria necessary in the establishment of a sound and effective internal audit function, we will relay the concepts back to the various principles outlined and then identify the lessons learned, which are covered in Section 1.

The proposed principles by the IIA for inclusion in the updated *IPPF* are as follows:

1. Demonstrate uncompromised integrity
2. Display objectivity in mindset and approach
3. Demonstrate commitment to competence
4. Appropriate position within the organization with sufficient authority
5. Align strategically with the aims and goals of the organization
6. Adequate resources to effectively address significant risks
7. Demonstrate quality and continuous improvement
8. Achieve efficiency and effectiveness in delivery
9. Communicate effectively
10. Provide reliable assurance to those charged with governance
11. Be insightful, proactive, and future focused
12. Promote positive change

Section 2: The Internal Charter—Reality or Fiction?

Introduction

The foundation for internal audit is embedded within the functions charter. A charter is defined as the document outlining the principles, functions, and organization of a corporate body. The internal audit department charter will typically begin with the definition of internal auditing. Leading practice charters can be readily obtained. Those charters outline the concepts and standards defined by the profession. However, how often have you seen charters that are rarely followed in practice? When considering this question, ask when the last time the details outlined in the departmental charter were reviewed with management and the audit committee? This question goes beyond the typical process of periodic approval of the charter by the governing body. Consider whether you have needed to refer to the charter or present it to process owners to support the department's relevant authority to execute a project. If so, what was the reaction of the process owner or management? Did they accept the charter statement as reality, or were you required to take additional steps to execute upon your obligation?

We have discussed the significant challenges faced when dissecting the definition of internal audit and determining the functions ability to abide by the definition. It is just as important to take a detailed and transparent evaluation of the department charter. Audit groups should examine the specific attributes defined in their charter, review those elements with management and the audit committee, and critically evaluate their ability to execute on each element in an independent and objective manner.

Challenge 5: Internal Audit Charter

Attribute Standard 1000 speaks to the need for an internal audit charter. Specifically, the standard provides the following interpretation:

> The internal audit charter is a formal document that defines the internal audit activity's purpose, authority and responsibility. The internal audit charter establishes the internal audit activity's position within the organization, including the nature of the chief audit executive's functional reporting relationship with the board; authorizes access to records, personnel, and physical properties relevant to the performance of engagements; and defines the scope of internal audit activities. Final approval of the internal audit charter resides with the board.
>
> **Institute of Internal Auditor Standards 1000—Interpretation**

This standard identifies the internal audit charter as a formal document that outlines the internal audit activity's purpose, authority, and responsibility. Important elements of a charter may include the following:

- *Establishing the internal audit activity's position within the organization.* This includes the nature of the CAE's functional reporting relationship with the board.
- *Authorizing access to records, personnel, and physical properties relevant to the performance of engagements.*
- *Defining the scope of internal audit activities (e.g., compliance, financial, operational, governance, etc.).*
- *Defining the nature of assurance services provided to the organization.* If assurances are to be provided to parties outside the organization, the nature of these assurances should also be defined in the internal audit charter.
- *Defining the nature of consulting services that the internal audit function will provide to the organization.*

Major sections of a typical charter will include the following:

- *An outline of the internal audit organization structure.* Structure includes the manner in which the function is established including administrative and functional reporting lines. Other important aspects related to structure include requirements for professionalism of individuals within the function. This section will typically refer to the internal audit standards and guidelines as well as the profession's code of conduct.
- *Department's overall authority and responsibility.* This component includes responsibility assigned to the function including:
    - The scope and responsibility of the function for examination of the organization's processes
    - The manner in which the department will develop the annual audit plan
    - Expectations for independence and objectivity
    - Responsibility for consulting and advisory services as well as special investigations and fraud evaluations
    - Responsibilities for quality assurance activities

- *Communication methods for internal audit.* This section will detail the expectation for communication among the internal audit activity, management, and the board. These responsibilities include the reporting and working relationship between the internal audit function and the external audit function. Other elements include:
    - Formal reporting requirements to process area management and the board
    - Responsibilities for communicating impact on resource limitations
    - Responsibilities for reporting and monitoring identified deficiencies as well as follow-up activities
- *The nature of audit committee relations.* This section will address the responsibilities of the governing group assigned to oversee internal audit. Elements within this section should also be identified within the governing body charter. Typical responsibilities of the governing body as it relates to internal audit include:
    - Approval of the internal audit charter
    - Approval of the risk-based internal audit plan
    - Approval of the internal audit budget and resource plan
    - Communications from the CAE on the internal audit function performance relative to the plan
    - Approval of decisions regarding the appointment and removal of the CAE
    - Approval of the salary and incentive for the CAE
    - Inquiry of management and the CAE to determine whether there is inappropriate scope or resource limitations for internal audit

Since the internal audit charter serves as the basis and foundation of the function, the information outlined within the charter should be carefully considered and evaluated prior to acceptance by the organization. For internal audit groups who work toward compliance with the *Standards*, it is important to include aspects outlined in the professional guidelines. However, it is just as important to ensure that the organization is able to fully execute each aspect outlined within the charter. Organizations should be cautious when blindly accepting formal charter documents that are deemed leading practice. The inability to execute upon charter elements can result in an inefficient internal audit function and undue risk exposure to the company. To illustrate this point, consider the following scenario.

Charter Scenario Acme Inc.—Acme Inc. is a publicly traded company that has traditionally maintained a very small internal audit function. The responsibilities of the group have been to support the external audit process and to perform Sarbanes–Oxley work. In this instance, it may not be effective for the organization to utilize a charter that outlines expectations for the internal audit group to be involved in risk assessments, consultancy projects, fraud evaluations, or other special projects. Although theoretically this is a standard of the profession, the organization's approach and expectations of the internal audit group may never provide for the ability to actually execute on these charter aspects. Including these aspects within a charter and knowing that they cannot be executed is an example of fiction over reality.

Challenge 5 Potential Actions: Internal Audit Charter Audit committees who understand the *Standards* and who believe in their value may be able to exercise their oversight authority through direct interaction with the CAE on functional responsibilities. However, without audit committee support and buy-in, the CAE may find challenges when attempting to garner the appropriate level of authority in any individual area. To fully execute their fiduciary duty related to the internal audit charter, the CAE should address the following:

- *Ensure adequate organizational positioning.* If lack of appropriate organizational positioning impedes the efficiency of the internal audit function and its value to the organization, the CAE must identify the most appropriate method to communicate this concern to the audit committee and to senior management. However, be cautious when simply expressing concerns without providing alternative solutions. A strong leader will be able to recommend potential alternatives for mitigating the issue they perceive exists.

- *Ensure the internal audit charter is reality, not fiction.* The CAE must closely examine the internal audit charter and determine whether the document is truly fact or fiction. A document that contains policy statements that are not embraced or upheld by the organization is not worth the paper it is written on. A legal professional may relay that writing a policy or a charter that cannot be followed may actually put the company at risk. If the company is regulated by an outside body who periodically reviews the internal audit function, having a charter that only represents leading practice recommendations and is not truly executed with identifiable actions can result in unwanted questions and accusations.
- *Establish a compliant approach to the Standards.* Openly communicate with management and the audit committee when instances arise that put the internal audit function at risk for not complying with the *Standards*. Explain the potential risk that noncompliance may present to the organization. Ultimately, if the internal audit charter outlines responsibilities as defined by the *Standards*, the function must have the appropriate level of support and buy-in to effectively execute on those responsibilities.

Challenge 6: Positioning and Authority

Principle 4 proposed by the IIA cites that the function should maintain "appropriate positioning with sufficient organizational authority." The principle relates to various components included in the internal audit charter, and the importance of validating the audit charter is fact, not fiction.

Proper organizational positioning for the CAE and relevant authority for his/her position is an ongoing topic for evaluation and debate. *Standard 1100* of the Professional Practice Framework states:

> The chief audit executive must report to a level within the organization that allows the internal audit activity to fulfill its responsibilities.
>
> **Institute of Internal Auditor Standards 1100**

The wording utilized within this *Standard* allows for significant interpretation by the organization. There are many alternatives for reporting lines and reporting responsibilities. The varying alternatives can prove to be effective or ineffective depending on how the organization administers the process.

The IIA encourages the administrative reporting line for the CAE be directed to the CEO. However, benchmarking studies continue to indicate this is not the predominant practice. Current practice continues to represent that the majority of CAE reporting lines are routed to the CFO. Alternative options are reporting lines that extend to the chief legal officer, corporate compliance officer, or corporate administrative officer.

Some organizations consider the concept of internal reporting lines as a minor issue. In reality, any of these reporting lines can be effective as long as the CAE is able to maintain objectivity, independence, and authority in all aspects of performing the job. If the CAE is unduly influenced because of alternative reporting lines, the organizational positioning should be questioned and brought to the attention of the audit committee.

Examples of true functional reporting to the audit committee would entail independent relationships that are unfiltered by management. The word unfiltered is extremely important in asserting independence and organizational positioning. However, the fact that internal audit is considered a part of the organization often prevents companies from maintaining a single reporting line from the CAE to the audit committee.

Reporting line options can be debated and further examined; however, the key lies in the CAE and internal audits' ability to maintain independence, objectivity, and ultimate authority when it comes to execution of responsibilities. The function must be able to independently and frequently speak to senior management, the board, or the audit committee. If functional reporting lines require the CAE to obtain approval of management prior to any communications with the audit committee, independence and objectivity can be impaired.

Another consideration of organizational positioning relates to the CAE's ability to gain the appropriate information on strategy and business planning. If the CAE is not considered a part of the senior leadership team and does not have the ability to gain a seat at the table, they will continue to face challenges when attempting to understand the overall strategy and direction of the organization.

On the surface, the principle of appropriate positioning for internal audit may seem to be directed at the reporting line of the CAE. However, the positioning of the internal audit department itself within the organizational structure is a critical element for providing internal auditors the opportunity to deliver true value to the organization. The manner in which internal audit is positioned within the organization may imply expectations related to authority or responsibility for the function.

Appropriate organizational positioning speaks to the ongoing challenge internal auditors face in asserting their independence and objectivity. Adequate independence is required to enable unrestricted evaluation of organizational process activities. Internal audit standards assert that since the primary customer of internal audit is the entity charged with oversight of management's activities (the audit committee), auditors should be able to effectively execute their role. In reality, internal auditors are a component of the overall company culture. Their work and actions are impacted in many different ways by the actions of management. Auditors engage in the daily activities of the organization. Pay, bonus, and organizational standing are determined by the very individuals internal auditors are expected to be independent from. Regardless of administrative reporting lines, this unrelenting factor can create difficulty.

Although the audit committee is considered an oversight authority for internal audit, in reality, many of the functional responsibilities for oversight of internal audit are aspects that may be strongly controlled by management. Let's examine a couple of scenarios related to organizational positioning and authority. As you review these scenarios, consider how the questions may apply within your organization.

Scenario 1: Organizational Positioning and Authority ABC's internal audit charter includes information about functional responsibilities to the audit committee. The wording in the charter reflects guidelines outlined in the *Standards* and incorporates the requirement that the audit committee approve the internal audit charter. The *Standards* outline specific activities that the audit committee should strive to be engaged in. These activities are to assist in the appropriate organizational positioning and perception of independence for the internal audit function.

Although ABC Company has included the relevant *Standards* requirements within their charter, each factor presents a challenge to the internal auditor as well as the audit committee when attempting to execute. Elements such as approval of the CAE's salary and/or approval of the appointment or dismissal of the CAE are often areas of contention with management. From a reality viewpoint, management views the hiring or termination of employees as their responsibility. In addition, compensation is a very delicate issue and follows specific protocols outlined by the organization. With this in mind, ABC's audit committee has become complacent in their responsibilities in this area. They rely on information provided by management and the company in order to execute their oversight responsibilities. They also rely strongly on the external auditors to provide advice and counsel regarding many processes including the internal audit function. Concepts such as approving the budget of the internal audit function or making inquiries of the CAE regarding resourcing are issues that may be executed with strong management suggestion and as such are considered more form over substance.

ABC's committee members have a strong relationship with the company's executive management. Although they understand that, in principle, they should use their independent judgment when executing their functional responsibilities, the committee has a multitude of oversight requirements to address in order to appropriately execute their role. This results in the need to prioritize responsibilities. Often, some of the aspects relating to the oversight of internal audit are viewed as ancillary responsibilities that are deferred to management's judgment.

ABC's experience with oversight of the internal audit function is not unusual. Many audit committees place significant reliance on senior management outside of the CAE when questions arise regarding charter guidelines. In many companies, the charter approval processes for board activities are handled by the corporate compliance office or the legal department. Although *Standards* suggest that the internal audit charter should be developed with strategic input from the audit committee, the reality is that charters are typically developed by management personnel. Internal audit must take a transparent look at the individual elements in their charter and ensure that they are executable in their organization. In other words, the CAE must ensure that charter statements are reality and not fiction.

When charters are initially developed, they may outline the expectation of management for how the internal audit function should be managed and organized. For organizations that are not publically traded, this concept can be a significant source of debate and contention. For the internal audit function to adequately meet the principle of appropriate positioning with overall organizational authority, the CAE should address the following:

- Maintain authority over recommended changes to the internal audit charter.
- Ensure the audit committee understands their oversight responsibilities for internal audit and the specific activities that may be involved with executing appropriate oversight.
- Work with the audit committee to ensure confidentiality of communications.
- Periodically discuss with committee members the challenges that may result from meeting some of the requirements. Stress the overall value that can be provided to the organization when these attributes are clearly articulated and executed.

Scenario 2: Organizational Positioning and Authority Acme Inc. is reviewing the compensation structure of their management. The CAE's compensation is included within this review. The CAE's compensation has been determined according to the organization's predefined human resource process and benchmarks. The salary will vary depending on the CAE's job grade level within the organization. Individuals who have held the CAE role at Acme Inc. in the past have retained titles such as directors, vice president, or compliance officer.

A functional responsibility suggested by the *Standards* is that the audit committee approve the compensation of the CAE. However, Acme Inc.'s management does not believe this responsibility is one that requires audit committee input.

In the instance of Acme Inc., management has taken the position that the audit committee should not have input to the salary structure of the CAE. In many organizations, the audit committee may receive information on the CAE's salary and provide verbal approval; however, many CAEs would indicate that it is a rare event when their salary determinations are a factor of the independent opinion and suggestion of the audit committee. When was the last time the CAE of your organization had a private and transparent discussion with the audit committee regarding benchmark statistics on CAEs' comparable salaries? Many CAEs would not attempt to broach this topic due to the political sensitivities that may be inferred by management. However, think about the other side of the equation. Has the audit committee requested the CAE to provide benchmark statistics on typical CAE salaries in order to evaluate whether the position is being remunerated commensurate with industry expectations? If not, are they fulfilling their fiduciary duty related to the oversight of internal audit? Granted, this is a very sensitive topic, but the questions point to the importance of ensuring that your charter is factual. If the internal audit department charter includes the statement that "the audit committee will approve the salary of the CAE," you must question how this responsibility is being executed adequately and in the best interest of the organization. In addition, the execution of this responsibility should entail more than a simple approval of a salary level based on management recommendation.

Now that we have reviewed a couple of scenarios that may impact the CAE's positioning and authority within an organization, let's examine some potential actions that may assist the CAE in solidifying their authority role.

Challenge 6 Potential Actions: Positioning and Authority In order to facilitate effective positioning and authority, internal audit must build and maintain strong relationships throughout the organization. There are many actions that can enhance relationships. Some potential considerations include the following:

- *Allow the CAE to facilitate periodic meetings with senior management of various business areas.* These meetings can be utilized to work and gain an understanding of risks and challenges managed within the business.

- *Consider establishing subject matter experts within the audit group who can work to establish strong relationships with specific process areas.* This will allow audit professionals to gain additional exposure to process owners and provide a broader coverage of one-on-one relationships with management.
- *Allow the CAE or audit management to provide routine internal control, risk management or emerging risk issue updates for business area staff meetings.* The updates can be informational on objectives and focus of the internal audit function or provide relative updates to the process area on new aspects of internal control that may impact compliance or regulatory issues.
- *Ensure process owners understand the authority and responsibility provided to internal audit by the organization.* Consider sharing aspects of the internal audit charter with auditee management prior to an engagement commencing. Also, ensure that the audit team has appropriate representation from internal audit management to reinforce aspects of authority and responsibility.
- *Establish procedures for internal audit management to periodically assess the organizational culture for perceptions on respect and objectivity garnered by the department.* If certain process areas are deemed as challenge areas to execute reviews, internal audit management should be involved in setting the tone for individual audits. This may entail meeting with auditee management prior to audit initiation or establishing some type of communication process that will allow management to understand how the audit is progressing and allow internal audit management to proactively address any questions of process area management.

Section 3: Internal Audit versus Quality Assurance Functions

Introduction

There is an increasing trend for companies to consider the credential of a six sigma black belt as a critical skill for the CAE. Having this credential can provide a strong skill base for the CAE role; however, it is important that the internal audit function maintain a distinct and separate objective from what would be expected with a six sigma or other quality assurance function.

The role of a quality assurance function is to develop procedures and systems in collaboration with other departments ensure all deliverables are of consistent good quality. Quality assurance is proactive in that it aims to prevent defects or problems from occurring. The International Standards Organization (ISO) developed the ISO 9000 standards for a quality management system. ISO Standards provides the framework that governs how a consistent, training-driven quality system should function. ISO 9000 defines quality assurance as a part of quality management focused on providing confidence that quality requirements will be fulfilled.

The concepts of quality assurance and internal audits are very distinct. Quality assurance projects can manifest itself through a number of operational policies and systems. Audits projects are more specific. They are systematic investigations of a specific area. Audits may dig into any area of a company, including accounting, human resources, and even quality assurance programs. It is important that organizations have a clear understanding of the difference in these terms. Quality assurance may be a part of everyone's job in some companies, whereas it is distinctly separated in others. Although many quality assurance functions follow standards as outlined by ISO, *Standards* outlined by the internal audit profession place more stringent protocols around ensuring independence and objectivity and providing assurance to third parties.

Internal Audit versus Quality Assurance—The Reality

When there is not a clear understanding of the *Standards* and their importance to the execution of internal auditing, organizations may begin to confuse the concepts of quality assurance and internal audit. This can lead to significant difficulties for the internal audit group when attempting to meet *Standards* and expectations. A quality assurance group will approach reporting of observations in a different manner than internal audit. This can include who the report is delivered to, how the report is written, and how issues are measured or ranked. When management confuses the concept of quality assurance projects with the internal audit function, they may assume that the internal auditors are not required to report certain findings to the audit committee or even issue written reports on findings. The delineation between the activities of quality assurance and internal audit should be made distinctly clear. Internal auditors can execute upon quality assurance reviews; however, management must understand how these vary from assurance activities and the requirements to report specific control gaps and findings.

Mini-Audit Functions

An interesting phenomenon in the world of corporate America is the manner in which organizations develop mini-audit or assurance functions that can be correlated to periodic management monitoring or quality assurance processes. Consider the example of organizations that maintain specific environmental, health, and safety auditors. These auditors may work directly within the business unit. They establish and execute on regular facility reviews or audits to ensure the company is meeting environmental health and safety standards and expectations. This also occurs in process areas such as information security where professionals regularly monitor transactions and periodically execute random testing to ensure procedures are being followed and information security systems are adequately maintained. Another example may relate to quality assurance areas established for organizations that maintain call centers. Often, there is a separate and distinct quality group that randomly monitors customer calls for quality assurance. The difference between these quality groups and internal audit is the requirement of independence along with the requirement of reporting issues to the board and audit committee. These mini-audit functions may be embedded within the organization with professionals who possess a strong background in the technical aspects of the process. However, acknowledging that these are typically management monitoring processes, some may question whether significant findings that are identified during these reviews should be reported through to internal audit or to the audit committee. Ask yourself a few questions related to mini-audit processes that may exist in your organization:

- How comfortable are you that the issues identified during the normal course of a quality assurance area's work are appropriately remediated?
- Do you believe that issues which may rise to any level of significance are elevated to the proper individuals within the organization to ensure proper oversight?
- What position would your audit committee take if they felt that issues being identified directly in the business areas are of significance that would otherwise be reported if identified by internal audit?

Audit committees can fall into a false sense of security when they assume that all significant issues occurring in the organization identified will be brought to their attention by internal audit. This will only occur if internal audit has the opportunity to review the area or has been made aware of the issue. In the case of mini-audit functions, internal audit may not be made aware of the findings identified. This can result in the findings remaining at the business unit level with no notification to senior leaders.

This discussion is not to assert that all mini-audit areas or quality assurance areas should have a reporting line to internal audit. However, there may be some logic in identifying a process where internal audit has some connection or insight into the activities and observations of these mini-audit or quality assurance areas. The purpose would be to ensure that internal audit has a level of understanding regarding the reviews and projects performed. In addition, internal audit would have greater insight into issues that may arise from these reviews. In some circumstances, internal audit groups have worked with other process areas to ensure an understanding of the organization's definition of risk tolerance. The purpose is to ensure that if these mini-audit areas identify a control issue that may breach corporate tolerance, they understand that the issue is one that should be communicated to senior management, internal audit, or even the audit committee.

This may not be a process your company would embrace, but it is certainly a concept worth discussing with your audit committee. As an example, consider how the audit committee may react to the following scenario.

Scenario: Mini-Audit Process

ABC Company is a large manufacturing organization with operations spread throughout the United States. The organization is structured into distinct business units that focus on various aspects of the manufacturing process. Typically, each business unit executes on multiple manufacturing projects for various customers. The organization assigns each project an operations manager and project controller. During the course of a large project, the project controller identifies discrepancies in submitted expenditures. The project controller believes there is strong evidence that inappropriate expenditures have been submitted by operations management. He informs the project manager and the head of the business unit. As the issue is further examined, they find that the inappropriate expenditures extend to other projects that certain personnel have worked on over the past several years. Initial calculations project that the inappropriate expenditures could exceed $5 million. The project manager, controller, and head of the business unit decide they will evaluate the issue internally, but they will not engage any assistance from the corporate accounting area. Even if the issue turns out to be an incident of fraud, the expectation is that the issue will be handled by management within the business unit. The head of the business unit does not want his peers to know that this type of issue has occurred under his area of responsibility.

Based on the scenario described, do you believe this is an issue that should receive audit committee attention or, at the very least, internal audit review? What if the incident turns out to be some type of illegal fraud that later must be revealed to the audit committee or becomes public through other communication channels? Would the audit committee have expected to be made aware of the issue sooner?

In most companies, this would be an issue that deserves not only audit committee attention but also independent review. However, based on the scenario given, it is likely that unless the issue is reported through an anonymous method, or someone within the corporate arena becomes aware of the issue, it will not receive appropriate attention at the corporate level. Although we would like to assume that management understands that this type of behavior is inappropriate, we must also understand the tendency to want to handle issues quietly and internally. When organizations maintain diverse business units and operating areas, the leaders of those areas may feel responsible for managing issues internally. They may be under the assumption that managing the expenditures on projects within their realm of responsibility is part of their daily task. It may not occur to them that the inappropriate expenditures occurred due to control breaches or poorly designed processes. In addition, they may fall under the assumption that since the issue was discovered internally, it is up to them to manage and mitigate the issue.

Ultimately, the decision about how these issues are handled will relate to the manner in which the organization delegates authority to its business unit leaders. The point of the scenario is to illustrate how it is possible that issues can occur within the daily performance of responsibilities, which are in essence control issues that should be considered for communication to individuals outside of the business unit.

Challenge 7: Internal Audit versus Quality Assurance

Organizations that are not publically traded entities or that do not have governmental, regulatory, or debt requirements may not require an organized internal audit process. In these situations, the organization may perceive the internal auditors as quality assurance professionals.

Challenge 7 Potential Actions: Internal Audit versus Quality Assurance The CAE must ensure that the organization can distinguish between an internal audit function and a quality assurance function. A CAE who enters a new function and observes actions that may infer a lack of understanding of the variance between quality assurance and internal audit must clarify the variance with management and the audit committee.

Assume that a professional is placed in the CAE role but does not have previous experience with internal audit. However, the professional has a six sigma black belt credential. Both the CAE and the audit committee should carefully evaluate how the aspects of the CAE's experience within quality assurance will translate and be managed within the *Standards*.

The bottom line is—call the function what it is. If it is a quality assurance function, then this is how it should be referred to. If it is an internal audit function, there will be expectations by debt holders, regulators, customers, and shareholders, among others, that the function operates in accordance with guidelines and principles established by the profession.

Section 4: Management Expectations versus *Standards*

Introduction

Does the management and audit committee have a strong understanding of the *Standards* and how they apply to your function? Consider how you might answer the following questions:

- Does the management understand that *Standards* and guidelines exist to guide the work of the profession?
- Is there an understanding of the expectations established by the profession for individuals who reside within an internal audit function?
- Does the management understand the implications of a quality assurance review of internal audit and how the review is conducted?
- Is the management aware that internal auditors are bound by their individual code of ethics and responsibilities?

Let's evaluate specific *Standards* and discuss the challenges that may be faced when working with management to gain acceptance and buy-in of the function. Within our discussion, we will also evaluate alternatives that the CAE and internal audit group can consider when working with management to balance their expectations with the standard requirements.

Management Expectations and the Standards

Within the profession there are two terms utilized when referring to the *Standards*. These terms are defined as follows:

- *Attribute Standards* address the attributes of organizations and individuals performing internal auditing.

- *Performance Standards* describe the nature of internal auditing and provide quality criteria against which the performance of these services can be measured.

It is critical that management have a basic understanding of both categories of *Standards* and their requirements for the profession. For management to accept the *Standards* as value-add, they must understand why the guidelines were developed. Management can gain assurance that the *Standards* were developed to ensure effectiveness and efficiency of the internal audit function.

It is important management understands that the *Standards* are principle-focused, mandatory requirements consisting of:

- Statements of basic requirements for the professional practice of internal auditing and for evaluating the effectiveness of performance, which are internationally applicable at organizational and individual levels
- Interpretations, which clarify terms or concepts within the statements

A key phrase to recognize is the utilization of the term mandatory requirements. This can be one of the greatest challenges that an internal audit must address. It is not unusual that management is unaware that the *Standards* actually exist and that they are considered mandatory requirements for individuals who practice within the profession. Organizations may take the position that the *Standards* are not promulgated by a law-making body, and as such, they are only suggested guidelines. This position contributes to the ability of management to maintain that they alone know what is best for their organization and how the internal audit function should operate. However, for internal audit to operate in accordance with professional *Standards* and guidelines, they must be able to exhibit that they comply with the *Standards* promulgated by the profession. If they do not comply, then the question must be asked as to whether the function is truly an internal audit process or a quality assurance process.

Certified Internal Auditor

Similar to other professions, the IIA has established a certification referred to as the Certified Internal Auditor (CIA). However, as opposed to other professions that issue formal licenses such as lawyers, doctors, or certified public accountants, there is not a license to practice issued for a CIA. This contributes to the difficulty encountered when attempting to exert official independence. Although *Standards* suggest and recommend independence, there is no official licensing body with authority to enforce issues or assess fines and penalties when an organization does not recognize the independence concepts.

Although the *Standards* are strong guidelines for the profession, management may not place the same official blessing on these documents as given to guidance provided by professions that issue licenses controlled by a legislative body. In order for the internal audit function to be able to effectively execute their responsibilities and act in a manner that includes objectivity and independence, they must maintain the ability to relay their observations and judgments to the audit committee without undue bias or pressure from management.

For purposes of analysis, we will focus first on the *Attribute Standards*. In theory, management would need to accept and understand the relevance of the *Attribute Standards* to effectively adhere and comply with the *Performance Standards*.

Challenge 8: Attribute Standards Integrity and Ethical Values

Challenge 5 addressed how the *Attribute Standards* impact the internal audit charter. Let's now evaluate how the same *Standards* impacts the auditor's integrity and ethics.

An important underlying principle for internal auditors is the concept of maintaining integrity in line with the code of ethics and *Standards*. Many organizations include the trait of integrity as one of their core values or principles within their own code of ethics. The trait of integrity can sometimes be taken at face value and not given an adequate level of focus and attention.

One of the 12 principles proposed for consideration when updating the *Standards* includes the concept of maintaining uncompromised integrity. This requires a consistent and agreed-upon definition of integrity. The *Standards* refer to integrity of internal auditors through the *Code of Ethics and Statement of Responsibilities for Internal Auditors*. The current IIA Code of Ethics identifies four separate principles which the auditor must demonstrate in order to properly meet the expectations of the code. Those principles are as follows:

- *Integrity*. The integrity of internal auditors establishes trust and thus provides the basis for reliance on their judgment.
- *Objectivity*. Internal auditors exhibit the highest level of professional objectivity in information about the activity or process being examined.
- *Confidentiality*. Internal auditors respect the value and ownership of information they receive and do not disclose information without appropriate authority unless there is a legal or professional obligation to do so.
- *Competency*. Internal auditors apply the knowledge, skills, and experience needed in the performance of internal audit services.

To gain an understanding of the challenges internal audit and the CAE face, take a step back and further evaluate the literal definition of integrity:

- Integrity is steadfast adherence to a strict moral or ethical code.
- Integrity is the state of being unimpaired; soundness.

In the simplest form, integrity may be thought of as doing the right thing when no one is looking. Further evaluating the definition of integrity professionals can begin to see the inherent challenge that may exist. The definition assumes that the professional will accept the stated morals and beliefs outlined by the organization. Morals and beliefs of professionals may vary significantly. They are impacted by culture, religion, race, sex, and technical knowledge as well as other influences. One professional's view of the proper moral or ethical code may be very different from the manner in which the next person views the issue.

The first citation of the definition of integrity includes steadfast adherence. This presumes that regardless of a person's individual morals and beliefs, he/she will strictly adhere to those outlined within a particular code of conduct. However, as we've mentioned, behaviors can be impacted by personalities and beliefs. This makes the assumption of steadfast adherence difficult to ensure. Let's illustrate this thought process with the following scenario.

Integrity Scenario—Parents work to instill morals and ethical concepts in their children's value systems. You may have observed that siblings who are reared within the same family setting may have very different views on integrity and morality. Although they may be schooled in the same concepts within the family setting, the manner in which they personally internalize and take action on those concepts is impacted by peer pressure, psychological makeup, and their own development of rationalization. In addition, individuals come from different walks of life, cultures, religions, and ethnicities. Chapter 1 discussed how the ethical versus legal line can be very gray. The actual width of the gray line can hinge on any number of variables. The lesson learned is that integrity and respect are closely tied to personal morals and beliefs. It can be very difficult to change or alter a person's morals. This doesn't mean it can't be done. But it does mean that the person should have a very deep and full understanding of the intentions behind the words. If individuals view colleagues or other employees acting in a manner they do not interpret as having integrity, they will rationalize the reasons why the term does not apply to them.

From an internal audit viewpoint, having regular, open, and transparent conversations with personnel and staff regarding the morals and integrity expected when performing the role is critical to setting the right tone for the department. The CAE will face many variances in how professionals, both internal and external to the department, interpret expectations surrounding integrity. From a departmental viewpoint, the CAE must understand cultural, generational, and other dynamics that exist in the department. They must ensure that all professionals have a clear understanding of expectations of behavior. A simple example might relate to a departmental policy directing professionals to avoid speaking about audit issues outside of the audit team. Internal auditors may feel that audit issues are open for discussion with all personnel in the department. Periodically, the auditor may believe it is appropriate to obtain input from other area management on the issue. This is a process that may be acceptable in some circumstances while not being appropriate in others. The auditor must ensure that the inquiry is completed with utmost integrity and respect. If individuals view the discussion of audit issues as an unnecessary form of communication or some type of accusation, the auditor will create significant challenges for the department and the CAE.

Ultimately, the CAE must be able to appropriately communicate and define the concepts related to uncompromised integrity. Those concepts must be well understood within the internal audit department as well as throughout the organization.

Challenge 8 Potential Actions: Attribute Standards Integrity and Ethical Values The succinct statement of uncompromised integrity is one that requires strategic focus and dedicated action. As is often stated with tone at the top, action speaks louder than words. To encourage and enable uncompromised integrity, CAEs must:

- Work to ensure that personnel within the function can exhibit the traits and skills required to demonstrate uncompromised integrity.
- Lead by example and be able to appropriately explain their recommendations when challenged by the management.
- Ensure that management and the board have a complete understanding of the internal audit profession's expectations of uncompromised integrity for executing the role.
- Facilitate and encourage mutual respect and integrity. This applies to that given to management as well as that provided to the internal auditors. Without mutual respect and integrity, any professional will have difficulty adhering to the stated principle of uncompromised integrity.

Challenge 9: Attribute Standards Proficiency and Due Care

The requirement of proficiency and due care provides other unique challenges to the internal auditor. The broad wording applied may leave room for interpretation. Following are the specific attributes related to proficiency and due care:

> Engagements must be performed with proficiency and due care.
>
> **Institute of Internal Auditors Attribute Standards 1200—Proficiency and Due Care**

> Internal auditors must possess the knowledge, skills, and other competencies needed to perform their individual responsibilities. The internal audit activity collectively must possess or obtain the knowledge, skills, and other competencies needed to perform its responsibilities.
>
> **Institute of Internal Auditor Attribute Standards 1210—Proficiency**

> Internal auditors must apply the care and skill expected of a reasonably prudent and competent internal auditor. Due professional care does not imply infallibility.
>
> **Institute of Internal Auditors Attribute Standards 1220—Due Professional Care**

In order for the internal audit department to add value to the organization, they must maintain an adequate level of resources, knowledge, skill, and appropriate internal audit tools. This is where the concept of proficiency and due care becomes important. The ability to fully execute on proficiency and due care would require the CAE to have full authority over the establishment of the internal audit budget as well as the ability to recommend and pursue additional resources or staffing. In some instances, the CAE may not have the final word when it comes to setting the internal audit budget or appropriate resourcing. This can impact the department's ability to execute on proficiency and due care.

One of the twelve principles identified by the IIA as qualities needed of the internal auditor is cited as principle 3, commitment to competence. In order to be able to effectively comply with proficiency and due care, auditors must maintain a commitment to competence within their functions. If a CAE does not have ultimate authority over their own internal budget, they can be significantly hampered in their ability to manage commitment to competence. Although the standards suggest that the audit committee has input to the internal audit budget and overall resourcing, in reality, this is often an issue that can be referred to as form over substance. Large organizations utilize complicated and detailed methods when developing annual budgets. Process areas are often given departmental targets related to future year budget expenditures. These targets can be based on previous year expenditures combined with corporate projections for future year revenues. In addition, depending on the CAE's organizational positioning, their departmental budget may play a role into a larger business unit budget that is controlled at a higher level of the organization. Essentially, these factors can contribute to constraints on the ability for the CAE to attract and retain top talent and to expand the function to meet objectives as outlined within the *Standards.* Inevitably, this will impact the internal audit groups' ability to maintain a dedicated commitment to competence.

Some professionals view the principle of commitment to competence as one where individuals have the proper credentials for the role. In other situations, commitment to competence extends to ongoing learning and training of organizational professionals. Many organizations experience challenges in this area especially in times of economic constraints or resource limits.

Commitment to competence for internal audit must extend to both concepts. The proper credentials, skill, and background are certainly important attributes for the internal audit professional. However, the importance of ongoing education and learning cannot be understated. These principles all impact proficiency and due care of the function. The profession of internal audit continues to evolve. Auditors must maintain knowledge of internal audit standards, new and emerging audit evaluation techniques, and ongoing changes that may occur in the business economy or in their individual industries.

Challenge 9 Potential Actions: Attribute Standard Proficiency and Due Care Commitment to competence is a significant aspect of the proficiency and due care standard. Actions the CAE can take to enhance this trait include the following:

- *Work to ensure consistency within the function and enable professionals to maintain certain competencies and qualifications that provide full value to the organization in the performance of internal audit responsibilities.* This concept extends beyond simple certification criteria such as the certified public accountancy, certified internal auditor, certified information systems auditor, or other credentials. Personnel must be able to obtain relevant and timely continuing professional education for more than just the purpose of maintaining their certification. Continuing professional education extends to the concept of commitment to competence.
- *If the CAE does not have ultimate control over the departmental budget they must speak to management regarding the implications.* The inability for the CAE to manage his/her departmental resources and budget may place restraints on the ability to uphold the principle of commitment to competence.
- *Take time to evaluate the particular educational needs of your staff.* Tailor professional training to assist the auditor in advancing their skill set and knowledge in a way that will benefit both the individual and the organization.

The other aspect of proficiency and due care pertains to organizational authority. Appropriate organizational positioning speaks to the ongoing challenge internal auditors face in asserting independence and objectivity. Adequate independence is required to enable unrestricted evaluation of organizational process activities. Actions that the CAE can take include the following:

- *The CAE must periodically speak to senior management and the audit committee regarding the positioning of the internal audit department within the organizational structure.* This topic should not be left to annual reviews or yearly charter updates.
- *If organizational positioning impacts the effectiveness of internal audit, the CAE must address the issue with management.* Organizational positioning is often a critical element to the effectiveness of internal audit. The CAE must be able to transparently and openly speak to management about how organizational positioning impacts effectiveness of work.

Challenge 10: Attribute Standards Quality Assurance and Improvement

The final *Attribute Standard* relates to quality assurance and improvement programs. The IIA has established procedures for expectations for quality assurance reviews. Quality assurance reviews of internal audit are meant to provide management and organizations further assurance of the efficiency and effectiveness of their internal audit groups. *Standards* state that external assessments should be conducted at least once every five years by a qualified, independent reviewer or review team from outside the organization. Organizations that undergo the recommended quality assurance reviews must ensure they apply appropriate procedures when addressing any identified performance issues. The *Standard* related to quality assurance states:

> The chief audit executive must develop and maintain a quality assurance and improvement program that covers all aspects of the internal audit activity.
>
> **Institute of Internal Auditor Standards 1300**

Challenge 10 Potential Actions: Attribute Standards Quality Assurance and Improvement Has your organization undergone an external quality assurance review? Do you maintain an effective internal quality assurance process for your department? There are no reliable current statistics to reference when determining whether organizations are applying this standard. From a corporate perspective, the reality is that organizations may see the review as a costly procedure that may or may not provide relevant value to the company. If the organization is not required to maintain an internal audit department, they may not view the requirement as one that is relevant. In addition, for small internal audit groups, the exercise of performing an external quality assurance review may not be pertinent based on the manner in which the function operates. The challenges faced by internal auditors to adequately meet the *Standards* can be further complicated when attempting to abide by and execute on guidelines. If the internal audit function experiences difficulty with aligning their processes to the *Attribute Standards*, they will face an even steeper hill to climb when attempting to abide by the *Performance*

Standards. Actions that the CAE should consider include the following:

- *Ensure the organization understands the true value of a quality assurance review*. The CAE must appropriately communicate with management and the audit committee the intentions of the review and the potential benefits to the organization.
- *Provide information and benchmarks on the benefits of a quality assurance review*. The CAE should provide to management leading practice statistics regarding the benefits that can be found by undergoing a quality assurance review.
- *Develop a plan to remediate findings that are identified in a quality assurance review*. When undergoing a quality assurance review process, the CAE should ensure they have an effective plan in place to timely remediate any findings that are presented.
- *Consider performing an internal quality assessment*. The CAE should evaluate the potential to perform an internal quality assessment review that will allow the department to evaluate potential gaps that may exist within their processes and proactively address those gaps prior to an external quality assessment.

Next, we will dissect the major areas of the *Performance Standards* and evaluate the various challenges that may be faced when attempting to abide by these standards.

Section 5: *Performance Standards*

Introduction

Performance Standards speak to the requirements for managing the internal audit function. The specific *Standard* states:

> The chief audit executive must effectively manage the internal audit activity to ensure it adds value to the organization.
>
> **Institute of Internal Auditors Performance Standards 2000**

Evaluation of the *Performance Standards* at face value may demonstrate how management perceives the job of the CAE. Because the standard states "to ensure it adds value to the organization," management may take the position that the CAE must manage the function to the extent management believes it adds value to the organization. However, closer examination indicates that the CAE is responsible for much more than the concise wording that the *Standards* may indicate.

Challenge 11: Performance Standard 2000

The *Standards* cite details about the expectations of the CAE when managing the internal audit function. These include:

- Requirements for establishing a risk-based audit plan
- Communication of the plan, department resource management
- Establishment of internal policies and procedures
- Coordination of efforts with other functional groups
- Reporting to senior management and the board

CAEs can face significant challenges when attempting to align management expectations with those outlined in the *Performance Standards*. Consider the following scenario.

Scenario: Jitterbug Company Jitterbug Company is a family-owned clothing manufacturer experiencing exponential growth. The company just completed an initial public offering and is in the early stage of establishing an internal audit function to ensure that they meet Securities and Exchange Commission (SEC) expectations. Organization management is composed primarily of family personnel who have come up through the business. The company executives and managers have no experience with internal auditors. However, because of debt requirements, the company has been required to have external audits and as such is familiar with the external audit process.

Jitterbug Company requests advice from their external auditors on the procedures required to set up an internal audit function. Their external audit firm is a small regional firm whose business typically deals with smaller organizations that do not have an internal audit function. In order to provide management guidance in this area, the external auditors obtain copies of the internal audit standards and provide generic suggestions on how the function should be organized. For reference on how the activity should operate, management is referred to the following *Performance Standards*:

- *Standard 2000*—Managing the Internal Audit Activity
- *Standard 2100*—Nature of Work
- *Standard 2200*—Engagement Planning
- *Standard 2300*—Performing the Engagement

Management meets with their newly appointed audit committee and reviews the *Standards*. After review and discussion, management arrives at the following recommendations for the planned internal audit function:

- The company will hire a head of internal audit who will report administratively to the CFO and functionally to the audit committee.
- Management interprets the *Performance Standard* requiring "internal audit to provide value to the organization" as an area where the organization has full control over the scope of how the function will be established. Management decides that the function will focus 80% on Sarbanes–Oxley work and the other 20% on operational audits deemed relevant by management.
- Management interprets standards 2100, 2200, and 2300 as a typical processes that any department would need to abide by. They decide that the newly hired internal audit director will be responsible for developing departmental procedures.

The actions taken by Jitterbug Company on the surface appear reasonable in light of their current business situation. The challenge will come into play when the head of internal audit is hired and begins to attempt to execute on his/her responsibilities. Since the company has not had previous experience with an internal audit function, it will be incumbent on the new internal audit leader to establish the proper control environment and tone to ensure that management understands the full scope and expectations of the function. Jitterbug Company may be able to employ some of the following listed potential actions identified in our Challenge 11.

Challenge 11 Potential Actions: Performance Standard 2000 We will use the outlined scenario to identify potential actions that the CAE may take to resolve challenges with this *Standard*. These include the following:

- *Clarify the purpose and meaning of the Attribute and Performance Standards.* The following are specific clarifications the CAE may wish to address:
  - Work with management to provide education on the expectations of *Standards* of the profession.
  - Focus on the concepts of objectivity and independence as well as the interpretation of how the function should or could add value to the organization.
  - Present management and the audit committee with facts surrounding the evolution of the internal audit profession after the Sarbanes–Oxley years.
  - Address with management the expectations of spending 80% of audit resources on Sarbanes–Oxley work. Although in the initial years of the function, this may be a critical component of how the function should operate, if the CAE hopes to evolve the function, management must understand the full scope of possibilities for internal audit work.
  - Discuss with management and the audit committee the concepts of providing risk management, governance, and consulting assurance work.
- *Establish the proper tone for the function with management and the audit committee.* The Jitterbug scenario indicated that the organization had no previous experience with internal audit. In addition, they were previously closely managed through family connections. Most likely, there is a strong established culture within the organization tied to relationships built by the management structure. The CAE will come into the organization as a new infusion into the culture. Following are some considerations the CAE may wish to address:

- Look for ways to address the importance of independence and objectivity as well as authority and accountability for the new function.
- Communicate to management the importance of transparency and open discussion with the audit committee.
- Affirmatively address the issues of the *Standards* and the requirements of independence and objectivity. This is needed to establish a solid basis for the future of the internal audit function. Depending on the CAE's organizational positioning and authority, the act of exerting independence may be difficult. These challenges are very real and should be proactively addressed with management and the audit committee. The ability to successfully address these items will require the CAE to gain buy-in and respect from the management structure and the audit committee.

- *Position the internal audit function for success.* A new internal audit function is always a challenge to develop. Following are considerations for positioning internal audit for success:
  - Understand and evaluate the organization's past and evolving culture. This may assist in proactively identifying any perceptual challenges that may exist when establishing the function.
  - The CAE must understand the expectations of management and the board and be prepared to reconcile those expectations to the *Standards*.
  - Understand any regulatory requirements that may be placed on the company based on its industry or business model. The CAE will need to understand any exposures that internal audit reports may have to external regulatory agencies.

Understanding these aspects of the organization and then establishing a path to enable effective implementation of the *Standards* will be strategically important to how well the *Standards* are accepted and embraced.

Section 6: *Standards* and Report Writing

Introduction

The duty of formal reporting is one of the basic responsibilities of internal audit. Reporting protocols are executed in many different ways. Some utilize formal report templates that are structured based on risk. Other functions may utilize a memo format that is focused on individual audit findings. Still, other functions may utilize reports that outline issues and allow for management response to control gaps.

The *Standards* do not specify the exact manner in which the results of engagements must be communicated. This chapter will discuss challenge 12 as it relates communicating results.

Challenge 12: Performance Standard 2400 Communicating Results

The *Standard* for communicating audit results is also a guideline that has broad implications.

> Internal auditors must communicate the results of engagements.
>
> **Institute of Internal Auditors Performance Standards 2400**

The purpose of the *Standard* is to provide enough flexibility to be able to adequately meet organization needs. However, the *Standards* do provide guidelines for information that should be included within the formal communication. Subsections of *Performance Standard 2400* outline specific aspects that should be included within the communications including the engagement's objectives and scope as well as applicable conclusions, recommendations, and action plans. In addition, *Performance Standard 2410.A1* indicates:

> Final communication of engagement results must, where appropriate, contain the internal auditors' opinion and/or conclusions. When issued, an opinion or conclusion must take account of the expectations of senior management, the board, and other stakeholders and must be supported by sufficient, reliable, relevant, and useful information.
>
> **Institute of Internal Auditors Performance Standards 2410.A1**

The specifics outlined within *Standard 2410.A1* are an area that can be of greatest challenge or contention with management. Many internal audit departments do not provide an opinion or conclusion to their internal audit reports. The reality is that operational management may inherently have difficulty with formal opinions issued by internal audit. They may correlate this concept to a formal external audit opinion of the financial statements.

Internal audit departments who attempt to issue formal opinions may find this protocol will lengthen their report issuance time. Although in theory, internal audit should be able to independently issue reports, most groups work with management to gain acceptance to issues and work toward management's agreed to solutions. The assignment of an audit report ranking can create significant contention on issues and their relative significance.

Challenge 12 Potential Actions: Performance Standard 2400 Communicating Results With the many challenges that can arise when attempting to abide by *Professional Standard 2400*, there are many actions the CAE may want to consider to address the challenges.

CAEs must carefully consider their process for assigning overall opinions or report rankings to audit reports. If this is considered an approach the internal audit function will take, internal audit management should establish strong protocols and procedures to ensure that the ranking and reporting process is effective. These may include the following:

- *Establish a clear outline of the categories of rankings and related definitions for each rank.* Audit groups that use concepts such as "acceptable," "unacceptable," "pass," "fail," or other generic terms without describing those classification and the manner in which they impact the organization will create issues with management. There must be a clear definition of each category with clear evidence of how the ranking is measured.
- *Predetermine the input management will have on assessing the overall report ranking.* The CAE must consider whether management pressure can influence a ranking.

- *Avoid defining rankings that are so disparate that reports end up being primarily classified as neutral.* This can infer that the audit process is not effective.

If an audit report is classified as unacceptable or high risk, ensure internal audit can explain the impact to the organization. The highest measurement should not be at an extreme that would mean a material issue has been found. Generally, internal audit should identify issues before they reach that level. However, when taking this approach, the CAE must ensure management understands the implications of a high-risk ranking. In other words, can a qualitative or quantitative impact be assigned based on the ranking? More information on report rankings will be covered in Chapter 6.

Section 7: Realities of Embracing Risk-Based Auditing

Introduction

A basic underlying theory of risk-based auditing is to align the audit with the objectives, risks, and goals of the enterprise. If the internal audit group is to provide true value to the organization, they must focus on those risks that could prevent the organization from meeting their overall goals. The fifth principle identified by the IIA as a required principle for internal auditors is to "align strategically with the aims and goals of the enterprise." This section will begin to discuss Challenge 13 related to risk-based auditing. Further information on risk-based auditing will be covered in Chapter 5.

Challenge 13: Risk-Based Auditing

In considering the principle relating to alignment with the goals of the enterprise, the internal audit group should evaluate their ability to execute and perform complete risk-based auditing. The question that must first be discussed is the definition of what is considered risk-based auditing and how it should be applied within an organization.

Professionals have varying definitions for the term risk-based auditing and the various processes and procedures that should be included within the scope of the definition. Typically, most individuals will agree that risk-based auditing is a style of auditing that focuses upon the analysis and management of those risks that are most significant to the organization. A risk-based approach would attempt to review those risks that may prevent the organization from achieving its objectives. It would seek to identify the greatest potential impact risks and focus review or analysis in that area. We will discuss the challenges embedded in the various phases of risk-based auditing in Chapter 5. In this section, we will further elaborate on the concept of how management views risk-based auditing versus how it may be defined by internal audit as initially discussed in Lesson 4, Chapter 1.

Challenge 13 Potential Actions: Risk-Based Auditing To properly facilitate an effective risk-based audit function, management and internal audit must have the same theories on the definition of risk-based auditing. The following are considerations for addressing this challenge:

- *Internal audit and the organization must have a common understanding of the concepts of risk-based auditing and how it will impact the organization.* A company that views internal audit as a pure compliance or operational function may take the approach that the auditors are present to perform Sarbanes–Oxley compliance testing or potential operational validation of inventory or asset processes. Although these areas are within the scope of internal audit, management and the audit committee must understand the basic concepts surrounding the broader concept of risk-based auditing and determine whether their function will embrace that concept.
- *Determine the impact of risk-based auditing on departmental resourcing.* If the function chooses to exercise a complete view of risk-based auditing as well as assurance and compliance work, the resourcing and audit plan will be dramatically different than a function that chooses to direct their efforts toward an isolated or specific purpose. In the end, the decision to embrace risk-based auditing will impact internal audit resourcing as well as the audit plan.
- *Define the required skill set for internal auditors.* In order to align work with organization goals, internal audit must have the experience and skills to provide the broad-based definition

of internal audit including financial, compliance, operational, consulting, and assurance activities.

- *Understand the organization's goals.* If the internal audit group is to execute on complete risk-based auditing, a strong insight to the goals of the organization is required. That understanding can be obtained in a multitude of ways:
  - If the CAE holds a seat at the table, this seat will provide internal audit with insight into strategy concepts and discussions of the organization. Without having a seat at the table, internal audit will need to search for other methods to obtain strategic insight.
  - Companies that maintain an enterprise risk management process may have strategic insight into organizational goals and strategies. In these circumstances, it would be important for internal auditors to maintain a connection and understanding of the enterprise risk management process. This alignment and connection can help ensure that the risks identified in the audit plan also address the risks that the organization may view as a threat to their strategic objectives.

Often, internal audit groups who are not fully supported in their attempts to execute complete risk-based auditing find that management contends that "internal auditors do not fully comprehend our business," or "internal auditors are not qualified to audit strategy." Very few audit departments actually audit the strategy of their company. As such, the following considerations may assist in meeting this challenge:

- *The CAE and the internal audit group must understand the company's short- and long-term strategy and objectives.* Having knowledge of this piece of the puzzle will allow the CAE to properly prioritize risks and issues as they are identified.
- *Determine how internal audit can obtain relevant information that allows them to fulfill the principle of strategic alignment to the goals of the organization.* The concept of the CAE obtaining a seat at the table will be further discussed later. However, recognizing that CAEs who have a direct reporting line to

the CEO are in the minority, the internal audit group must identify other unique and innovative methods to be able to obtain the knowledge of organization strategies and emerging risks and goals.

Section 8: Internal Audit as Governance Pillar

Introduction

A portion of the definition of internal audit addresses the responsibility for involvement in the governance component of the organization. As previously discussed governance principles are often those that are managed by compliance or legal individuals. In the abstract context, governance is a theoretical concept. It refers to the actions taken to oversee how procedures and processes are applied as well as the processes of decision making among the individuals involved in solving a particular problem or issue. This section will cover challenge 14 related to internal audit's role in governance. Additional information about governance-related concepts will be covered in Chapter 5.

Challenge 14: Internal Audit's Role in Governance

Since governance processes have typically been considered those which reside at a different level in the organization, management may question what role internal audit should play in these processes.

The graphic in Exhibit 2.1 depicts internal audit as one of the outside pillars that help support the overall structure for the organization. The illustration depicts that internal audit is an important pillar to support the structure and framework of the organization. Utilizing this graphic can help provide the proper reference to management when explaining internal audit's role in governance processes.

Challenge 14 Potential Actions: Internal Audit's Role in Governance One of internal audit's purposes is to provide advice and oversight to the board of directors. This responsibility provides the relevant support for the importance of internal audit's involvement in governance

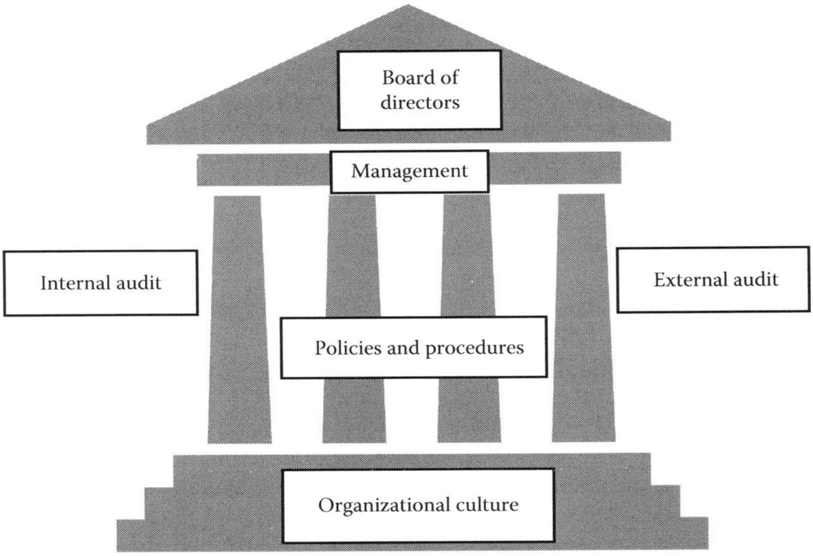

Exhibit 2.1 Governance structure.

processes. The CAE can address challenges to meeting this *Standard* by considering the following:

- *Outline the primary focus for internal audit in governance activity.* Since internal audit has not traditionally played a strong role in this area, management inherently may resist the inclusion of internal audit within the process. Outlining the primary focus for internal audit may assist in paving a road toward inclusion in this critical area. When management understands the responsibilities of internal audit as defined by the profession related to governance work, they may be more open to accepting observations in this area.
- *Outline the role internal audit can take in risk management processes and how this applies to the overall objective of governance.* Management should understand how internal audit applies the concept of risk management within audit methodology and how being an active participant in various risk management processes can contribute to a strong overall governance program.
- *Outline the role internal audit can take in preventing, detecting and deterring fraud.* This responsibility may be viewed in varying ways within organizations. However, one of the responsibilities

of internal audit is to ensure they assess the risk of fraud within the audit process. Ensuring management understand the *Standards* auditors are held to regarding fraud may assist in adding this attribute to the overall governance framework.

- *Outline how internal audit can provide valued input into the creation of the audit committee agenda.* The development of the audit committee agenda is often handled through the CFO or the legal officer in conjunction with the audit committee. However, *Standards* indicate that the CAE should provide input into the audit committee agenda. Discuss this concept with management and provide insight into how this responsibility can be a positive enhancement to the company's governance program.

Summary

Each organization's perspective regarding internal audit's role in governance will vary and may hinge on industry, culture, organizational maturity, past experience, and a multitude of other variables. Internal auditor's capabilities are evolving and maturing. CAEs must be able to provide management and the board with appropriate guidance regarding the proper role for internal audit within a company's governance structure. In addition, they must ensure that the guidance provided can be adequately executed.

Focus on aspects of governance work that will provide ultimate value. From a profession viewpoint, governance work may include reporting critical management control issues, suggesting questions or topics for the audit committee's meeting agendas, and coordinating with the external auditor and management to ensure that the committee receives effective information. However, some of these roles may be areas in which management or the organization is not prepared to accept assistance. An example may be the process of suggesting topics for audit committee agendas. Compiling of audit committee agendas is often managed by the CEO, CFO, and the audit committee chair. Some internal audit groups are able to provide suggestions or input to the agenda. However, in many instances, internal audit is not considered as a source for information topics. The CAE must have an understanding of how the organization sees the various governance roles related to the board. There may be a time when the internal audit group can provide valued input into the audit committee agenda; however, the CAE must understand the avenues to reach that point. Establishing a strong relationship with the audit committee, management, and the external auditors may be the first step in gaining the respect and trust that would be considered important in various elements of governance.

Consider internal audit's role in enterprise risk management, ethics, fraud, and board oversight. In recent years, the IIA has advocated more formal evaluation of corporate governance particularly in the areas of board oversight of enterprise risk, corporate ethics, and fraud. An organization's maturity, tone, and culture regarding risk management, ethics, and fraud will often dictate the level of involvement acceptable for internal audit. The CAE must be able to appropriately evaluate each of these areas, identify the required skill sets and capabilities needed to provide relevant input, and provide management and the audit committee with transparent communication about the potential role for internal audit.

3

Building an Internal Audit Team

Introduction

In today's advanced and dynamic business culture, internal auditors possess a wide variety of technical backgrounds that extend from accounting, finance, operations, engineering, and legal. The nature of the organization, its business strategy and focus will dictate the specific skills and attributes that are most beneficial for the internal auditor in each organization. When internal audit efforts are focused on operational processes, organizations may find that individuals with operational or technical backgrounds are the most effective personnel. Organizations that focus on financial processes may require accounting or financial expertise for the audit team. Regardless of an individual auditor's specific skill set, the concept of building an effective team is a critical element for building an effective internal audit organization. Having individual skilled professionals with strong technical abilities is important when determining staffing needs, but CAEs must not overlook the importance of creating a culture of teamwork. An atmosphere where each professional works to contribute to an overall goal for the organization can provide greater value than a group of highly skilled workers who do not understand the concept of working cohesively toward a goal. This chapter will cover the following challenges within each of the indicated sections:

- Challenge 15: Internal Audit Team Structure
- Challenge 16: Department Sourcing Methods
- Challenge 17: Resourcing to Address Significant Risks
- Challenge 18: Defining the Required Skill Set for Internal Auditors

- Challenge 19: Internal Audit as a Management Training Ground
- Challenge 20: Outsourcing
- Challenge 21: Co-Sourcing
- Challenge 22: In-Sourcing
- Challenge 23: Maintaining Appropriate Skill Sets

Team First and the Leader Within

One of the most important teaming lessons I learned came from watching my 18-year-old high school senior in his defining moments as a varsity football player.

In the fall of 2012, his football team was expected to be a strong contender for the state playoffs. His class had many natural-born athletes who provided the team with a strong competitive advantage. The coaches recognized the talent of this group early on and envisioned the potential for these boys to excel as a team. They strategized methods to instill the concept of "team" and discourage an atmosphere of individual accomplishments (not everyone could be on the starting squad). The alternative was having strong individually skilled players working toward their own goals rather than those of the team. From the start of football camp in July to the end of the playoff season in November, everything became focused around the team. The boys were like a band of brothers. They did everything together from eating meals to watching game films, lifting weights, and even a trick-or-treat outing at Halloween. The team-building process paid off exponentially.

The team entered the 2012–2013 football season with 33 seniors on the varsity squad. In the first game of the season, several of the natural-born athletes were injured. Thanks to the team concept, other players stepped up to the plate to fill the void. The boys continued to focus on the team goal and not on their own individual aspirations. As my son and other less skilled players were put into unfamiliar positions, they would rely on those natural athletes (leaders) on the sideline to provide buddy coaching during the game. Over the course of the season, the backups as well as the natural leaders put their pride aside for the betterment of the team. The goal was to keep the team competitive until the first-team players could rejoin the squad during playoff time. What was surprising was the maturity and development of the backup athletes.

A specific demonstration of teamwork occurred in a high-profile rivalry game. Our team was set to kick the winning field goal, a mere chip shot for our kicker. Unfortunately, the kick was blocked, and the team lost in the final seconds. The emotion of the loss was overwhelming. The kicker remained on the field in despair. All of a sudden, one of his teammates ran from the sidelines, grabbed his buddy, and walked him to the sideline while speaking words of encouragement. What a remarkable team gesture. This player put his emotions aside and ran to support his friend. It wasn't until the boys reached the sideline that I noticed the number of the player who helped the kicker; it was my son. What struck me was the ability of my son to seize a moment in time and display the team philosophy. His actions in that moment displayed the ability of a young athlete coached in the team concept rise to the occasion and become a leader for his friend.

At playoff time, the coaches faced a new dilemma. The backups had proved their worth and matured much quicker than many anticipated. The issue became, do you bench a player who has excelled on the field for the natural-born athlete who was ready to return to the lineup? The lesson here was how these 18-year-old boys put their individuality aside and bonded as a team. You don't have to be a natural-born leader to do that. But you do need to have a passion for a goal, a desire to put others in front of yourself, an attitude of team and the desire, and ability to take action even in the face of adversity. In today's world filled with competitive edge, maybe we need a few more team players to help our leaders point us in the right direction.

So what does football have to do with internal audit? I relay the scenario to demonstrate the undeniable power of culture and team. Effective teaming requires the right setting, culture, openness, and recognition of cultural makeup and talent and of course departmental leadership. As a CAE or an internal audit manager, you may have a staff of top-rated stars, or you may have a mixed staff of individuals with strong technical skills and others with strong soft skills. Your challenge is to bring those individual traits together to form the proper team components that will assist your function in achieving their overall goal.

Individuals who have been in an organization that has merged or been acquired by another company may have experienced a similar situation when working with the team concept. In the early stages of an organizational merger, there is a period of time where the culture is referred to as Company A and Company B. It takes work and effort to combine the cultures and form an effective team atmosphere. Managers and leaders who have worked through these situations can attest to the importance of team building and forming a cohesive organization. This example points to the importance of culture and departmental tone.

Section 1: Internal Audit Resourcing, Staffing, and Building a Team

Challenge 15: Internal Audit Team Structure

Each internal audit function will define the departmental structure that best meets company needs. The structure may hinge on how the function is sourced and the expertise of the individuals within the function. Structures have been impacted in recent years by the influx of professionals with varying technical backgrounds. In addition, the heightened attention to compliance and financial areas has resulted in the need for additional supervision and oversight of areas such as those with a dedicated focus on Sarbanes–Oxley compliance. In the years prior to Sarbanes–Oxley, advancement through the internal audit function may have depended on time spent within the function and specific technical capabilities and roles. However, this model has dramatically changed and is often dependent upon the skill or trait most valued by the individual organization.

A report released by the IIA in March 2014 indicated that a growing number of new CAEs are recruited from outside the internal audit profession. This is occurring as organizations look for diversity of business skills (The Institute of Internal Auditors Audit Executive Center; Pulse of the Profession survey released March 24, 2014). The survey showed that 42% of CAEs in North America held positions outside of internal audit immediately prior to becoming a CAE. The survey acknowledged the trend provided a new energy and perspective along with deep business knowledge for the CAE role. However, the opposite spectrum was the rotated CAEs lacked internal audit experience and in many instances knowledge of the *Standards*.

The infusion of CAEs from outside of the profession raises concern regarding adequate understanding, knowledge, and application of the *Standards*. Typically, individuals who rotate into internal audit from outside of the profession do not have a strong understanding or appreciation of the *Standards* prior to accepting the position. This can create challenges once they become familiar with the requirements and expectations especially those associated with independence and objectivity.

Although there are wide variety of titles for job levels within, typically, organizations define the ranks of their internal audit team in several categories:

- *Staff auditor*. These individuals typically have the basic skills required to review organizational procedures, processes, and operations. Their responsibilities may entail performing interviews, detailed testing, analyzing and documenting information, and performing compliance and operational reviews under the direction of another staff member. Staff auditors can have a variety of backgrounds and skill sets extending from financial to operational, compliance, and legal.
- *Senior auditor*. These individuals will have some level of business experience. They will be tasked with leading the performance of audits and supervising staff as well as planning and coordinating audit work. Senior auditors may also have a variety of backgrounds similar to those of staff auditors.
- *Supervisors or managers*. These individuals are more experienced in the discipline of internal auditing and should be familiar with the *Standards*. They will be responsible for supervising or managing individual team members as well as audits. They may also have responsibilities that extend to maintaining relationships with senior-level management of the organization. These roles continue the trend of having varied backgrounds. In addition, they will have some exposure and experience in managing professionals.
- *Director or CAE*. This person is tasked with the oversight and execution of the internal audit function. They are responsible for the development and execution of the audit plan as well as communication with senior leaders and the audit committee. This individual should have management experience, a strong understanding of the *Standards*, and high ethical values. Years ago, this position was one that many organizations felt required a certified public accountancy credential. In today's

business, the CAE may possess a multitude of credentials including certified public accountant (CPA), certified internal auditor (CIA), certified fraud examiner (CFE), chartered global management accountant (CGMA), certificate in risk management assurance (CRMA), certified information systems auditor (CISA), among others.

Although the listed certifications are some of those most frequently held by CAEs, there is also an increasing trend of CAEs who are being placed within the role from outside of these certifications. These individuals may possess credentials such as total quality management or six sigma certifications. With the increase in quality assurance specialists entering the CAE role, it is important for management, CAEs, and audit committees to understand the variances in how quality improvement functions may operate versus internal audit. We discussed a segment of this phenomenon in Chapter 2. These variances can result in different staffing needs and requirements. Let's consider a specific scenario.

Scenario: ABS Company ABS Company is a privately owned organization operating in the United States and internationally. Company revenues are $14 billion with an employee base of over 7000. Over the past 10 years, management has attempted to establish an internal audit function but has struggled with a model that best meets organization objectives. The organization has experienced significant turnover within the internal audit function as well as within the CAE role.

Management views the role of internal audit as one that primarily supports the external audit. Internal auditors have typically experienced significant management pressure when attempting to execute financial or operational reviews. Past CAEs have experienced significant challenge when attempting to execute upon independence and objectivity. The CAE's reporting line has been directed to the CFO. Each CAE who has held the role over the years has been informed that it is not acceptable to speak to the audit committee without permission of the CFO.

The company has hired its sixth CAE in the last 8 years. The new CAE is informed by the CFO that there is an expectation is to raise the standards of the internal audit function. He is directed by the

CFO to implement a risk-based focus for internal audit. However, he is informed there are specific elements that will not change including the following:

- The function will continue to dedicate 40% of their time to the external audit.
- The CAE is not allowed to issue reports independently. CFO approval must be obtained before releasing reports.
- The CAE is not allowed to speak to the audit committee without approval of the CFO and CEO.
- The CAE has no control over the departmental budget. His budget is managed by the CFO.
- No changes are allowed to the audit plan unless approved by the CFO. Certain process within the company areas are considered off limits for audit consideration.

After a few months, the CAE leaves the company due to difficulties he has encountered with independence and objectivity. Upon his departure the company decides to place a long-time internal operational manager in the CAE role. This manager has process improvement background but no internal audit experience. The new CAE choses to manage the function similar to a quality assurance function. Is this the proper action given the circumstances?

When analyzing this scenario, consider the various factors outlined. The company has experienced past difficulty when placing individuals within the CAE role who have background in internal audit an understanding the *Standards*. The new CAE has the advantage of being considered a long-time insider who understand the operations of the company. Since the company has no requirements to maintain an internal function, it is within the purview of management to dictate how the function will operate. The previous turnover trend could be contributed to the company's attempt to hire individuals who have an understanding and dedication to the *Standards*. This focus may not be in line with management expectations.

The scenario as described presents many challenges that may be viewed as presenting a lack of independence and objectivity. These include functional reporting line, inability to independently issue reports, lack of communication with the audit committee, lack of authority over the departmental budget, and lack of authority over the annual audit plan. The company's decision to place an operational individual into the CAE role may be the most effective step for their organizational objectives. However, management and the audit committee should recognize this action is a departure from internal auditing *Standards*. Unless the department is operating with full independence and in line with *Standards*, it should not be labeled as an internal audit function.

In addition, the company must consider how it is representing the existence of their internal audit function to outside parties (e.g., debt holders, creditors, customers). If the new CAE operates the function as a quality improvement group, there are certain aspects of conducting work that may not be in line with the *Standards*. If this is the case, the company should consider representing the function as a quality assurance group rather than an internal audit function.

Challenge 15 Potential Actions: Internal Audit Team Structure Internal audit management must take into consideration many factors when building a team and aligning it with the organization's expectations and objectives. The act of building a team is much like constructing a building. It doesn't happen overnight. The right infrastructure and framework must be in place to ensure that the team (building) is sound. Compare the task to the scenario I relayed about building a football team. The act went far beyond identifying skilled players. It took cohesion, dedication, care, understanding, and great leadership. As you build your audit team, or work to restructure the team, keep in mind the following concepts:

- *Teams need a strong leader who can pave the way.* The word leadership, when associated with the concept of team, can be anything from a sports team captain to a work team leader. In the case of a sports team captain, the term is often associated with the most talented or inspirational team member. In the case of work team leader, the term may refer to a person who has achieved a skill or personal leadership level. There are many articles and studies on the concept of leadership. What makes a good leader? A bad leader? A toxic leader? An energetic leader? A charismatic leader? You may have your own experiences on being a leader and seeing the leadership process at work. Leadership involves an abundance of traits and skills that are meshed together in a manner that inspires and excites other team members. The CAE is the team leader for internal audit. Their tone, work ethic, integrity, ability to care for the team, and overall support and attitude toward the process will impact the effectiveness of the team. CAEs as team leaders must first understand and support the *Standards* of the internal audit profession. They must then find ways to instill that knowledge and support through to management and the audit committee.

- *Teams require an established goal to know when they've reached the finish line.* If a football team didn't know where the goal line was, points would never be scored. Many internal audit groups lack a strong vision of the goal line. There is a big difference between third down and 1 yard to go versus third down and 20 yards to go. Internal audit teams must know their ultimate goal and understand the path to reach that goal. Teams who are continually being questioned regarding not just their audit plan, but also, their audit methods will ultimately begin to question themselves. This creates a poor atmosphere and—one that does not inspire members to give their all. The team goal should be more than simply completing the audit plan. The CAE should work with their team to set a departmental mission statement and goal. Ensure that the mission statement isn't so broad sweeping that its intent is difficult to understand. For instance, a mission statement that indicates the department will provide ultimate value to the organization does not guide the team members on how that ultimate value will be reached.
- *Teams must follow the rules of the game.* Rules provide a sense of order to a process. In sports, we understand that when rules are broken, there are penalties to pay. In life, when rules (or laws) aren't followed, there are consequences. Teams must have rules to ensure that all members understand the path to the goal. Rules allow teams to refrain from wandering too far from the path. Take an example of establishing a rule regarding audit project hours. Assume that your department has a rule that indicates that once the team has expended 20% of the budgeted project hours, they must revisit the plan to

ensure they can complete the scope of the project within the budgeted hours. Any requirement for additional project hours must be approved by the CAE. This rule is to maintain a sense of order around project hours and keep the team from wandering too far from the path. Another rule may be that all work papers must be reviewed by a supervisor prior to final issuance of a report. This rule is to ensure findings relayed in the written report are appropriately documented and supported. All teams need rules. The CAE must ensure relevant rules are identified that are important to maintaining a disciplined audit methodology. This will provide ultimate value to your organization.

- *Teams need a fan base.* Where would our pro football teams be if they couldn't fill those 80,000 seat stadiums on Sundays? The point is, even an internal audit team needs to have the proper support through a fan base or auditees who believe in the process. The ability to establish strong relationships with strategic personnel within the organization (both senior level and business level) can be critical to how well your team will function.
- *Team players must be skilled with an attitude of putting the team first.* We've reviewed the concept of having a group of individually skilled players and the need to be able to form that group into a strong team with one goal. If you are a CAE who has experienced difficulties with team dynamics, take a close look at the individual team players. Understand the variances in personalities, gender, age, and moral and personal beliefs. It is important to find the glue that can bind the various players together. If a senior member of the team has the attitude that they alone knows the best path, you will have a difficult time rallying the whole team to a common goal. Team members must understand and respect the views of each individual. They must learn to listen before they speak and to evaluate the opinions and ideas of others. In the end, the team leader or CAE will have the ultimate say; however, the ability to allow other members of the team to voice their views and opinions will be a strong component of building a strong team.

- *A good team has a backup plan, and sometimes, it is necessary to call an audible.* Team dynamics can turn quickly. It is the nature of the beast. Teams are composed of individuals. Individuals have different opinions, views, political, and personal touch points, attitudes, and sensitivities. In addition, life happens. You never know when a member of the team will go down with an injury. It is important to plan for the unexpected. Examine your resources, and know your backup plan especially on large projects. Also, build a team process that allows for an easy outlet to express concerns or issues. If team members feel they are being silenced on an issue, they may choose to run off the reservation.
- *CAEs need to build personal confidence in team members.* For any team to excel in their job, they must have a sense of personal confidence. This is a trait which some people may refer to as an inherent trait while others contend it can be learned. Whatever the case, the internal audit team must exhibit and maintain a sense of self-confidence in their job and their actions. Sometimes playing the role of internal auditor is difficult. You are always being questioned by management regarding your observations. You also may work hard to phrase your inquiries in a politically correct manner, yet you come away from the meeting feeling as though the process owner was questioning your abilities. This can dramatically impact self-confidence and the ability to excel in responsibilities. CAEs must pay attention to these attributes and work with employees to instill and maintain a strong level of confidence in their work and abilities.

Life is a series of roller coasters. Not everyone will succeed each time they attempt something. There is always some example of individuals who have endured unimaginable stress, yet they have somehow lived through the incident and are able to continue with their lives. Then, there are those who have difficulty coping, and the issue ends up defining their existence. The question becomes, how can we each personally adapt to stressors we may encounter and utilize the stressors as learning situations to enhance our future lives?

Whether it is the popular high school girl spinning tales about another girl or the supervisor continually rejecting a professional's suggestions and ideas, these events can contribute to a person's overall sense of being. How it contributes is very much up to you as an individual.

In today's world, those who are able to work through these challenges and continue to maintain a level of confidence in their own abilities are probably the individuals who will, in the long run, live the most satisfying and successful lives. Notice that I didn't say "professional life." That is because we live in a world where the reality is that there is always someone else who has an impact on where our individual professional careers may turn or land.

A story of personal confidence involved the football hall of famer, Joe Montana, during Super Bowl XXIII. Trailing 16–13 with 3:20 left in the game, the 49ers had the ball on their own 8-yard line. Joe later noticed some of his teammates being unusually tense. But as usual, he was focusing on the game situation. Just then, he spotted the actor John Candy in the stands. As he entered the huddle, about to make the call, "Look," he said, "isn't that John Candy?" Imagine the surprise of his teammates with the Super Bowl on the line. But it broke the tension. Joe later relayed in interviews that everyone cracked a smile and relaxed. The result was a now-famous 92-yard game-winning drive with the winning touchdown coming with just 34 seconds remaining in the game.

The anecdote shows how powerful confidence can be on the actions of others and the ultimate outcome. Joe's teammates recall their belief and confidence in Joe and his ability to march the team 92 yards down the field. Imagine if he had walked into the huddle and yelled at John Taylor or Jerry Rice (who were both instrumental in the final drive) and said "You guys just aren't cutting it today! I've lost faith in throwing to you." That 92-yard drive probably would not have occurred.

What elements may assist a professional in gaining that personal confidence level, and what can CAEs do to facilitate this process? Consider the following:

- *Encourage the professional to believe in themselves.* If professionals lose confidence in their own abilities, the future road will be tough to travel. Managers must work with employees to attempt to ensure that the opinion of others do not define the person the professional will become. The professional is the only one who can make that decision because they must live with it.

- *Encourage professionals to listen to others.* Don't let the morals of others define individual existence and creep into a professional value system. Morals and beliefs are a very personal thing. It is important to listen and understand the point of view of others, but if they don't line up with your individual morals, maybe you are in the wrong place.
- *Ensure that professionals understand that they will not succeed at everything they try.* Failure happens to everyone but it is often just an obstacle we need to learn from. If everyone was a success at everything they did, what kind of a world would have today?
- *Help professionals move forward after a setback.* Easier said than done right? Well, we all make mistakes, and managers must acknowledge that fact. The only way professionals will learn is to experience mistakes. Michael Jordan, the legendary Chicago Bulls basketball star was once quoted as saying "I've failed over and over again in my life.... and that is why I succeed." Allow your staff to learn from the mistakes and move forward. Don't let the incident or the other individuals involved define how an individual employee's future will roll out. Those individuals won't be there, and they have probably made the same mistakes at some point in their lives. Help professionals understand that the worries of the working world should not consume their everyday thoughts and actions. If they do, the professional will become an unhappy, bitter person.

These are a few considerations the CAE may want to contemplate when building and sustaining a team. It is important to recognize and understand team dynamics and work to instill a cohesive bond between team members.

Challenge 16: Department Sourcing Methods

Organizations have varying views on the most effective method for sourcing professionals within the internal audit function. Numerous benchmark studies exist with guidance on the suggested number of auditors based on organization revenue size, asset size, or industry type. Recommendations within these studies can vary dramatically.

Many factors come into play when determining the appropriate staffing level for the internal audit function. These determinations include much more than simply outlining hours in an audit plan. The CAE must first identify the focus for the function and the expected resource allocation that will be allowed. When identifying the focus, consider the expectation of management and the audit committee. Is the organization a publicly traded entity or a private organization? These factors may dramatically impact how the team will be structured. CAEs must align their internal audit team with the objectives of the organization. In considering sourcing alternatives, consider the following concepts:

- The company industry and related scope of services expected to be provided by internal audit
- Geographical disparity of the operations
- Expected focus of the audit function as it relates to auditing the asset base of the company versus revenue assurance or compliance areas
- Expectations for involvement in Sarbanes–Oxley or other regulatory or compliance issues
- Time expected or required to support the external audit
- Expectations of the audit committee and management
- Potential for unplanned audit requests or special investigations (e.g., fraud work)
- Involvement expected in new business initiatives or systems
- Experience and skill set expected of staff including specialized expertise (e.g., information technology knowledge, engineering knowledge, six sigma, fraud expertise)
- Planned and potential for unplanned paid time off for staff
- Auditor productivity and chargeable hour expectations
- Auditor and management training and administrative time requirements
- Available budget dollars to obtain consulting or project assistance and to properly compensate internal auditors in line with professional guidelines and benchmarks

Typically, the CAE will have a staffing quota dictated by the organization. The staffing quota along with the available consulting budget will often drive the hours allocated to the annual audit plan. Whether these resources will be sufficient to evaluate significant risks as defined by the organization is debatable.

CAEs who work to ensure they have available resources to cover audit plan projects will often begin for each projecting chargeable time by auditor. Ultimately, they will arrive at an estimated number of available hours for an annual audit plan. Once a risk assessment is completed, the CAE must determine whether they will attempt to cover a higher number of risks and allocate fewer hours to each project or apply more hours to a fewer number of risks.

In a perfect world, the development of the annual audit plan would be supported by a bottom-up risk evaluation. The evaluation would utilize concepts of a complete risk-based audit approach to determine areas that should be considered for inclusion on the annual audit plan. This evaluation often includes many of the following considerations:

- Internal audit will work with management and the audit committee to identify risk tolerance thresholds acceptable to the organization.
- A risk assessment is performed for the areas that are considered within the realm of internal audit responsibility including operational, compliance or financial reviews. Management tolerance guidelines should be considered.
- Based on management and audit committee tolerance, internal audit identifies the most relevant and significant auditable risks that the organization may face.
- An assessment is made regarding the potential audit scope for each of the relevant risk areas identified.
- An estimate for special requests or investigations is developed.
- Based on estimated projects, hour scope, and special requests, a total number of auditable hours is determined.
- Auditable hours are equated to available resource hours to determine resourcing gap.

There may be considerations missing within this approach, but the theory is internal audit should perform a bottom-up analysis of potential audit areas. This approach would allow the audit plan to be developed based on risks to be evaluated rather than on the number of professionals currently sourced in the department. If auditable risk areas were in excess of available resourcing, internal audit and the audit committee would determine the appropriate plan of action. In some cases, additional internal audit resources would be added, whereas in other instances, internal audit projects might be outsourced or co-sourced. Unfortunately, this particular outline and protocol does not represent the manner in which many internal audit groups function. In reality, internal resources are often defined based on company parameters. CAEs must then fit the audit plan to those resources.

Challenge 16 Potential Actions: Department Sourcing Methods Once the organization has determined the allocated headcount for the internal audit function, the CAE must identify the most appropriate method to source professionals and determine the various skill and experience levels needed to execute the goals of the function. The considerations will take into account the methods that are available for organization of the department. The method selected may depend on the size of the audit function as well as the availability of resources in the geographical locations where the auditors will be placed. Various considerations are evaluated including the following:

- *Sourcing with experienced career auditors.* Many organizations find they have individuals who are considered career auditors. These individuals have chosen to dedicate their careers to the profession of internal auditing. Career auditors may provide the organization with a sense of stability in the function.
- *Mix of career auditors and transitional staff.* Not every professional who enters the internal audit function does so with the intent of becoming a career auditor. Many look at the position as a stepping stone to other areas within the organization. It is important for each CAE to understand the professional's expected career goals and career path. This will assist the CAE in planning for potential departures and providing appropriate mentoring to individual staff members.
- *Auditor rotation program.* An auditor rotation program involves rotating professionals from other areas of the organization through internal audit. The intent is to provide those

professionals with a broad-based experience through exposure to the various organization processes internal audit works with. These individuals can, in theory, be rotated out of the department and utilize their learnings to advance into other management ranks. Some organizations view a rotational program as exhibiting a commitment to competence.

- *Staff loan program.* Some organizations utilize a regular practice of providing operational or finance personnel to the audit team when specific needs arise. For instance, assume that the company is a manufacturing industry and chooses to execute upon a vendor audit of a major supplier. They may find it beneficial to utilize a professional from the operations group who has a strong understanding of the vendors' specific processes and procedures. This may be an acceptable method assuming there are no independence concerns.
- *Co-sourcing and outsourcing.* Pre-Sarbanes–Oxley, it was not unusual for organizations to regularly outsource their internal audit function to consulting firms or external audit firms. Aspects imbedded within the Sarbanes–Oxley legislation have now made it difficult for a company's external auditors to perform the role of internal audit for the company they provide financial statement attestation work for. The issue of co-sourcing and outsourcing will be further discussed later in this chapter. There are many processes that are still considered potentials for outsourcing or co-sourcing projects. Information technology expertise is a typical area where internal audit groups find it difficult to maintain the appropriate level of expertise and competence within the function. They may rely on outsourcing or co-sourcing to fill needs. Regardless of the method used, ultimately, the issue will revert back to available budget dollars to appropriately fund the expertise needed for the department.

The approach and its effectiveness can hinge on how the function is able to maintain consistency in the execution of their audits and procedures. The varying approaches can also have an impact on how individuals within the function view commitment to competence for internal auditors. Consider the implications of utilizing a rotation theory. This concept can make it difficult to develop adequate competencies as identified within the *Standards*. With personnel continually rotating through the group, consistency and efficiency can become a difficult concept to manage.

Since the passing of Sarbanes–Oxley, the internal audit profession is viewed as a professional choice for many employees. Individuals enjoy the experience of job responsibilities that continue to evolve and change. Individuals who choose to become career auditors are typically those who learn the various guidelines and practices outlined in the *Standards and Professional Practices Framework*.

Internal audit management and the CAE must carefully consider the benefits and challenges faced when utilizing any of these sourcing methods. Each method has its pros and cons. The manner in which each method impacts the organization will vary based on the goals and objectives of the organization and its expectations of internal audit.

Challenge 17: Resourcing to Address Significant Risks

Chapter 1 outlined 12 principles the IIA has proposed as necessary attributes for the internal auditor to possess. Principle 6 states that the function should "maintain adequate resources to effectively address significant risks." The phrase "to assess significant risks" assumes that the internal audit group can agree with management on which risks are significant to the organization as well as which risks internal audit has the ability and capability to evaluate. If the statement and principle are taken literally, this would require management and internal auditors to come to some agreement on significant risks in order to properly assess the resources required to address those risks.

When determining significant risks, the ability to properly identify the organization's risk tolerance and risk appetite is important. However, this is a concept that organizations struggle with quantifying or qualifying. The inability to determine risk appetite and tolerance makes the principle of "identifying significant risks" much more difficult to meet. We will delay the discussion of risk tolerance and risk appetite for now and focus on adequate resourcing and staffing for significant risks.

Staffing is an issue for many corporate back-office functions. In difficult economic times, organizations work with lean resources. When the economy is emerging from recessionary periods, the ability to grow a function to align with stated goals can take years. The ability for the internal audit group to maintain adequate staffing will strongly tie to the purpose, scope, and definition of the department's work as well as the company's economic standing.

Challenge 17 Potential Actions: Resourcing to Address Significant Risks The CAE is responsible to ensure internal audit is appropriately staffed to address significant risks. In order to arrive at this assessment, the CAE must work with management and the audit committee to ensure they have a strong understanding of the following factors:

- *The company's view and definition of risk-based auditing.* There must be a comprehensive and holistic understanding of the expectations of risk-based auditing. This understanding must translate from the CAE to management and the audit committee. It is critical that all parties understand how the theory will be applied in practice. Personnel within the department who are expected to execute the methodology should have appropriate training and understanding of the risk-based process including risk evaluation, analysis, and mitigation techniques.
- *Overall objective and charter of the internal audit group.* The CAE must be able to adequately interpret statements outlined by the internal audit charter regarding how the company perceives the responsibility and authority of the function. This includes a comprehensive understanding of the role that internal audit will take in aspects of risk management, governance, and fraud investigations.
- *Management's stated tolerance levels and their definition of significant risks.* To appropriately determine staffing needs, it is imperative that the function obtain a clear and transparent understanding of management perception of significant risks and related risk tolerance. In addition, the CAE must be able to determine the ability to actually audit identified significant risks. Not all risks are auditable. Concepts like strategy are certainly significant risk areas to the organization, yet strategy is an area that is difficult to apply audit techniques towards. The CAE must be able to reconcile these concepts to management expectations and evaluate how they impact potential resourcing issues.

- *Expectation for involvement in activities outside of the typical definition of internal audit services.* This may include activities for controls consulting on new business initiatives. Controls consulting is a proactive process. In some instances, management may feel it is not appropriate to involve internal audit in these up-front evaluations. Many factors impact this perception. The important concept is that the CAE understand how management views the role of internal audit as it relates to activities outside the typical assurance definition of the function. If controls consulting is embraced by management, and there are numerous critical business initiatives on the horizon, the CAE should consider this need when defining the appropriate level of departmental resources.
- *The expertise and skill level of personnel sourced in the function.* This includes whether the department has technical and operational experience that extend further than financial reporting. These technical skills may include areas of information technology, operations, engineering, finance, or even legal. The CAE must be cognizant of the required skill levels to adequately execute upon planned projects. If an audit is planned, and the skill set is not currently housed within internal audit, the work may need to be outsourced to specialists.
- *The expectations for a true internal audit function versus a quality assurance function.* This includes understanding whether the department will function as an internal audit group that will abide by *Standards* or whether they will function as a quality assurance function focused on management efficiency and improvement initiatives. The CAE must understand how management views the function and ensure that internal resources are appropriately aligned.
- *Understand the staffing history of the function.* The CAE must be able to individually assess the stability and staffing history of the function. If the function is one that has experienced difficulty in retaining personnel, the CAE should work to identify the root cause of the issue. The reasons for staffing inconsistencies can extend from a lack of understanding of the role of internal audit by management to internal management issues that have occurred within the department.

Understanding staffing history is an important component in effective recruitment and staffing of the function. Consider the following example of staffing issues.

A CAE relayed an experience where he discussed staffing difficulties of the internal audit group with his audit committee. The committee members seemed to believe the frequent turnover in the function was due to the inability of the organization to put the right individuals within staff roles. The CAE questioned the committee members further regarding their perception. He explained the function had typically recruited experienced internal auditors, CIAs, and internal control specialists. However, the audit committee felt the recruitment process did not adequately consider the culture of the organization. The CAE spoke to the committee about his concerns regarding the lack of independence he had observed while working in the function. He cited instance of the inability to work directly with the audit committee, and the significant resistance of management toward many aspects of the *Standards*. The audit committee members were surprised the CAE would infer this might be a possibility. The CAE explained difficulties he had personally encountered in his first 8 months of employment. However, the audit committee deferred to management to determine whether there was any merit to the CAE's opinion. The CAE left the meeting feeling that the audit committee refused to recognize what seemed to be right in front of their eyes. In this instance, the function continued to undergo fluctuations and changes. Management had a strong impact on how the function operated, and the audit committee placed reliance on the management. Ultimately, the CAE moved to another position, and the function continued to experience many changes. However, the CAE had done what he could to express his concerns and observations to those responsible for the governance of the organization. In addition, he attempted to speak to the external auditors about the dilemma but did not receive any support. In essence, he fulfilled his fiduciary duty and in the end moved to another position in the company due to his concern that the function could not operate in accordance with *Standards*.

This story illustrates the importance of effectively examining the staffing history of the function and addressing what might be the contributing factors to challenges experienced. CAEs who do not feel they can speak up and address the issue with the governance body are not fulfilling their individual fiduciary duty. This can be easier said than done, and the CAE must be able to deal with any fallout or ramifications that are presented.

Section 2: Skills Requirements for an Effective Internal Auditor

Introduction

Internal auditors are increasingly being called on to exhibit and provide a variety of technical skills. These capabilities include hard skills such as accounting, information technology, and engineering knowledge as well as soft skills such as communication and leadership.

Many corporate managers find that candidate traits they evaluate during the interviewing process actually evolve as the manager gains more experience in the corporate setting. As a new manager, it is not unusual to focus on technical skills or educational accomplishments of candidates. Later, as the manager gains additional experience in the corporate setting, he/she often considers the importance of a prospective employee's soft skills. Depending on the specific position being sought, the manager may place a stronger emphasis on soft skill capabilities when making the hiring decision. Performance is more than exhibiting the technical skills to solve a problem. Traits such as communication, networking, corporate politics, and the ability to apply constructive feedback are important to an individual's ability to effectively execute responsibilities. In addition, advancements in information technology and social media have changed the landscape of corporate protocols and the skills that individuals within the profession must be able to exhibit.

Communication can be the foundation of learning and skill advancement. In today's business environment, e-mail, Instagram, Twitter, instant messaging, and many other communication methods can be easily overused or misused. In the old days, communication meant face-to-face meetings or formal memos. In today's world, a great deal of day-to-day business is conducted via e-mail or some other social media. Although some professionals see e-mail as the evil of all communication, it does allow for more immediate transmission of information. Young professionals have come through the educational system during a time when social media and advanced technological communication techniques have surfaced. These professionals see this instant communication as the way to do business. However, if not used properly, it can create an atmosphere of misunderstanding or lack of accountability. Professionals sometimes use the tool very liberally and find out later that the message sent was interpreted differently than intended. It is important for professionals in today's business to understand that face-to-face communication is still the most effective process for important and sensitive issues. It is difficult to read body language and facial expressions over e-mail.

Another dynamic that impacts today's workforce is departmental relationships and teamwork. Professionals must understand that these skills involve dynamics that include work goals, job assignments, peer competition, job positioning, work arrangements, and past experiences. For departments that maintain a multi-generational workforce, managing those relationships can dramatically impact the department's ability to be successful in various environments. From a teamwork perspective, the young professional may be accustomed to working in teams within the educational setting. In these instances, they are working toward a joint goal of a letter grade on a project. In the workforce, the team may have a shared goal, but there are underlying dynamics that may create political sensitivities. Teamwork can be perceived and viewed differently depending upon the project outcome, organizational culture, and structure and team makeup.

These factors will create additional challenges to formulating a cohesive team. It is the CAE's responsibility to be able to effectively identify and manage these various aspects to ensure their team can be productive and efficient regardless of makeup.

Technical versus Soft Skills

Many articles and white papers outline expected skills for the new professional. In May 2013, Ernst & Young commissioned Forbes Insights to conduct a global survey of CAEs. The study focused on how internal audit's shifting mandate has impacted the skill requirements for staffing. The report titled "Key Findings from the Global Internal Audit Survey 2013" provided strategic insights into required skill sets. The findings included:

- Increased expectation for internal audit to provide stakeholders with business insights while also serving as a strategic advisor to the organization.
- Increased expectation for internal audit to be involved in identifying, assessing, and monitoring emerging risks.
- Acknowledgment that current resources are lacking critical skills in the areas of data analytics, business strategy, deep industry experience, risk management, and fraud prevention and detection.
- Respondents ranked the following issues as the top 5 emerging risk areas:
    - Economic stability (54%)
    - Cyber security (52%)
    - Major shifts in technology (48%)
    - Strategic transactions in global locations (44%)
    - Regulations around data privacy (39%)

Additional survey information ranked specific skill sets that respondents felt were imperative to internal audit. Interestingly, all of the skills that were cited and ranked focused on technical skills rather than soft skills. The skills as ranked were as follows:

- Financial audit and accounting
- Internal controls
- Operational audit
- Compliance and regulatory knowledge
- Risk management
- Data analytics
- Business strategy
- Deep industry experience
- Fraud prevention and detection

The listed skills are undoubtedly important for the internal auditor's toolbox. Many of the listed skills require business acumen and organization understanding and knowledge. The typical skills of a young professional coming from the educational realm may not include these attributes with any degree of proficiency. The young professional may possess the accounting and control understanding, but often, the application of the technical skills requires organizational knowledge, experience, and maturity. The skills listed in the Ernst & Young survey do not focus on many of the soft skill attributes such as communication and professional presence.

Internal audit professionals are expected to operate with the same agility their companies need to exhibit amid ongoing external volatility. Technical skills remain necessary, but they may not be sufficient on their own. The most effective internal auditor possesses a broad range of non-technical skill attributes in addition to deep technical expertise. On a professional level, internal auditors must have the intellectual ability to accept and absorb new information and evolving processes. They also must possess the flexibility that will enable them to juggle priorities and effectively respond to rapidly changing business conditions.

These abilities speaks to a professional's personal makeup and demeanor rather than pure technical skills. Individuals who can display a trait of flexibility and adaptability are often those who have a personality that is open to constructive feedback and change. They are individuals who are not easily frustrated and can maintain an open attitude toward new ideas and changing needs and demands. They must be comfortable with professional, open, and transparent communication with a multitude of individuals throughout the organization. In today's world, adaptability is not only considered a nice to have competency; it is considered a competitive advantage for becoming a leader of the organization. All of these skills speak to the concept of developing a true team approach to executing work. CAEs and internal audit leaders who are able to facilitate a team atmosphere within their organizations may find many synergies in providing overall value to the organization.

Balanced Skill Set

In 2012, Robert Half sponsored a study on the top 5 skills sought by recruiters for internal auditors. This survey showed the recognition of a combination of both soft skills and technical skills (Robert Half's study "Top skills for internal auditors," 2012). The respondents ranked the skills as follows:

- Analytical and critical thinking (72%)
- Communication skills (57%)
- Information technology general skills (49%)

- Risk management (49%)
- Business acumen (43%)

This study provides a good indication of the importance of soft skills to the internal auditor. Although most respondents ranked analytical and critical thinking as a top skill, a strong percentage recognized the strategic importance of communication skills. In addition, the concept of business acumen made the list of critical skills. These skills recognize the need for internal auditors to possess strong analytical and thinking skills for proper evaluation of risks and controls. The need to be able to effectively communicate findings utilizing proper business language and acumen is also recognized. Each of these can be a critical element to ensure that the communication of observations and findings contain merit.

Other very important soft skills are those that go much further than communication techniques. Some of these skills may be those that are embedded within individual personalities and thought processes. These would include aspects such as the following:

- Natural inquisitiveness that encourages professionals to continually exercise their professional skepticism to the level that they are satisfied with the reasoning behind answers to basic questions.
- The ability to continually pursue an answer to the extent that there is a clear picture of the issue at hand.
- The ability to adapt and change as the situation requires.
- The ability to recognize, accept, and respond to diverse thinking styles, learning styles, and cultural qualities.
- An open mindset that allows the professional to evaluate various rationalizations without being jaded or influenced by their own personal or moral beliefs.

Each of these factors speaks to the importance of recognizing the need for a balanced skill set within the internal audit function.

Challenge 18: Defining the Required Skill Set for Internal Auditors

The challenge for internal audit management is to identify the proper mix of skill sets that meet the goals and objectives of their individual functions. There is no secret formula or checklist that will provide

CAEs with a perfect guideline for staffing their departments or determining the required skill sets. However, having an understanding of the types of skills that auditors may need to employ is important to being able to appropriately staff and source any audit function.

Challenge 18 Potential Actions: Defining the Required Skill Set for Internal Auditors Although there may not be a standard checklist for determining the right combination of skill sets for the internal audit team, there are questions that can be considered when formulating staffing options. These questions may provide insight into those skills that may be of greatest need for auditors at various levels within the function.

- *What is your company's organizational hierarchy?* An organization that is extremely structured with specific lines of authority may require the audit team to have similar departmental reporting lines. Organizations that value detailed hierarchies may inherently expect specific protocols for communication of audit issues. This may require maintaining individuals within the internal audit department who are experienced in the culture and political communication expectations of the organization. In these instances, the audit department may have a greater need for managers or supervisors with some level of organizational background and perceived respect and trust. They may be individuals who are strong communicators with personal attributes that contribute to the attainment of personal integrity within the organization.
- *In what industry does the company operate?* Industries can be distinct and varied and may require distinct and varied skill sets for the internal auditor. Consider the following scenarios:
    - Organizations such as credit card agencies have a strong prominence of data-centric information. These organizations may require auditors with specific data analysis and information technology expertise.
    - An organization in the health care industry deals with sensitive personal information and may have a strong need for auditors who understand elements of information privacy laws and associated technological applications.

- An organization that works in an industry where technology is less advanced may have a strong need for proficient operational auditors who understand various aspects of the business operations.
- An organization that has highly technical engineering processes may require individuals with an engineering background to efficiently execute on operational audits.

Internal audit management must ensure that it is able to match staffing needs to the requirements of the industry.

- *Are there cultural nuisances of the organization?* Placing political sensitivities aside, there are certain industries and businesses in which gender preferences may reside. These preferences could be tied to the nature of the industry or to the nature of the specific profession the industry is in. As an example, companies in certain industrial manufacturing organizations or possibly mining operations are typically those that have been dominated by the male gender. Although in today's business, we would like to believe that gender should not be a consideration when it comes to communicating an issue, the fact remains that it may be. This is not to say that departments should walk the gender line of only sourcing the department with individuals of the male or female gender. It is also not to assert that communications should come from certain individuals based on gender. However, it does provide audit management with some insight into providing the proper support for individuals who are tasked with executing work and communicating findings. Similar to the concept of not sending a young auditor to the CEO of a company to report a wrongdoing, audit management should be mindful of how they assign personnel to specific audits as well as how and when they are communicating specific issues. Ensuring that the audit team has the appropriate balance of expertise and knowledge will help pave the way to a positive outcome.
- *Is the organization multi-cultural or located in wide geographic areas that may include international locations?* The internal audit group may have a need for individuals with a diverse cultural background or even individuals who are multi-lingual. There

may also be a need for consideration of individuals who have the ability to adapt and adjust easily when working within various areas of the company. Large organizations with operations that span various countries recognize that operating environments and processes can be extremely different. A process in one area of the company may require adjustments to be effectively implemented within another area of the company. Auditors must be cognizant of these nuisances and be able to make interpretations as to when adjustments are appropriate due to cultural or regional variations. This contributes to the ability to recognize, accept, and respond to diverse thinking styles, learning styles, and cultural qualities.

- *What is the physical location of the audit team?* In instances where a company has diverse geographical facilities, it is important to understand the potential need to source professionals in the specific location or maintain the ability to source appropriate travel to cover audit requirements. If the audit team is centrally located and requires significant travel, there are a multitude of considerations that internal audit management should evaluate. This may include the ability for staff to engage in required travel, the need for work permits or passports, as well as the ability to fund related travel cost that may be incurred.
- *What is the organization's expectation for the scope of internal audit responsibilities?* We've discussed the concept of how internal audit may execute on the responsibilities outlined by the profession related to governance, compliance, risk, fraud, and consulting arrangements. For internal audit management to appropriately staff their organization, they must be able to openly address the question and expectations of how the function will operate within the organization. If the organization does not deem internal audit as an area that will provide substantial support to risk management processes, the need for internal auditors with a detailed understanding of enterprise risk management may not be a skill set that is at the top of the list for the department. Alternatively, that does not mean that internal audit management should not have a solid understanding of the aspects of the area. It simply points to the mix and sourcing of other staff within the function. Another

example may relate to the internal audit department's involvement in fraud evaluations or investigations. If the organization does not include internal audit within these processes, the need to have forensic investigators or CFEs may not be a skill set that is specifically required. However, as outlined within the *Standards*, internal auditors are not expected to have the technical expertise of forensic auditors, but they are expected to have an understanding of fraud red flags. This is important to be able to understand and identify potential situations that may surface. Internal audit management must be able to effectively outline the responsibilities that are expected of the function as well as those that are anticipated for the growth of the function. These responsibilities and attributes can then serve as a road map for the most beneficial skill sets for sourcing internal audit staff.

Section 3: Internal Audit as a Management Training Ground

Introduction

Early in this chapter, the challenges and benefits of a rotational theory for internal auditors was examined. Although management continues to assert the benefits of the rotational theory, studies point to cautions for companies when exercising the approach.

The IIA compiles an annual benchmarking study referred to as Global Audit Information Network (GAIN). The study presents statistics on various aspects of internal audit including staffing size by industry type as well as staffing size by revenue or asset base. Often, the true predictor of a staffing model hinges on management's expectations and definitions of the objectives of their internal audit function.

A prospective CAE relayed an experience when interviewing with a new company for a position as the head of internal audit. He was interviewing with the CFO of a large public company. Early in the interview, the CFO explained that the company had experienced difficulty in building a sustainable and value-oriented internal audit function. He posed the question to the candidate, "What is your view of a staffing model for internal audit?" Before the candidate could respond, the CFO commented, "Our company does not believe in career auditors or leaving professionals stuck within internal audit."

The comment took the prospective candidate by surprise. His experience with internal audit had been that in order to build a sustainable and value-oriented function, the department should be staffed with individuals who had an interest in the internal audit profession. He acknowledged the benefits of building a function with diverse skills and backgrounds. He understood the potential benefits of staff rotation, but he did not view a tenure in internal audit as one that would be characterized as "stuck" in a role. The candidate's response to the CFO's question was he felt that there should be a proper balance between rotational staff and career auditors. He went on to express that many professionals who chose to work in the function consider it a professional career similar to any other accounting or finance role. The candidate did not end up advancing in the interview process and later relayed that he learned that the CFO did not agree with the his stated perception of staffing internal audit. This story illustrates that management's view and perception of the role of internal audit and the individuals staffed in the function can have a strong impact on any staffing model.

A study released by researchers from the University of Georgia, University of Arkansas, Texas A&M University, and Brigham Young University in October 2011 focused on the effects to financial reporting quality when using internal audit as a management training ground. The results suggest the use of internal audit as a management training ground may impair the function's ability to improve financial reporting quality. This was the first study to investigate the effect of this practice on financial reporting quality. While prior research has examined its effect on objectivity and perceived objectivity, this study used archival data to test and find that the effects extend beyond the internal auditor to the impairment of financial reporting quality. The study was limited to data collected between 2000 and 2005. It noted that although it was a tumultuous time for publicly traded companies, there was no reason to believe that the events of the time period would be correlated with the use of internal audit as a management training ground. The study concluded that companies should consider the potential costs of using the internal audit function as a management training ground and, if adopting this practice, should ensure that the appropriate compensating controls are in place to mitigate such costs.

A separate study released in June 2013 evaluated whether the objectivity of internal audit was compromised when the internal audit function is a management training ground. An experiment conducted with 74 internal auditors examined the effects of using the internal audit function as a training ground for future senior managers. The study evaluated the internal auditors' willingness to resist current management's aggressive revenue recognition policies, assuming that internal auditors expect to move into senior management positions in the future. It also examined whether increasing the power of the board of directors would reduce threats to internal auditors' objectivity. This was the first study to empirically examine whether training grounds influence internal auditors' objectivity. Results of the study indicate that internal auditors are less objective (i.e., they are more likely to side with management's aggressive revenue recognition policies) when they expect to move into senior management positions relative to when internal auditing is not used as a training ground. It also found that empowering the audit committee further decreases the objectivity of internal auditors. The results suggested that board power can have unintended consequences on the behavior of internal auditors.

When comparing these studies with the March 2014 IIA reported trend of bringing CAEs into the organization from outside the profession, questions surface regarding the overall ramifications to the function and the ability to meet the definition of internal audit as outlined by the profession.

Challenge 19: Internal Audit as a Management Training Ground

Regardless of empirical studies and reports, the impact and ramifications of utilizing internal audit as a training ground for management must be something that organizations strongly consider. The organization must examine the intent of the rotational process as well as the benefits and challenges. The ultimate impact, similar to other concepts we have discussed, may be related to how the organization views and positions the internal audit function as well as the CAE role.

Challenge 19 Potential Actions: Internal Audit as a Management Training Ground Prior to embarking on a dedicated rotational audit program, management should consider their objectives for prospective program as well as the overall implications to the organization. A CAE whose organization is considering a rotational program should be able to address the following questions and arrive at the conclusion that the program will not impair the department's overall independence and objectivity. Questions to consider may include the following:

- *What is the staffing size of the internal audit function?* Many internal auditors have experienced management declaration that "The auditors don't know my business" or "We are always training the auditors." The CAE is responsible for adequate staffing and execution of the audit function. This includes ensuring the type of rotational program is providing a benefit to the organization and to the internal audit function. Although department size isn't the only factor to consider, it can provide some indication of whether a rotational program is something that is beneficial to the organization without unduly impairing the internal audit function's ability to sustain a value-oriented service. Organizations with large internal audit groups may be more adept at managing a rotational auditor program. These organizations may have an established infrastructure of audit management and senior staff who can mentor and guide rotational auditors in their execution of responsibilities. Organizations whose internal audit function is limited in size may find that a rotational auditor program can significantly impact their ability to sustain any type of consistency in performance. CAEs must ensure their departmental infrastructure is appropriately established to adequately manage and maintain a rotational program. Without the proper infrastructure, the department may experience high levels of turnover, variances in performance metrics, and inconsistency in job execution.
- *What is the expected tenure of the rotational program?* An important factor that may impact the success or failure of a rotational audit program is the expected tenure of the assignment. The tenure of a rotational assignment can vary depending on the purpose for the rotation. Many professionals will agree that the first 6 to 12 months of any new job is a learning

experience. With this in mind, management must understand that making rotational assignments for tenures less than 1 year may not be beneficial to the organization or to the individual. The department will spend significant time and effort training the new professional on procedures and processes. It can take several assignments before new auditor becomes comfortable with the internal audit process. Since an individual audit can span many weeks or even months, professionals may be in the initial stages of grasping the overall concepts of internal audit and the *Standards* within their first year. This is when a professional's training provides payback to the function. Programs that rotate individuals out of the function within or at a year may result in unintended performance consequences for internal audit. If the rotational program is in a small audit group, audit customers may feel as though the department lacks consistency in performance. Separately, audit management may feel they are in a continual training cycle and unable to adequately address emerging risk areas should be addressed by company. CAEs must ensure rotational assignments are of sufficient tenure to ensure the professional has received the appropriate understanding and training in the internal audit process. However, the program must also balance the impact that continual change in personnel will have on the overall performance of the department.

- *What are the current capabilities of the function?* Because of the wide variety of skill sets needed within internal audit, sourcing and maintaining those skills on a consistent basis can be a challenge. Often, departments consider utilizing "guest" auditors or temporary rotational auditors who have a specific skill that can benefit a particular project. An example may be when an internal audit group is conducting a business partner review. It may be beneficial to utilize operational individuals to assist in some of the detailed work of the audit. The operational individuals can contribute strategic knowledge to the process through their understanding of the business partner's processes or business. In these instances, a rotational or guest auditor process can be beneficial. However, it is important that individuals utilized for these roles are properly supervised and mentored to facilitate adequate objectivity in performance of audit work.

These are just a few considerations when determining whether utilizing internal audit as a management training ground is efficient for your organization.

Section 4: Outsourcing, Co-Sourcing, and In-Sourcing

Introduction

Sourcing models have experienced dramatic swings in popularity depending on the business environment. In the years prior to Sarbanes–Oxley, the concept of outsourcing was very prevalent. Many external audit firms specialized in outsourcing internal audit functions in which they also executed the external financial audit. In addition, the firm may have been involved executing work in multiple areas of the company such as providing tax services, due diligence work, benefit plan reviews, or other consulting-related work. Shortly after the Enron downfall and the passing of Sarbanes–Oxley, the pendulum swung the other way, and external audit firms found they were no longer allowed to outsource the internal audit function for a company where they performed the external audit.

Regardless of trends in the past years, evaluating each of these possibilities can provide insight into benefits as well as challenges. In order to understand what may be the best approach for your company, it is important to briefly revisit these models. Throughout my career, I've worked within four separate internal audit functions and consulted with several others. I've seen each of the following models work with success in some environments, while facing significant challenges in others. The success or failure of any particular sourcing model was often due to how management viewed the process. In other instances it related to how the functions managed their staffing and communication. Let's briefly review some of the benefits and challenges of each method as well as considerations that CAEs and internal audit management may want to evaluate when faced with these particular scenarios.

Challenge 20: Outsourcing

The outsourcing model is one in which typically, the internal audit function is performed solely by an outsourced firm. This could be another accounting firm (outside of your current external auditors) or another specialty consulting firm. The concept has some benefits as well as challenges. The benefits include the following:

- Cost is predictable and normally managed close to proposed budget.
- Outsourced firms typically have access to leading practice methods or specialist that can be used in certain areas.
- There is normally some support when unexpected situations occur, and additional work requires additional resources.

The challenges of the process include the following:

- It is difficult to predict the skill level of the resources that will be provided. Often, companies find they are dealing with professionals who have little to no experience in their industry.
- There tends to be a high turnover rate in personnel among these firms. This turnover can impact the effectiveness of consistency of services.
- Individuals from outsourced providers are viewed by the company as outsiders. It can be difficult for internal audit to build a nurturing and trusting relationship.

Organizations that have previously or who currently employ the outsourcing model may experience each of the listed benefits or challenges. Information gathered from personal observations as well as quality assurance reviews with various functions seem to indicate that from the internal audit perspective, an outsourced model may be ranked third on the list of most effective. This may be due to several factors including:

- Concern about the ongoing revolving door of auditors that are staffed in the function.
- The continual learning curve of new staff assignments.
- The lack of a complete and holistic understanding of the business by the outsourced auditors.

- The inability of the outsourced auditors to establish close relationships with process owners.
- The perception of the cost involved when outsourcing.

Of course, we can't overlook the benefits, which include:

- The expertise that stands behind the firm providing the resources.
- The access outsourced firms have to leading practice information.
- An existence of truly independent outlet for questions.

In the long run, it is difficult to maintain any consistency of service when trying to build respect and a reputation with stakeholders if the audit team is continually changing. As an example, one CAE relayed an experience when utilizing a fully outsourced function. One of the measurement metrics was to track dollars saved from the internal audit process. The CAE explained that it was interesting to watch the significant amount of time spent by personnel to justify or extrapolate dollar savings on soft control issues. His observations was that the outsourced firm was working to justify dollar savings that equated to their outsourcing fees.

In some instances where a company chooses to outsource their internal audit function, they may have recently completed an external quality assessment review. After the review, the assessor's firm is able to convince management that their team can complete the activities much more efficiently and less costly. This can contribute to their need to justify savings found. But the question must be asked, can these projected savings be realized?

Challenge 20 Potential Actions: Outsourcing The term outsourcing will typically mean that the full function is sourced and managed by an external firm. However, there may be someone internally in the organization who will coordinate information and potential work or communications with the outsourced firm. This person could be someone from the finance and accounting area or possibly an internal employee whose primary responsibility is to coordinate work and plans with the outsourced firm. If your organization is considering an outsourcing model, or possibly you are currently utilizing an outsourcing model, there are a few considerations that should be considered by the audit committee to ensure that this process is most effective for the organization. These may include the following:

- *Analyze true cost versus benefit of the process.* When firms are able to sell their outsourcing services, they will outline cost considerations and justify those with their ability to be truly independent and more efficient than internal employees. The justification may include their ability to access numerous subject matter experts, tools, and personnel. These factors are certainly benefits of outsourcing if the model is right for the company. However, audit committees and management must not overlook the offsetting soft elements that may impact whether outsourcing is truly providing the benefit proposed.

  Outsourcing comes with more than monetary costs. Companies who outsource all of their internal audit work are losing certain benefits that may be hard to quantify. Firms will focus on the related benefits they are providing to the company through outsourced work. However, companies should evaluate the identified benefits to determine if there are ancillary challenges that may come along. Consider the following stated benefits of outsourcing and the related rationale of viewing the statement from the other spectrum:

  - *Outsourcing allows companies to focus their attention on core business activities.* The opposite side of this argument is that outsourcing internal audit means you are bringing in individuals who may not be familiar with the core business activities they are being audited. The company loses the ability to utilize in-house knowledge of internal auditors who have worked for the company and understand the culture, processes, and business strategy. There is significant benefit to building internal audit expertise in-house. The synergies that are created through consistency in resources provide strategic value to the organization. Of course, this is assuming that the internal audit department is able to maintain consistency in staffing and resources. Often, the reason organizations look to outsourcing is due to the inability to maintain consistent staffing within internal audit. The audit committee and management must determine the value they expect from the internal audit function. The argument of allowing personnel to focus on core business activities is contrary to the position that the internal audit profession promulgates. The function is considered a profession and provides value to all core business functions when operated efficiently.

- *Outsourcing provides the benefit and access to subject matter experts.* This may be one of the most solid arguments for outsourcing. External firms have ready access to individuals with subject matter expertise that may be needed for various audits. However, the subject matter expertise comes with a cost. If the expertise is one of a very technical nature that is difficult for an internal audit department to maintain in-house, the services also may be more costly than anticipated. The alternative to full outsourcing is a co-sourcing model. Through co-sourcing, the company gains the advantage of the subject matter expert while retaining the ability to transfer knowledge to in-house employees to use in future reviews. The consideration to evaluate with this argument is the company's position regarding building and maintaining subject matter expertise in-house to allow for synergies in future audits.
- *Outsourcing protects the company from disruption of service compared to employing an internal specialist and then having that specialist leave.* Outsourcing firms may take the position that when you employ a specialist internally, you create reliance on that person, and when he/she leaves, you suffer a disruption to the business. However, this argument can also be viewed through a different lens. Many outsourcing firms experience their own difficulties with maintaining consistent resources and experts. You may find that you are utilizing a multitude of experts with the same technical skill on similar audit areas. This occurs because the firms have their own challenges with turnover. So, in essence, you may not be obtaining the consistency initially represented by the firm. The consideration to evaluate is which method is most reliable for the company. If the outsourced firm has a strong reputation for maintaining and assigning

consistent resources, the argument may be valid. However, if the outsourced firm cannot provide the company with some assurances regarding the consistency of resources, the argument may not be as solid as presented.

- *Outsourcing firms may contend that employing someone with the experience and qualifications to perform an internal audit role is expensive, and trying to recruit cheaply may result in retaining poorly qualified employees.* This argument may be used to justify the cost benefit. The validity and accuracy of the statement will hinge on how the company views internal audit. Often, outsourced firms assign personnel to work based on availability. Projects may be staffed by individuals who have not worked with the company in the past and do not necessarily know the intricacies of the company's business. As we have covered, the profession is evolving, and there are many qualified individuals in the market who have a strategic interest in the role of internal audit. Audit committees and management must again evaluate where they place the value in expertise. If the company views internal audit as a value-oriented function, there is a strong argument for ensuring that your recruiting and retention processes are strong.
- *Outsourcing ensures true independence.* As outlined in Chapter 2, independence and objectivity are more complicated than simple reporting lines. Although the statement that an outsourced firm has organizational independence when performing the function may be true, there are still the concepts of functional independence as well as utilization of objectivity. Organizations that are looking to outsource their internal audit functions and reference the concern of independence should look within to identify the core root of that concern. If the concern is due to management pressure on internal auditors, the simple act of outsourcing may not solve the situation. If management feels they can influence the findings of an audit, they may feel the influence extends to whoever performs the review regardless if it is an internal employee or a consultant.
- *Long- versus short-term objectives.* The concept of whether outsourcing is a relevant sourcing alternative for internal

audit may depend on the company's short- versus long-term objectives. If the organization is undergoing significant change, the need to outsource internal audit may relate to requirements for certain skill sets or even relevant resources. The trend of outsourcing versus in-sourcing continues to evolve and change. The direction a company chooses to move in relationship to sourcing their function should have a semblance of a longer-term plan. Audit committees and management should consider how they wish to posture the function both in the short and long term. This decision may impact how the sourcing plan is managed.

When evaluating the need for outsourcing, companies should ensure they view the alternatives through a critical lens and understand both sides of the potential proposal. Outsourcing can be an appropriate sourcing method for certain companies or even at certain points in the evolution of a business. In other instances, outsourcing internal audit can prove to be more costly than viewed in a pure financial sense.

Challenge 21: Co-Sourcing

This model is typically used when the organization maintains a core staff of internal auditors and sources externally when specialty experience is required. Another alternative is when the co-sourcing program is closer to an outsourcing program where there is only one internal individual who assists in coordination of the resources with the external firm. Challenges and benefits of the process include the following:

- The benefits of a co-sourced function are very similar to those of an outsourced function, with the additional benefit being there is some semblance of internal representation in internal audit that can be the catalyst for developing relationships within the organization.
- The challenges are similar to outsourced functions; however, with co-sourced functions, some of the knowledge transfer occurs to the internal representative(s). This assists with the challenge of frequent turnover within the external firm.

A senior audit professional relayed their experience working with a co-sourced function in the days prior to Sarbanes–Oxley. The function was co-sourced by the company's external auditors. The auditors performed the company's tax work, benefit plan review, and many of their due diligence projects on new acquisitions. In addition, although there were several internal auditors employed by the company, the director of internal audit was a member of the external firm. This situation had many dynamics. Prior to joining that company, the professional relaying the example had worked for a company where internal audit was fully in-sourced. In the initial years with the co-sourced function, the professional indicated he had many questions and observations. However, since the director was a member of the external firm, there was no process established to allow any of the internal employees to speak directly to management about observations or questions.

The professional indicated that in many ways, the co-sourced model worked well. The company had access to experienced individuals who were able to bring a talent to the table that would not have been available to the function if it were in-sourced. In other situations, difficulties were encountered due to the co-sourced arrangement existing with the firm that conducted the external audit. Internal employees found when questions were presented about being involved with financial reviews or other aspects the external auditors were involved with, the internal team was told it wasn't needed. The company also experienced difficulty in developing a true sense of teamwork. Although the co-sourced firm made several attempts at teaming, there appeared to always be an inherent us versus them attitude. The professional relayed that many of the internal employees felt that the co-sourced employees from the firm were viewed as having an advantage or leg up for the better assignments. Whether this perception was true, it was difficult to resolve. The professional relayed that the primary benefit he felt was obtained was the access to the leading practice information of the firm along with access to subject matter experts for information technology or data analysis.

Challenge 21 Potential Actions: Co-Sourcing When evaluating the benefits and challenges of a co-sourcing model, consider some of the following:

- *What is the purpose for the co-source decision?* Pinpointing the reason for moving to a co-source model is an important factor for staffing decisions. It is also important to realize that a co-source arrangement is different from a loan staffing arrangement. With a co-sourced arrangement, the group is looking for a specialized skill that may not be maintained in-house. Of course, it isn't limited to specialized skills. The arrangement can be beneficial to provide additional staffing during times of business constraints. Having a clear and definitive outline for your co-source arrangement will ensure that you maintain adequate controls and metrics around the process. Co-sourced auditors should be measured just like the internal staff is measured. Metrics to consider include:
  - Did the auditors stay within expected timing?
  - How were their reports and recommendations received?
  - How well do the personnel fit into the culture?
  - How do the post-audit surveys of co-sources staff compare to in-sourced staff?

  The CAE or internal audit management must be able to answer these questions and many more to ensure their co-sourced arrangement is effective.
- *How will the co-sourced firm source the specialties needed for the work?* Different consulting firms maintain different expertise. Some firms focus heavily on data analysis, whereas other firms may be subject matter experts in operational process such as health and safety or environmental. Ensuring the proper needs and skill sets for the co-sourced staff will ensure proper access to individuals that can provide the greatest value to your organizations. In some situations, companies work with one particular co-sourced provider to manage their projects. Depending on the skill sets of that firm, this may or may not be the proper solution. Companies may need to consider having multiple agreements with firms that can provide varying services and specialties.
- *How will the co-sourced work be managed?* Don't overlook the aspect of proper oversight and management of individuals from the co-sourced firm. Your internal audit group will most likely prefer to have reports written in the department's

typical style. That may mean ensuring that the co-sourced auditors understand the internal audit methodology and rating system for reports. In addition, will there be an internal employee assigned on the review to work with the co-sourced auditors? This may provide for some assistance in communications and facilitation of work.

- *How will reports be issued on the co-sourced work?* This can be a more significant issue than some may believe. The CAE must address the following questions:
    - Will the co-sourced firm independently issue their reports to management?
    - What input does the internal audit function have on the manner in which the reports are written, ranked, or worded?
    - How are the reports actually delivered to management, and who is responsible for monitoring the issues and findings?

  All of these aspects are important to consider in a co-sourced arrangement.
- *Will there be a transfer of knowledge to in-sourced auditors?* Ultimately, in a co-sourced arrangement, the consultant auditors should work to transfer some level of expertise and knowledge to the internal auditors. The CAE or internal audit management must establish a protocol within their audit methodology to facilitate this knowledge transfer. A consideration is to have a member of internal audit serve on the audit team or possibly a simple debriefing of the issues and findings post conclusion of the audit. In order for internal auditors to obtain a strong understanding of processes, it is important that the co-sourced process not be executed and completed entirely within a vacuum.
- *How is the decision made as to which projects will be co-sourced?* This speaks to the effectiveness of audit planning. When the CAE is developing the annual audit plan, they may identify the need for specialty expertise such as information technology, engineering, governance, or compliance aspects. The determination of which projects will include co-sourced consultants is important to establish the proper timing for the audits as well as the ability to secure the proper resources.

- *What teaming concepts should be addressed to integrate co-sourced auditors with internal auditors?* This consideration should not be overlooked. If the co-sourced relationship is to be sustainable and ongoing, the CAE or internal audit management must make strides toward building processes that encourage teamwork between the internal staff and the external consultants.
- *How will communication of co-sourced audit reports be delivered to the audit committee?* Internal audit management may choose to have co-sourced reports delivered independently to the audit committee. In other instances, the CAE will manage the communication. It is important that the CAE work with the audit committee to determine their level of comfort with each approach.

These are a few of the considerations internal audit management should address within a co-sourced audit relationship. Co-sourcing can be very valuable in many respects. But the CAE has additional dynamics when establishing a proper working environment and the proper organization perception of the internal audit group.

Challenge 22: In-Sourcing

In-sourced function occur when the company retains internal employees to source the department. The benefits of this process include the following:

- Internal employees are viewed as part of the organization culture. This can facilitate the establishment of close relationships with the process owners.
- Internal employees have a dedicated interest in learning about the company's overall operations. This will assist in performing later assigned reviews.
- Overall, the cost of in-sourcing a function (when balanced appropriately) can be a greater benefit than outsourcing. Internal employees are contributing to the bottom line of the company and learning the company processes that will enable them to be more efficient in their roles. They take a vested interest in the results.

The challenges of this process include the following:

- If the function is seen as training grown or possibly viewed as an area with little respect, there may be high turnover in the area.
- If the function is highly valued, there may be long-term career auditors who become complacent in their role if not properly managed.
- Depending on management's tone regarding internal audit, the concept of objectivity and independence can be difficult to execute as an internal employee.

A CAE relayed their experience of moving from a co-sourced function to a fully in-sourced function. The process took several years to work through issues and develop an atmosphere of team. In the end, it was accomplished but there were many stumbling points. The in-sourced team learned that during the co-sourced years, management did not place significant value in the recommendations or findings of internal audit due to the narrowed focus of the work. Once the company moved to an in-sourced model, the audit committee stepped to the plate to provide the in-sourced function with the support needed to allow the department to become a value-oriented function. The committee acted on its fiduciary responsibilities and regularly spoke with the CAE and encouraged open and transparent communication. Even during tough political times within the organization, the audit committee stood behind the internal auditors to solidify their position. This isn't to say that the team didn't have problems with management. They continued to struggle with some of the same dilemmas that many departments struggle with including gaining respect and acknowledgment of authority. It wasn't until the CAE reporting line was moved to the CEO that the internal audit group was able to effectuate a strong value.

In another situation, a CAE of a very large nonpublicly traded company led an in-sourced function. The group was staffed sparsely. Certain information technology work was outsourced. The model did not work well for this organization due to management preferences and pressure on how they believed the internal audit group should function. Several previous CAEs of the same company had expressed to the audit committee their difficulty executing the work with independence and objectivity. However, their communication was not embraced by management or the audit committee. In this instance, the company had a stronger need for more of a quality assurance function.

Challenge 22 Potential Actions: In-Sourcing Considerations that internal audit management should make when examining the in-source model may include the following:

- *Is overall staffing adequate?* One of the strongest arguments for outsourcing or co-sourcing is the consultant firm's ability to obtain resources when needed. Internally sourced functions face similar dilemmas as other corporate departments. Individuals may take paid time off or family leave; they may look to move into different parts of the organization or outside of the organization. All of these instances can result in a staffing deficiency. In some situations, long-term auditors may become stagnant in their positions and are not as motivated and productive as required. These issues require the CAE to stay abreast of the needs of the company and its relationship to the resourcing of the audit group. The existence of long-term auditors is not a bad thing. But if the auditors become complacent in their duties, the CAE must be able to address their work products and habits. In addition, paid time off or disability is an issue that is difficult to control. CAEs must be cognizant of vacation days, potential sick days, holidays, and other factors when estimating their annual audit plan for the year. They cannot assume that all employees will have 2080 chargeable hours in a year. They must consider time off for vacation, sick leave, and other reasons. This may mean that the CAE should establish a backup plan in the event they lose personnel from the department or even for a period of time.
- *Does the department have the relevant expertise?* This will impact commitment to competence. We discussed earlier the concept of providing auditors relevant training. There are many methods to obtain training, and CAEs and internal audit management must ensure they work to continually improve the skill set of staff. Even when internal budgets are constrained, this

should not prohibit internal audit from conducting their own in-house training for auditors as well as assigning mentors to individuals to help them gain the experience needed to adequately perform their job. There may be circumstances where a review arises, and there is not an internal resource available or qualified to perform the review. A good example is a forensic evaluation. The CAE must have the ability to closely examine these instances and reach out to obtain resources that may not be available within their department.

- *Is there concern of independence and objectivity?* When evaluating the in-sourced model, the CAE must be able to obtain relevant information regarding how the staff has experienced management reactions and/or pressure. If there are valid concerns of objectivity and independence, the CAE must have alternative methods to address the issue. As was stated previously, even an outsourced firm can experience pressure from management where independence and objectivity can be impaired. The CAE must openly address any challenges they see when attempting to execute on independence and objectivity. This is a key attribute for internal audit to perform effectively.
- *Is the organization capable of maintaining a consistently sourced function that retains skilled internal auditors?* There are many cases of internal audit groups where staffing is extremely thin and not in line with benchmarks. In these instances, the department is hampered in their ability to provide adequate and consistent services. Many organizations exist where the staffing numbers for internal audit was determined when the department was initially formed. Unless the staffing decision is periodically evaluated to ensure it meets company needs, the internal audit function can find themselves in a predicament of narrowly scoping audit areas to attempt to cover risks in order to complete the audit plan. Consider the scenario of an organization that has typically sourced with a handful of auditors. Now fast forward 5 years, the business has expanded twofold, but the audit department does not change in staffing size. In this instance, the CAE must be able to ask the "why" question and determine whether the group is able to adequately cover the risks of the organization.

Summary

The CAE should be prepared to evaluate each consideration for sourcing models and determine the best path for given current and future goals of the organization. Regardless of the method in place, a periodic review should occur to ensure that the method is effective to meet the organization's long- and short-term objectives. When challenges arise, the CAE should openly discuss those challenges with the audit committee. Don't allow the audit committee to simply ask the question, "Is internal audit properly sourced?" As the CAE, you must be prepared to provide the committee with a transparent opinion that outlines both the benefits and the challenges of sourcing. For the audit committee to execute their fiduciary oversight of the department, they must understand all aspects of the issue. It is difficult for them to understand the process when they only receive quarterly reports.

Section 5: Internal Audit Skill Sets and Knowledge

Introduction

The audit team should be able to obtain the proper skills as well as maintain those skills. How often do we hear "There is no room in the budget for training?" Another statement may be, "We are saving our training dollars until the end of the year." When year-end arrives, there is no time to attend training, or the budget dollars have been restricted because of company mandates.

Challenge 23: Maintaining Appropriate Skill Sets

As a manager within an internal audit group several years ago, I did not have the opportunity to attend professional training events outside of local IIA chapter meetings. At one point, another manager and I were able to convince the CAE that it was important for us to attend a professional convention. We came away from the convention with a host of ideas and new initiatives. Over the years, I have been a strong proponent for auditors to obtain the proper amount of exposure through training classes. Some of these classes were basic auditor skill courses. I witnessed exponential value for when auditors were given the opportunity to learn and observe in different atmospheres. It was beneficial for the auditors to hear and learn how other groups managed their audit documentation, planning, fieldwork, and reporting process. In addition, they would return from the training and provide a briefing to the internal audit group. Many ideas on advancements and changes for the group came from these interactions.

Challenge 23 Potential Actions: Maintaining Appropriate Skill Sets Internal audit management must work towards critical evaluations and considerations on actions to ensure their teams are adequately staffed. Following are some specific thoughts to contemplate.

- *All internal auditors must retain some level of ongoing education.* For auditors in highly technical industries, training on industry background and operations can be important to appropriately execute operational audits.
- *Understand any requirements for regulatory compliance reviews.* For auditors who are faced with these types of reviews, it is important to understand relevant legislation or compliance requirements. Also, having access to emerging changes in compliance regulations is important.
- *Allow networking with peers and industry professionals.* Understanding how other internal audit functions operate can provide significant value. For new initiatives like continuous auditing, enterprise risk management, fraud evaluations, or governance processes, ideas from other experienced internal audit groups can help springboard your organization to the next level.
- *Maintain a strong process around internal department training.* Members must understand process and protocols for executing and reporting audits. As a CAE or internal audit manager, your ability to execute periodic internal training classes which discuss areas such as audit methodology, report writing, communication, and leadership skills is important to provide auditors with the proper set of tools to execute their responsibilities.
- *As a CAE, ensure you establish processes to instill confidence within the staff.* Personal confidence can be a defining factor

in a professional's individual success or challenges. It begins at a very early age when we work for the approval of our parents, then teenage peers, and later supervisors. There are many educational courses on leadership where the topic of confidence is covered. CAEs must work to instill confidence in their team members. When a working atmosphere is hampered by an unhealthy attitude and individuals who are only concerned about their own well-being, the result can be devastating to other team members.

Summary

Building an effective internal audit team requires the ability to critically evaluate many aspects of the organization culture, needs, strategy, and focus. However, it also requires instilling the proper concepts of teamwork into the everyday responsibilities of the auditors. A department's ability to obtain the value-added status will greatly hinge on their ability to cohesively and effectively source and manage the proper set of skills balanced with the appropriate teaming concepts, customer relations, and audit methodology.

4
Audit Plan

Introduction

When you hear management state "The internal auditors should develop an independent risk-based audit plan" what is your individual reaction? Is it reasonable to believe that internal audit can independently and separately develop a risk-based audit plan? *Standards* address the need for internal audit to develop a risk-based audit plan. However they recognize the importance of gaining input from management and the audit committee on risks critical to the business. *Standards* also address the need for the CAE to periodically reassess the audit plan with management and adjust plan to the business needs. This concept recognizes that management understands the business and the risks of the organization. It is critical to gain management insight and input when determining components of the internal audit plan. Considering these directives, a well-developed risk-based audit plan is the product of input from management, the audit committee, and internal audit's various evaluations.

CAEs commonly express the concern that management's expectation is for internal audit to independently determine the audit plan. This expectation may be due to management view on the concept of independence of the internal audit function. When CAEs or audit management run into this dilemma, it is advisable to provide information to management about the *Standards*. Share with management the concepts of the professional *Standards* and the position on development of a proper risk-based plan. It may assist in paving the way toward a more comprehensive understanding of the most effective methods for audit plan development as well as the internal audit profession's definition of risk based auditing.

The *Standards* include the requirement to obtain input from senior management and the board to develop a comprehensive plan. As previously discussed in Chapter 2, an underlying theory behind risk-based auditing is to align the audit processes with the objectives, risks, and goals of the enterprise. The concept of applying risk-based auditing will be further examined within Chapter 5.

When considering the need for alignment of the audit plan to the goals of the enterprise, the internal audit group must evaluate their ability to execute complete risk-based auditing. A company that views internal audit as a pure compliance or operational function may take the approach that the auditor's responsibility is to perform Sarbanes–Oxley compliance testing or potential operational validation of inventory or asset processes. Although these areas are within the scope of internal audit, they may not be areas that would surface as most critical when developing a risk-based audit plan. If the function chooses to exercise its full definition of risk-based auditing as well as assurance and compliance focus, the resourcing and audit plan will be dramatically different from a function that choses to direct efforts toward an isolated or specific purpose. In the end, the decision to embrace risk-based auditing will impact internal audit resourcing the audit plan and the value proposition of internal audit.

To execute on complete risk-based auditing, a strong insight to the goals of the organization is required. Challenge 15 in Chapter 2 discussed how allowing the CAE to have a seat at the table will provide insight into strategic discussions. However, other methods also exist. These methods may include:

- A process to allow for regular updates to the audit plan based on evolving risks.
- Regular meetings with the CEO and business unit management to discuss the organizations business strategy.
- Individual meetings with the audit committee to understand their views on initiatives of the business.
- Exposure to any risk assessment processes conducted by other personnel within the company. This includes risk assessments of areas such as fraud, emerging risks, technology, ERM and operations.

To properly measure and prioritize risks and execute risk-based auditing, the CAE and the internal audit group must understand the company's business and have the relevant expertise to execute on critical risk audit areas. They must also understand the organization's short- and long-term strategy and objectives. Having knowledge of this piece of the puzzle will allow the CAE to properly prioritize risks and issues as they are identified. To be able to effectively execute on these tasks, the internal audit group must have access to information that allows them to fulfill the principle of strategic alignment of the goals of the organization. Recognizing that CAEs who have a direct reporting line to the CEO are in the minority, the internal audit group must identify other unique and innovative methods to be able to obtain the knowledge of organization strategies and emerging risks and goals.

In this chapter, we will cover the following challenges:

- Challenge 24: Audit Plan Time Frame
- Challenge 25: Audit Plan Resource Allocation
- Challenge 26: Audit Plan Development Approach
- Challenge 27: Audit Plan Results
- Challenge 28: Enterprise Risk Management Assessment
- Challenge 29: Executing the Enterprise Risk Management Process
- Challenge 30: Enterprise Risk Management Reporting versus Internal Audit Reporting

Section 1: Developing an Independent Audit Plan

Introduction

Developing the internal audit plan can have many challenges. Important factors include determining auditable risks, the audit plan time frame, resource allocation, plan development approach, and overall methodology.

Challenge 24: Audit Plan Time Frame

In today's business, the concept of annual audit plan is somewhat of a catch 22. With the rapid change of business and risks, it may be difficult to foresee all of the relevant issues that should be examined over a twelve-month period. Many groups spend significant time working through management interviews and risk assessing their audit universe to develop an annual plan. This activity may begin several months before the new fiscal year. To assume that an audit plan developed this far in advance of the organizations fiscal year as well as assuming assessment of the plan will be fully relevant twelve-to-fourteen months later may be a bit optimistic. Risks are ever changing. Business is ever changing. There must be a method to allow the audit plan to appropriately evolve and adjust with these changing conditions.

Challenge 24 Potential Actions: Audit Plan Time Frame There are alternatives to an annual audit plan. A challenge to adopting one of the alternatives is convincing management of the need for change. When there is an existing process that has been in place for a long period of time and has been accepted as the *status quo*, it may be difficult to get parties involved to accept a change. Management tends to like an annual audit plan because it allows them insight into what to expect for the coming year. If the internal audit group were to suggest an adjustable plan or possibly a quarterly plan, they may receive pushback due to management's concern of the unknown. In today's environment, internal audit must consider the relevance of adopting a different approach to annual audit planning. Some considerations may include the following:

- *Establish an initial audit plan which is segmented by quarters. The plan could then be updated on a quarterly basis.* This approach may help manage the process of transitioning away from the annual audit plan theory. By identifying an initial annual plan and then prioritizing the projects by quarter, the audit team can take the opportunity to reevaluate risks on a quarterly basis and propose updates or changes to the plan based on the evolving needs of the business. The procedure more closely matches the objective of aligning audits to the most critical business risk.
- *Establish a 6-month rolling audit plan.* By decreasing the time frame for the audit plan, there is greater likelihood that the projects executed will be timely and in line with business objectives. At the end of each quarter, internal audit would

add an additional quarter of audit projects to the plan. This process would allow the company to make appropriate adjustments based on evolving needs.

- *Establish an annual plan, and utilize priority category rankings.* This approach allows the audit group to develop an annual audit plan; however, it requires an assessment and prioritization of audits that may be of higher priority risk. Assume priorities are assigned as follows:
  - Priority 1: Audits that are assessed as high-risk areas and are expected to be completed within the first 6 months of the audit plan year.
  - Priority 2: Audits that are assessed as moderate risk. These projects would be expected to be completed within the plan year. However, if other projects surface that are deemed more significant, a priority 2 audit may be replaced with the newer project.
  - Priority 3: Audits that are assessed lower than the moderate risk level for audit plan purposes. These are audits that may be routine cycle audits or compliance reviews that could be deferred to a later time if business requirements dictate. In the event that a higher-risk issue arises, these audits would be the first removed from the audit plan. It is important to note that Priority 3 audits do not mean they are low-risk audits. The approach requires application of an assessment of risk to the category of audits identified to be included in the plan for the coming year. Priority 3 audits would be those that present a lower threshold risk or concern around the timing of their execution.

Using a priority-based approach allows the audit team to reassess risks on a quarterly or semiannual basis and make recommendations to management and the board for changes to the audit plan. If utilizing this approach, the audit team should gain agreement from management and the audit committee regarding the priority-level assignments as well as the transition of any individual audit on or off the plan.

Challenge 25: Audit Plan Resource Allocation

Individuals who have been involved in developing an audit plan may realize the concept can be more of an art than a scientific method. Companies have their individual protocols for identifying, prioritizing, and evaluating risks and then determining which risks are relevant to be included in the upcoming plan. *Standards* dictate the need to build a risk-based audit plan. To effectively execute on this process requires understanding and a clear definition of the company's expectations regarding the amount of time allocation internal audit will give to each respective area of the business. This may include either the business unit areas or financial, compliance, and operational areas. We've noted how many organizations place the responsibility for Sarbanes–Oxley compliance and testing within internal audit. This can consume a significant amount of audit time. In other instances, time may be allocated to assist the external auditors in their annual attestation work. Again, this can consume a significant portion of the audit plan. The CAE must first evaluate the organizations expectation for allocation of internal audits time to various areas. As an example, let's review a scenario:

Scenario: Audit Plan Resources The internal audit group is comprised of 10 internal auditors and 1 CAE. Internal auditors are expected to obtain 1650 chargeable hours per year. The CAE is expected to have 600 chargeable hours for the year. This information provides the CAE with audit plan hours of 17,100 available to allocate to the annual audit plan (10 auditors times 1650 hours plus 600 hours for the CAE). In addition, the internal audit group is expected to spend 2000 hours on Sarbanes–Oxley work and 1500 hours on the external audit support.

Given these constraints, there are 13,600 hours left to spread between other identified risk areas.

Assume the company expects the audit hours to be evenly split among operational, financial, and compliance audits. The CAE is able to determine this expectation results in each area being assigned approximately 5700 hours (13,600 divided by three). The hours allocated to Sarbanes–Oxley and the external audit are considered to be hours attributable to the financial area. This would mean 2200 financial hours are left to allocate (5700 minutes 1500 hours for compliance work). If the assumption is that the predetermined compliance hours are deducted from the total available hours, then the audit team would split the remaining 13,600 hours evenly among operational, compliance, and financial areas.

This methodology may not necessarily comply strictly with a risk-based audit approach. In a risk-based audit approach, the evaluation of risks is made at the overall corporate level and would not necessarily assume that the organization will split hours evenly among financial, compliance, and operational audits. However, since we are discussing the reality of how many internal audit groups must function, it is important to recognize the challenges that are faced.

Challenge 25 Potential Actions: Audit Plan Resource Allocation With the scenario given above, internal audit must ensure they understand how the organization expects the function to allocate available audit hours. For organizations that are segregated into distinct business units, the expectation may be for internal audit to spend a proportionate amount of time on each business area in relation to that area's contribution to the organization's revenues. In other organizations, the segregation of distinct business units may take a different approach. Management may prefer that internal audit spend a majority of their time on more significant business areas that present the strongest risk to organization. In any event, following are some important considerations when identifying how the hours in your audit plan will be allocated:

- *Gain agreement from management regarding how internal audit hours will be allocated.* Ensure that you have a clear road map regarding the expectations of management and the board. Understand whether the hours will be allocated on the basis of organizational business areas or financial, compliance, operational, and regulatory processes. In some cases, management may deem one area as having a stronger level of significance than others based on their individual risk prioritization. Internal audit must understand these expectations and be able to reconcile the approach to their individual risk-based audit approach.

- *Complete a holistic risk assessment, and independently evaluate whether the hours allocation is relevant based on the assessed risk to the organization.* Once you have an understanding of how management expects internal audit to allocate resources, compare that allocation to the results of your top-down risk assessment. Evaluate whether internal audit hours are being appropriately focused on the highest risk areas. If the risk assessment varies from the allocation expectations, the CAE should address concerns with the audit committee.
- *Understand management's expectations for internal audit to support the external auditors or perform Sarbanes–Oxley compliance work.* Many organizations still see internal audit as a resource for lowering external audit fees. In some cases, this may be a relevant use of internal audit's time. However, management must strongly consider the cost benefit of this approach. Often, internal audit support of the external audit process is relegated to lower-level compliance or substantive testing. Organizations which have completed a cost/benefit analysis of this approach have found that utilizing their internal professionals to perform lower-level external audit work is not an efficient use of time or resources. In addition, the work often does not provide the internal auditor with the most beneficial learning experience to ultimately add overall value to the organization. If management were to perform a cost/benefit analysis, they would often find that utilization of internal man hours along with overhead allocations does not provide the perceived benefit of lowered fees or costs. A brief example follows:
    - Assume internal audit dedicates 4 professionals to the external audit on a full-time basis in the final quarter of the year.
    - These 4 professionals have a combined salary of \$300,000. Considering the addition of benefits, the cost of the professional's time on an annual basis equates closer to \$400,000. The cost of assigning 25% of 4 auditors time to the external audit equates to \$100,000.
    - Savings from the external audit is stated as \$150,000. However, management must recognize the time and commitment of internal resources toward lower-level substantive testing.

Would this be considered an appropriate utilization of the internal audit team's time? The answer to that question will vary by company, but it is one the CAE must evaluate and discuss with management.

By focusing internal auditors on external audit substantive work, the company loses any value that can be provided when examining higher-risk priority issues for the company. This same theory applies to Sarbanes–Oxley work. Some organizations have moved toward establishing internal control functions to take on this administrative task. Management must evaluate the cost/benefit of expending internal audit resources in an area that may be a management control responsibility.

Challenge 26: Audit Plan Development Approach

Internal audit must have an established methodology to develop their annual plan in relation to the risks of the organization. With this acknowledged, internal audit is often challenged when preparing a risk-based audit plan due to a constraint on resources or the expectation by management for audit coverage of specific areas. In addition, internal audit may periodically face the dilemma of being asked to exclude a certain area of the business from audit plan considerations. According to *Standards*, this would not be an approach in line with risk-based auditing. CAEs must be prepared to address instances where management feels that certain areas are off limits, or other areas are typical areas for internal audit review. The ability to effectively address this challenge may lie in the relevance of your risk-based audit approach and ability to obtain buy-in from management.

Challenge 26 Potential Actions: Audit Plan Development Approach In order to gain appropriate support for audit plan development, consider the following actions:

- *Review with management and the audit committee the Standards and the concepts underlying a risk-based audit approach.* It is important for management and the audit committee to have an understanding of professional *Standards* and obligations. In addition, it is important they understand the importance placed on developing a risk-based audit approach that considers the full universe of organizational risks. An internal audit risk assessment that considers the complete universe of organizational risks will ultimately provide the organization with a stronger insight to the areas that should be audited.

- *Work with management and the audit committee to define organizational risk appetite and tolerance statements.* As discussed in Chapter 2 and later in Chapter 5 on risk-based auditing, it is critical for internal audit to work with management and the audit committee to gain an understanding of the organization's overall risk appetite. The ability to adequately outline and understand organizational risk appetite is a strong key to building a successful risk-based audit plan. Through the understanding of risk appetite, internal audit can appropriately evaluate and weigh the risks that have the potential to breach management appetite levels.
- *Develop the audit approach and methodology, and review and obtain buy-in from management prior to executing any work.* Providing management insight into the methodology and framework for identifying and assessing risks will assist in gaining an understanding behind the scope of the process and the considerations evaluated. By obtaining buy-in from management on the audit methodology and outline, internal audit will ensure the plan appropriately segments the business risks to provide for relevant allocation of internal audit available hours.
- *Create an initial risk analysis outline and review framework with management.* This step involves presenting the actual outline and format to management. It is important management has insight into information that comprises the audit plan. Consider the following scenarios that may be utilized within a methodology:
  - Utilization of specific criteria to evaluate process areas (e.g., risk for fraud, transaction volume/type, economic impact, operational efficiency).
  - Evaluation of areas by business segment or product line.
  - Development of a risk-based approach based on a financial statement assertion assessment.
  - Utilization of an approach that considers auditing based on asset verification or revenue/expenditure validation. (In many organizations, the internal audit function exists

as an asset verification function, whereas in other organizations, it may exist as revenue and expenditure examination function.)

Each of these scenarios requires appropriate understanding and buy-in from management. This will assist in mitigating any resistance that may arise later in the process.

Challenge 27: Audit Plan Results

Inevitably, at some point in an internal auditor's career, they may experience a disagreement with management regarding the significance or relevance of placing a particular audit on the audit plan. This can be a frustrating experience when the audit team has dedicated a significant amount of effort toward the development of a strategic risk-based audit approach. Many CAEs will express they have experienced incidents where management strongly contested a specific audit proposed by the internal audit group. In some cases, management felt the audit area was not within the purview of how internal audit responsibilities were defined for the organization. In other cases, management felt the area was already being adequately evaluated by the external auditors or some other quality function. The ability to work past management objections can depend on many factors including:

- The structure of the organization and the political implications
- Whether the organization is publicly or privately held
- The support received from the external auditors
- The independent relationship the CAE has with the audit committee
- The commitment to the internal audit mission by the organization

Challenge 27 Potential Actions: Audit Plan Results The CAE must consider what challenges they will face with audit plan recommendations and have a plan to address those challenges. Following are some considerations:

- *Perform your due diligence up front.* Ensure there is a transparent process for establishment of the internal audit plan. Obtain management buy-in for the process upfront. Review concepts including risk appetite considerations early in the audit plan development stage. Each of these actions will assist in mitigating many concerns that may arise late in the process.

- *Review the results of the internal risk analysis with the CFO/CEO prior to prioritization of any planned audits.* Taking time to review your analysis and assumptions with executive management is important. The ability to obtain management input regarding considerations for prioritization of audit projects will assist when opposition arises to proposed audit work.
- *Ensure that projects on the audit plan are within the purview of internal audit as outlined in the department charter.* The internal audit charter will define the responsibilities and authorities of the function. Assuming that the charter is a document that is fact and not fiction, internal audit should be able to rely on information within the charter to support their proposal of specific audits. However, as we have discussed, if the organization has specific expectations of internal audit's role, and if they have explicit expectations regarding areas internal audit will not evaluate (e.g., fraud, governance, ethics), internal audit may have a difficult time proposing a review in one of these areas. Acknowledging the *Standards* indicate that each of these areas is within the scope of the definition of internal audit; in reality, many organizations have very specific expectations regarding their functions. If the CAE plans to include an area on the audit plan that is not included in the internal audit charter, or if it is an area that has not typically been considered within the purview of internal audit, it will be important to set the stage and adequately outline justification and reasoning for including this area on the proposed audit plan.
- *Ensure that the proposal of audit projects is supported by available internal audit hours.* Inability to adequately estimate individual audit project time and reconcile the time to available internal audit resources will open the door for management challenges on whether the internal audit group can actually execute upon the proposed plan. Estimating audit project hours is another area that can be considered an art. In some instances, audit groups will scope their projects to the specific audit hours allocated in the plan. From a risk-based perspective, there

should be some level of expectation regarding risks that will be evaluated within the proposed audit area. This expectation should drive the proposed audit hours for the project. Absent an adequate up-front assessment of required hours for each project, internal audit will find they may have included on the plan that could not be adequately completed. This would not be considered in line with a risk-based audit approach.

- *Be aware of segmenting buckets of hours for special projects.* A typical process used by internal audit is to estimate a portion of hours that may be needed in the upcoming plan year for special projects or new initiatives. CAEs know that these special requests often arise during the year. However, it is important to have some logic and rationale behind how those hours are allocated. Audit management may immediately jump to past history. However, past history isn't always a good predictor of future events. The CAE must be able to support any allocated hours with a strong risk-based purpose or tie it to a strategic need of the business.
- *Reassess progress towards plan execution on a frequent basis.* A difficult situation can be created if internal audit does not appropriately keep management apprised of their progress on the audit plan. There are many instances where auditors have been required to scramble at the end of the year to finish audits included on the plan. This may result in a need to narrowly scope audits to allow for a check-the-box approach to completing the audit plan. Regardless of the type of audit plan developed (e.g., annual, quarterly, rolling), the CAE should periodically reassess progress toward completion of the plan. In the event there is an identified issue that may impede completion of the plan, the issue should be proactively addressed with management and the audit committee.

An interesting example that a CAE relayed was surrounding work on the internal audit plan for his company in the year 2001. Of course, this was the year of the 9/11 terrorist attacks. The CAE's company was located in the New York Manhattan district. As most can imagine, the devastation of that incident and the chaos caused to the businesses that were located in the Manhattan area resulted in many disruptions in workflow. In this instance, the

> CAE's audit plan was significantly impacted. Time was lost from relocation of corporate offices, family issues, travel constraints, and organization disaster recovery issues. The catastrophic nature of the event would lead most to assume the company management and the audit committee would understand many business processes were impacted, and this impact would extend to internal audit. However, as year-end approached, and the audit committee realized internal audit was significantly behind in their completion of the annual audit plan, the CAE came under significant criticism. The lesson learned is not to take anything for granted. Regardless of what you may believe is known, ensure that you timely communicate with the audit committee regarding any limitations on completion of the annual audit plan.

The CAE must proactively address any challenges that may exist when developing and executing the internal audit plan. This proactive work will assist in obtaining management and audit committee support and buy-in for the function.

Section 2: The Risk Assessment Approach

Introduction

How would your organization define the need for a corporate-wide holistic risk assessment? The literal definition of holistic denotes a meaning of concern with wholes rather than analysis or separation into parts. A corporate-wide holistic risk assessment is most effectively executed with the inclusion of strategic individuals throughout the business who have an understanding of various processes. Typically, internal audit's responsibility for risk assessment has been associated with the development of the annual audit plan. When Sarbanes–Oxley arose, the internal audit team often assisted in the development of a top-down accounting risk assessment for purposes of evaluating internal controls over financial reporting. With the emergence of enterprise risk management processes, many internal audit groups played a role in assisting to facilitate or participate in the company's entity-wide risk assessment. In addition, there is the aspect of fraud risk assessments. Depending on processes within the company and how the antifraud program is managed, internal audit may be involved in elements of assessing fraud risk.

There are many forms of risk assessment and many ways in which internal audit can add value. Internal auditors are process specialist. They have a wide and broad understanding of the organization and the many risks faced. Their ability to be involved in strategic risk assessment processes can provide management with great value and unique input. Yet, with this expertise, there are many cases where risk assessments are still conducted within their siloed processes. When enterprise risk management became an area of focus in business, companies looked to the *Committee of Sponsoring Organizations (COSO) Internal Control Framework* enterprise risk management model to provide a guidance for developing assessments. In some cases, internal audit had strategic input into the process, whereas in other instances, the company developed a distinct enterprise risk management function that administered and managed the enterprise risk management process. Whichever method your company utilizes, it is an important and critical that consideration be given to ensure the involvement of internal audit within any type of corporate-wide risk assessments. The ability to have input and knowledge of the risks evaluated through this process can add significant value and synergies to the creation of the annual audit plan and the company's individual enterprise risk management process. Inability to connect the two processes may result in overlap of responsibilities and varying levels of assessment and measurement. However, many audit functions face difficulty gaining acceptance as a part of the corporate-wide enterprise risk management process or even the corporate-wide fraud risk assessment. The challenges faced stretch from management's definition of the role of internal audit to specific organizational territorial issues. The CAE must work to gain insight and acceptance into these processes. In the end, the joint efforts will be most efficient for the organization. Let's review a few of the challenges that auditors may face when working to be involved in corporate-wide risk assessments.

Challenge 28: Enterprise Risk Management Assessment

There are several points of view within the business world regarding which departmental area should administer the enterprise risk management process. Enterprise risk management facilitation is similar to the concept of Sarbanes–Oxley compliance work. It is handled differently in almost every organization. Variations range from the establishment of a chief risk officer and an enterprise risk management group to full administration of the process by internal audit. In other organizations, management may view the process as being owned at the senior management or even board level. Many companies have developed lavish enterprise risk management teams and structures comprising lengthy risk registers, complicated likelihood and impact measurements, and detailed risk analysis and risk mitigation plans. The detailed administrative process of enterprise risk management can also be compared to the early days of Sarbanes–Oxley where organizations took a deep dive into the detail of documenting and testing multiple processes. In the end, many of these processes may not have had a significant impact on internal controls over financial reporting. As the years have progressed, many organizations have attempted to adjust their process or implement a bite-sized approach to enterprise risk management. Regardless of which stage your company operates, the critical concept of enterprise risk management is to identify those risks that could have the greatest impact to your organization's overall strategic objectives. It also requires the ability of the organization to grasp an understanding of new and emerging risks. These risks must be identified on a timely basis in order to establish appropriate mitigating actions prior to any significant impact.

As companies have built their enterprise risk management functions, many have separated the process from internal audit. In some cases, a distinct disconnection exists between the manner in which risks are assessed and measured by the enterprise risk management function and separately by internal audit. When this dynamic occurs, it can create significant questions on the part of management and the board regarding the adequacy of the internal audit process.

Internal auditors must find a way to maintain a seat at the table in the enterprise risk management process. The ability to understand how management examines risks and measures impact is of strategic value when developing the internal audit plan. In addition, internal audit should ensure that the audit plan addresses (to the extent they are auditable) those risks identified by the enterprise risk management team as most significant to the organization.

Challenge 28 Potential Actions: Enterprise Risk Management Assessment In the event the enterprise risk management process is separate and distinct from internal audit, there are several areas that internal audit should consider.

- *Understand the enterprise risk management team's methodology and process for the development of risk registers.* Gaining an understanding and appreciation for the measurement levels applied and the considerations used on risk tolerance and appetite can assist internal audit in adjusting and appropriately calibrating their audit plan.
- *Identify how the enterprise risk management team gathers information relative to risks.* Is it accomplished through interviews, facilitated sessions, or questionnaire input? Having insight into how information is collected can assist in understanding how the information will be compiled and utilized. In addition, if possible, having the ability to work with the enterprise risk management team as they conduct their interviews may provide some synergies when working on the audit plan.
- *Understand the impact, likelihood, and significance measurements utilized by the enterprise risk management team and the method in which those measurements were determined.* Enterprise risk management will often measure risks utilizing a scale that defines the highest-level impact as being catastrophic. Internal audit should not wait until an issue hits the catastrophic phase to initiate an audit or review. In addition, management may experience confusion around the variances in the scales utilized within the enterprise risk management process and the internal audit process. To address this concern, some internal audit groups utilize the enterprise risk management methodology when setting their internal audit measurement scale. They identify their threshold level as something much lower than the catastrophic level assigned by the enterprise risk management group. This allows internal auditors the opportunity to initiate an audit to identify potential control gaps. However, it is important that management understand the difference.

In addition, understanding the process utilized by enterprise risk management to define their measurement scales will be important when working with management to develop a risk appetite statement. Internal auditors should be able to reconcile their usage of risk appetite with how it is utilized within the enterprise risk management process. The ability to have a strong understanding of the enterprise risk management measurement process and translate it to the internal audit process can provide increased value to the organization.

Other important considerations include:

- *Identify how the enterprise risk management team stays abreast of emerging issues.* One of the important concepts of enterprise risk management is to establish a process that can be proactive when identifying risks that could threaten the organization in the future. Many companies maintain enterprise risk management councils comprised of senior leaders who meet periodically to discuss risks of the business and evaluate if any new or emerging issues may impact the business. The ability for internal audit to be involved in these sessions can enhance understanding of emerging risks. It can also provide proactive input into risks that may require focus from an internal audit perspective.
- *Understand how often the enterprise risk management team executes their methodology.* This can be important when approaching the audit planning cycle. Audit groups periodically encounter difficulty when attempting to execute their audit plan cycle. Process owners become disgruntled because they feel they have relayed the required information to another area. If internal audit can be involved in the enterprise risk management process, they will have a better understanding of the methods used and the information collected. This can be utilized to determine what additional information may be needed for the annual audit plan.

Challenge 29: Executing the Enterprise Risk Management Process

The execution of the enterprise risk management processes will continually evolve within organizations. As the organization's objectives and goals change, so will its focus on enterprise risk management activities. In the initial stages, much of the work may be focused on the identification of risks and measurement of their relative impact and likelihood to the organization. Once this process is complete, the focus will be toward maintaining an adequate process for management of risks and identification of emerging risks that could impact the organization. Depending on the stage of the enterprise risk management process, internal audit involvement can be varied.

Challenge 29 Potential Actions: Executing the Enterprise Risk Management Process In the early stages of the enterprise risk management process, internal audit can take a strong role in assisting with the identification of relevant risks to the organization. They can also be involved in the development of the measurement scales. Following are some actions internal audit teams may find of value when working with this process:

- *Involvement in identification of relevant risk registers.* Risk registers and the adequate identification of risk is an important aspect to enterprise risk management. However, organizations must be able to adequately manage their risk identification process and keep in mind the level at which risk identification should occur. Some organizations start at a high organization level, measure the top business risks, and then determine which of those risks are most relevant to evaluate at a deeper level. Other organizations attempt to identify the complete universe of risks at the onset of the project. The proper method will be determined by the organization. Internal auditors can assist management and the enterprise risk management team by providing their subject matter expertise on risk identification. This stage is one where the inclusion of internal audit can be a distinct value to the organization.
- *Involvement in the development of the relevant risk rating scales.* This process is critical to the enterprise risk management process. The potential for auditors to have input into the development of the measurement scales while also understanding the various measurements that are being utilized by the enterprise risk management team to define the scales is critical to the ability to apply concepts within the internal audit process.

- *Involvement in enterprise risk management interviews or facilitated sessions.* The enterprise risk management process can be facilitated through interviews, surveys, facilitated sessions or other methods. The utilization of facilitated management group sessions allows for consensus understanding, buy-in, and agreed to identification of ownership for the various risks. Allowing internal audit to observe the facilitated sessions or group interviews will provide the auditors with strong information for utilization in their audit planning efforts as well as individual audit project execution.

Challenge 30: Enterprise Risk Management Reporting versus Internal Audit Reporting

Management must understand that enterprise risk management reporting may take on various forms and formats that are very different from internal audit reporting. In theory, enterprise risk management reports should be reviewed by the audit committee. However, the reports are written in different formats and language from internal audit reports. Enterprise risk management does not have the same responsibility as internal audit related to the *Standards* and reporting of information. It is important that internal audit maintain an understanding of any reporting information provided to the audit committee by the enterprise risk management team. If the enterprise risk management team alerts the audit committee of a strong emerging risk, internal audit should be ready to address the issues and their potential involvement in any evaluation process.

Challenge 30 Potential Actions: Enterprise Risk Management Reporting versus Internal Audit Reporting Following are considerations for internal audit when working with the enterprise risk management group in obtaining report information:

- *Ensure that internal audit obtains copies of official enterprise risk management reports prior to their release to the audit committee.* It is important that internal audit be aware of risk issues they may be asked to review. If the enterprise risk management team reports an issue that is contradictory to a recently issued audit report, internal audit should be consulted to understand why the variance in results occurred.

- *Ensure that internal audit is aware of enterprise risk management's time requirements for reporting to the audit committee.* Internal auditors should understand the timing requirements for the enterprise risk management team to provide information to management and the audit committee. In some companies, the enterprise risk management team is distinctly separate from internal audit and may view internal audit as a competitor in relation to risk reporting. The silos of risk ownership must be eliminated, and both parties must be aware of when and what will be reported to the audit committee. This will minimize inconsistent reporting on risks to the audit committee.

The ability for the enterprise risk management team and internal audit to work jointly and cohesively is in the best interest of the company. The overall objective is to protect at company. That can only be accomplished through an adequate definition of roles and responsibilities and an understanding of how the functions can synergize and work together in the proper evaluation and assessment of risks.

5

Executing Internal Audit Responsibilities

Introduction

Through the first four chapters, we have evaluated the following:

- The lessons learned within a CAE role
- Understanding the definition of internal audit and executing upon the internal audit *Standards*
- Internal audit staffing and resourcing models
- Executing independence and objectivity as internal audit

Each topic is critical to understand before attempting to execute internal audit responsibilities. Within this chapter, we will cover concepts related to:

- Risk-based auditing
- Interpreting and understanding risk and control gaps
- Variance between consulting and assurance engagements
- Internal audit's role in governance and fraud processes
- Internal audit's role as educators

As we review each of these concepts, we will apply critical challenge questions for areas where internal auditors may face difficulties. This will provide ideas and alternatives for the most effective application of each concept. These challenges include:

- Challenge 31: Audit Planning Phase
- Challenge 32: Audit Process Area Control Structure
- Challenge 33: Using *COSO* as Part of the Risk-Based Audit Process
- Challenge 34: Understanding, Identifying, and Assessing Risk

- Challenge 35: The Concept of Tolerance versus Risk Appetite
- Challenge 36: Summarizing Results and Identifying Risk Mitigating Actions
- Challenge 37: Evaluating the Board of Directors
- Challenge 38: Internal Audit's Role in Fraud Awareness
- Challenge 39: Internal Audit's Role in Risk Assessment
- Challenge 40: Internal Audit's Role in Fraud Investigation
- Challenge 41: Internal Auditors as Consultants

Section 1: Aligning the Concept of Risk-Based Auditing

Introduction

Chapters 1 through 4 included various discussions on the importance of a strong understanding of risk-based auditing, how it is applied, and how management views the topic. As discussed, a risk-based audit approach starts with the need for internal auditors to understand the organization, its business environment, and the varying impacts changing business conditions may have on the entity. When referring to a risk-based audit approach, the internal audit team should clarify the scope of their reference and the manner in which they intend to execute upon the methodology. This chapter will deal with how internal audit could execute on a holistic approach to risk-based auditing that extends through the various phases of audit plan development, audit execution, and audit reporting.

Risk-based auditing can be considered a process itself. The process approach is most relevant once the specific audit area has been identified. Assume the audit area has been defined utilizing a top-down risk-based approach. The auditors are assigned a particular audit based on the assessment. Auditors who employ a risk-based approach will utilize the same risk methodology to determine the most significant risks to evaluate within the audit project. This will provide the relevant information needed to design and execute the required testing. In order to effectively execute on risk-based auditing, the auditor must be able to address each of the following issues:

- Ensure a complete understanding of the operational, financial, or compliance process in the relevant audit area and appropriately define the risks embedded.
- Discuss with management the business objectives of the area being audited and how those objectives will be achieved.
- Obtain a clear understanding of how the execution of processes within the area being audited are measured and monitored.
- Discuss risk appetite and tolerance with management and obtain an understanding of how boundaries for objectives within the area being audited are established.
- Begin with the objectives of the area being audited and move to understanding the threats and risks to the achievement of organizational objectives.
- Evaluate the procedures and processes used by management to mitigate and address the risks as well as any procedures utilized to identify emerging risks.

The following steps will further evaluate these concepts and address the challenges auditors may face.

Step 1: Understand the Process

To identify risks relevant to audit, the internal auditor must obtain a complete understanding of the entity and its operating environment. An experienced auditor's professional skill and judgment will be exercised when determining the specific information that should be gathered during this process. When applying risk-based concepts at the individual audit level, the auditor begins the assessment in a similar manner as used when developing the annual audit plan. Following are steps an auditor may take when attempting to understand the process for a specific area being audited:

- Understand and document how the nature of the industry impacts the objectives of the specific area being audited. Examine how those objectives contribute to execution of the business.
- Examine the ownership structure of the organization and determine how this structure impacts the personnel expertise needed within the area being audited.

- Understand whether aspects of the organizations regulatory environment impact the manner in which the area being audited performs their work.
- Determine how key strategic competitors of the organization impact work of the area being audited.
- Evaluate key reporting processes utilized by the area being audited to report critical information to management.
- Understand how the internal control environment operates of the area being audited.
- Evaluate what procedures exist to monitor critical risks of the audit area.

The internal auditor will collect information through inquiry of relevant professionals, observation and inspection of processes, and documentation. He/she will perform analytical procedures on key information related to the audit area being reviewed. Internal auditors typically refer to this stage as the planning stage.

Challenge 31: Audit Planning Phase

Planning is critical as step one in the risk-based audit process. This step ensures the audit is appropriately scoped and relevant information is gathered. Although auditors might consider the planning stage as a simple process where background information is obtained, they may also find a few imbedded challenges when executing upon this phase. Management may not understand the purpose for pre-audit interviews and data collection. In their eyes, it may be viewed as a time consuming process that does not add value to the audit. However, without proper planning and scoping, internal audit will experience many other challenges once they begin fieldwork.

As part of the planning stage, auditors must ensure management and process owners understand the purpose for the specific pre-audit protocols. Outlining the relevance of the planning activity to management in a way that allows them to understand the importance of adequate identification of risks will help ensure proper understanding of this critical phase.

Step 2: Identify the Control Structure

Auditors are familiar with the concept of identifying the company's internal control structure as it relates to Internal Control over Financial Reporting (ICFR). With the release of *COSO 2013*, the *COSO* Foundation has encouraged organizations to extend the concepts of the internal control framework to areas of compliance and operations. This recommendation provides an excellent opportunity for internal audit to align their risk-based audit process to *COSO 2013*. Within individual audits, process owners may not understand the need for utilization of a structured framework for internal controls. However, the *COSO 2013* framework can still be utilized as a guideline for conducting the audit and determining appropriate controls to evaluate. This approach will require internal auditors to evolve their audit process to incorporate all aspects of the five attributes of *COSO*.

Internal auditors often place the majority of their focus on the *COSO* control activity attribute. Benefits can be obtained by employing concepts within all five elements of *COSO* to each audit. By examining all elements of the area's control environment, risk assessment, control activities, information and communication, and monitoring activities, processes the auditors will gain a complete understanding of the effectiveness of the processes and procedures of the area being audited. Examining these individual attributes prior to advancing to the control identification and testing phase will allow the auditors to have a better understanding of how well the area's policies and procedures are developed, trained, and executed.

As a simple illustration, consider the concept of testing current policies and procedures. If the internal auditor has not examined policies and procedures to ensure they are relevant to the current business strategies (examining the effectiveness of the area's control environment), the testing process may not provide the information required regarding the efficiencies of internal controls. This is because the auditor is applying testing towards policies which may not be relevant or up-to-date with current objectives. Similarly, if the auditor has not evaluated how management assesses the risk of their area to ensure they are addressing the most significant issues (examining the effectiveness of the area's risk assessment process), potentially, an important element of the audit assessment has gone unidentified. The application of the *COSO* framework to an area being audited is depicted in Exhibit 5.1. The framework can be a strong tool for auditors to obtain an understanding of relevant controls. Following are suggestions for utilization of the process within the planning phases.

Challenge 31 Potential Actions: Audit Planning Phase When working to employ the full *COSO* framework to individual audits, consideration should be given to appropriate procedures for each phase of the audit. In the instance of the planning phase, auditors may want to evaluate the following considerations as they may apply to the specific area being audited:

- *Outline each component of COSO and examine relevant attributes for the area being audited, as described in the examples provided in Exhibit 5.1.* By examining each element of *COSO* within the audit planning stage, the audit team will be able to more effectively scope and plan the audit activities. They will have a better overall assessment of how well the control environment and operations structure work at the specific audit project level. Within Exhibit 5.1, each *COSO* component is outlined with various attributes that may be evaluated within an individual audit.

The illustration provides a concise view of the *COSO* attributes and concepts to consider within individual audits. Internal auditors can correlate the framework to individual audits by evaluating key phrases within the definition of each of the *COSO* attributes:

- *Control Environment*: The control environment "establishes" the policies/procedures and foundation for how the area being audited operates.
- *Risk Assessment*: The area being audited must "identify" relevant risks to the achievement of objectives in order to meet their individual goals and contribute to the organization's overall goals and objectives.
- *Control Activities*: The area's relevant control activities are those procedures commonly used to "execute" the individual processes.

Establish	Identify	Execute	Communicate	Evaluate
Control Environment	Risk Assessment	Control Activities	Information and Communication	Monitoring
Establishment of tone and ethics	*Identify risk*	*Execute controls*	*Communication through data and systems*	*Evaluate level of monitoring*
Management structure/philosophy/operating style	Departmental business	Compliance with area procedures	Process area general and application controls	Management monitoring processes
Organization structure	Objectives/goals and strategies	Controls over transaction initiation, authorization, process, and recording	Controls over spreadsheets	Override procedures
Establish policy/procedures	Metrics and measures	Process area physical controls	Internal communications	Supervisor reviews
Ownership/accountability training HR issues	Procedures to assess fraud in process area	SOD		Exception reports
	Remediation of identified control issues	Sign-offs and reconciliations		

Exhibit 5.1 *COSO* attributes applied to process-level evaluation.

- *Information and Communication*: Management of the area being audited verbally "communicate" goals and objectives as well as utilize the proper and most effective information processing systems to perform the responsibilities of the audit area.
- *Monitoring*: Procedures employed through the first 4 components of *COSO* are timely and efficiently executed by management through periodic "evaluation" techniques.

When applying the *COSO* attributes to a specific risk-based audit, the internal auditor should consider how each of the individual attributes contributes to the overall control structure and processes established within the area being audited. Typical considerations for each area would include:

- *Control Environment*: Consider the control culture of the area being audited. This would include elements that are typically considered within an entity evaluation. The internal auditors must apply the thought process at the individual audit area. Concepts to consider may include:
  - The manner in which policies and procedures are developed, maintained, reviewed, and updated.
  - The philosophy and operating style of management within the area being audited.
  - Adequate attention and focus to appropriate segregation of duties for risks within the audit area.
  - The tone of how the area is managed and staffed.
  - The existence of appropriate segregation of duties within the area being audited.
  - The manner in which aspects of ethics, respect, and integrity are exhibited by all personnel within the area being audited.
  - The presence of adequate commitment to competence for personnel within the area being audited.
  - The existence of adequate direction and training on procedures for employees within the area being audited.
  - Adequate supervision and monitoring of critical processes within the area being audited.
- *Risk Assessment*: Evaluate the method used to identify risks that may be relevant to the achievement of the objectives of the area being audited. This would include elements such as:

- The procedures utilized to identify and define risks that may threaten the achievement of objectives of the area being audited.
- The process for linking the goals and objectives of the area being audited to those of the organization.
- The inclusion of appropriate personnel, from the area being audited, in the assessment of relevant risks that may prevent that area from meeting objectives.
- Procedures to develop and execute metrics and measures within the area being audited in order to monitor for relevant risks.
- Procedures utilized to assess the risk of fraud within the area being audited.
- The manner and timing in which the area being audited chooses to respond to identified risks.

- *Control Activities*: Examine the individual controls relevant to the area or process being audited. This may include:
  - The manner in which policies and procedures are executed within the area being audited to ensure management directives are carried out.
  - Examination of specific controls related to the initiation, authorization, processing, and recording of the audit areas transactions.
  - Evaluation of relevant physical controls important to the area being audited.
  - Validation of procedures utilized to ensure appropriate segregation of duties for relevant processes within the area being audited.
  - Performance of required reconciliations, sign-offs, or tie-out procedures within the area being audited.
- *Information and Communication*: Understand those processes that are used to capture and facilitate communication throughout the area being audited as well as relevant information systems utilized to process data. Examples include:
  - Information processing systems utilized to transact the responsibilities of the area being audited.
  - The manner in which authority and access is granted to relevant information systems utilized by the area being audited.

  - Procedures utilized by management to verbally communicate responsibilities and authorities within the area being audited.
  - Procedures utilized by management to communicate relevant company information to employees of the area being audited.
- *Monitoring*: Evaluate those activities utilized by the area being audited to monitor activities crucial to the completion of their responsibilities. This may include:
  - Procedures utilized by management to ensure that relevant responsibilities are completed accurately and timely executed within the area being audited.
  - Examination of exception reports within the area being audited.
  - Procedures employed to address identified deficiencies within the area being audited.

Viewing the internal control structure of the area being audited in this fashion enables the internal auditor to identify relevant controls (if any) that may be in place and would be relevant to test. The auditor will also evaluate the following:

- Whether the absence of controls creates risk and, if so, whether the risk can be quantified.
- The extent to which the operating effectiveness of controls should be tested.
- Overall reliance that can be placed on internal controls within the area being audited.

These elements are all considerations that will occur during the planning and fieldwork stage. Auditors can use the *COSO* framework and apply concepts to the functioning of the particular area being audited.

The utilization of the *COSO* framework can also be extended into the audit reporting phase. Successful implementation of this portion of the methodology will require careful evaluation and a well-documented approach. In the event internal audit wishes to extend the utilization of the *COSO* framework to the reporting process, they might consider outlining sections of the report by individual *COSO* attributes. An example is shown in Exhibit 5.2. In this illustration,

<table>
<tr><td colspan="2">Control Environment: Represents attributes within the process that establish "tone at the top" including integrity, ethical values, policies/procedures, and competence.</td></tr>
<tr><td colspan="2">Control Environment analysis

+ The department manager has been in place for five years and is knowledgeable of the systems and control processes required for the department.
– Policies have not been updated, and personnel have not been trained on new procedures. Learning is ad hoc.
– Significant turnover in personnel has occurred within the function in the past twelve months resulting in inconsistency of execution of work and effective timing of payments. In addition, personnel within the function have been required to work significant overtime, which has increased the prevalence of turnover.</td></tr>
<tr><td>Risk analysis</td><td>Management actions</td></tr>
<tr><td>Policies and procedures risk

– Existing policies are based on older legacy systems and are not relevant to the new accounts payable automated system. In addition, authorizations have not been updated in line with new procedures.</td><td>– Example only</td></tr>
<tr><td colspan="2">Overall Control Environment assessment: Ineffective</td></tr>
</table>

Exhibit 5.2 Example accounts payable detail report—Section 1.

the detailed internal audit report is segregated into five sections, one representing each component of *COSO*. The section header describes the *COSO* component reported. Individual observations, both positive observations and control gaps, are listed within the report. At the end of each section, an assessment is given as to the adequacy of the particular *COSO* attribute for the individual audit area.

Accounts Payable Scenario To illustrate this process, consider an example where the audit team is performing an accounts payable audit. In their evaluation of the control environment, they find the policies and procedures for the department have not been formally updated for several years; however, the systems and procedures utilized to process payments have changed significantly. The department has utilized the knowledge of their personnel to manage changes that have occurred.

Internal audit may identify the lack of updated policies and procedures as a gap in the control environment. The lack of updated procedures creates risk to the process area in the event of employee turnover or inadequate supervision. This concern, along with additional observations made by the audit team regarding the lack of formal job descriptions, adequate training, and appropriate supervisor of personnel, may lead to assessing the control environment of the specific area being audited as either weak or moderate. The question to address is how to adequately report these observations. Exhibit 5.2 provides an example reporting template that could be used in the scenario discussed. This evaluation would be listed at the bottom of the section for control environment. If this assessment is made early in the review, the audit group may decide that detailed testing of the processes as documented would not be efficient. They may take a more substantive based approach to providing assurance that payments being made are accurately and timely processed and represent true obligations of the company. Alternatively, they may determine that it is important to report the observations of the control environment as a design flaw in the area's control structure.

Challenge 32: Audit Process Area Control Structure

Business and operations managers focus on accomplishing day-to-day tasks in the most efficient, effective, and timely manner as possible. Assume that the internal auditor were to pose the following question to auditees: "Tell me about your department's internal control framework or structure?" There is a strong possibility they will receive questioning looks or stares. Professionals often think of their jobs as the tasks required to complete work. They do not necessarily consider what controls may be imbedded within those tasks.

In Chapter 1, we outlined a scenario of an internal auditor questioning an administrative clerk. The clerk's individual responses to the questions were focused on the tasks performed without acknowledgment of control procedures. When beginning an internal audit of any area, auditors must be cognizant that internal control terminology may not be part of the area's daily business acumen. Utilizing a *COSO* based approach to conducting individual audits will require the auditor to ensure that management and the area understand the various concepts imbedded in a typical control framework like *COSO*.

Challenge 32 Potential Actions: Audit Process Area Control Structure To effectively utilize a *COSO* approach to executing individual audits, management must understand and embrace the concept of control frameworks. This includes:

- The ability to differentiate between daily tasks and imbedded controls within those tasks.
- The importance of management's responsibility to establish a proper tone and operating philosophy within the department. that stresses the importance of internal control.
- The ability of management to accept responsibility for assessing risks and develop monitoring techniques to pro-actively identify control gaps.
- The responsibility for timely and efficiently addressing control deficiencies identified in the work area.

Although all of these items may appear to be a given attribute to the internal auditor, management may not always be able to connect the dots. Auditors can assist in management's comprehension and understanding of control frameworks through pro-active education and awareness techniques. Some considerations may include the following:

- *Work with senior management to establish measurement terms to be used in audit reports.* When providing assessments on individual *COSO* attributes within each audit area, management should understand how each control attribute will be measured. An example reporting technique is provided in Exhibit 5.3. The categories used for each assessment stage in this example are "effective," "needs improvement," or "noneffective." The categories are further defined in relationship to the organizations business acumen. It is important to note the example categories provided may be different for each organization. Auditors should consider whether alternative words or measurements should be applied to their organization. The relevant term will vary by organization, and auditors must ensure they work to develop measurements that are best understood and accepted by their organizational culture. In some instances, auditors may choose to color code the risk categories as "red," "yellow," or "green." Although as auditors, this is typically considered a heat map approach. In some environments, management does not agree with the color-coding concept. Other alternative methods may include assigning priorities to each category.

COSO Attribute	Effective	Improvement Opportunity	Not Effective
Control environment: Establishment of tone/policies/procedures/operating style			
Risk assessment: Identification of process area risk and fraud evaluation			
Control Activity: Execution of individual control attributes			
Information and communication: Systems data and functional communication			
Monitoring: evaluation of process efficiency/effectiveness and remediation of control gaps			

COSO Definition	Description (EXAMPLE ONLY)
Effective	Attributes within this element appear effectively managed to a level reasonably consistent with management risk tolerance. Minimal probability exists that a control failure within this category, individually or combined with control failures in other categories, would have any notable impact on financial, operational or compliance results.
Improvement opportunity	Issue(s) identified indicating attributes within this element may not be effectively managed to a level below the "management alert criteria" category as defined by the organization's risk tolerance. If not corrected, probability exists that a control failure, individually or combined with control failures in other categories, would have an impact, though less than significant, on financial, operational or compliance results.
Not effective	Issue(s) identified indicate attributes within this element are not effectively managed to a level below the management tolerance. If not corrected, probability is strong that a control failure, individually or combined with control failures in other categories, would have at least a significant impact on financial, operational or compliance results.

Exhibit 5.3 *COSO* audit process area evaluation example: accounts payable.

- *Utilize the pre-audit conference to review COSO 2013 concepts and principles with management of the area being audited.* Work to ensure that management understands the individual five attributes as well as 17 principles of *COSO*. Auditors may also correlate the points of focus utilized by *COSO* to responsibilities that are relevant to the daily tasks of the area being audited. Explain the connection of those tasks to establishing a sound control environment for the area being audited.

- *When conducting interviews with the area being audited, focus on more than the individual controls that will be tested.* Consider performing control environment questionnaires that ask management and process area personnel open ended questions that can provide insight into elements of the various points of focus listed by *COSO*. Some example questions may include the following:
  - *How does your department evaluate the potential that something may occur within the process that would prevent you from performing your responsibilities timely and effectively?* This question would provide insight into the manner in which the area assesses departmental risks.
  - *How does management of the area being audited communicate employee's responsibilities and the manner in which those responsibilities are executed?* This question would provide insight into how area management establishes the proper tone for the department.
  - *What job tasks exist to supervise responsibilities within the area being audited to ensure that work is performed effectively?* This question may provide insight into how management executes their responsibilities related to monitoring activities.
  - *When personnel identify something that may not be working correctly, are those issues timely brought to the attention of area management? If so, how does the area being audited approach or mitigate the issue?* These questions would provide information related to how management handles the remediation of control gaps or deficiencies when they are identified by employees.

An additional reporting approach may be a visual depiction of the overall effectiveness of each *COSO* attribute evaluated for the area. A potential example was discussed and illustrated in Exhibit 5.3 which discussed the accounts payable scenario.

Challenge 33: Using COSO as Part of the Risk-Based Audit Process

Utilizing a detailed *COSO* assessment approach to individual audit areas will provide additional challenges to the internal auditor. Management may not be receptive to having internal auditors provide an opinion on processes related to control environments or risk assessment procedures within individual audit areas. To properly execute this type of assessment, auditors would be required to evaluate aspects of the process area's tone at the top and management philosophy and operating style. This can be a judgmental assessment and one in which management does not feel is within the purview of internal audit. In some instances, internal audit groups who have attempted to employ this approach have experienced resistance from management. They have been faced with justifying why it is important to evaluate individual area's control environments or even the purpose for trying to understand management's individual strategic process for identifying risks. Internal audit groups who choose to utilize this methodology must be prepared to provide justification to management regarding the benefits of the approach. In addition, if the audit group extends the utilization of the *COSO* framework to the manner in which findings are reported, additional explanation and documentation will be required.

Challenge 33 Potential Actions: Using COSO as Part of the Risk-Based Audit Process The existence of a well-defined and documented audit methodology is important for any internal audit group to consistently and effectively execute audit work. Utilizing a *COSO* approach within a risk-based audit process requires full documentation and procedural outlines within the audit methodology. Documentation should include the benefits of utilizing the approach. This approach can be a difficult one for both the audit group and management to transition to. When presenting the approach to management, provide information regarding the strategic benefits that would be obtained by utilizing the approach. These may include the following:

- *A more holistic assessment of individual audit areas and their compliance with the COSO attribute.* This can be helpful information when compiling evaluations for Sarbanes–Oxley purposes. The individual assessments can provide further support regarding the company's overall evaluation of the *COSO* attributes and the company's compliance with the 17 principles.
- *The COSO approach would allow auditors to evaluate individual control environments within the entire organization.* It would

allow for a deeper understanding of adequacy of policies, processes, and procedures that underlie specific control activities. If gaps are identified within the control environment of a specific audit area, the auditors can apply a go/no-go approach to the individual audit.

- *The approach assists in setting* standards *for the organization for understanding and adhering to COSO.* Establishing this process as part of a risk-based methodology will assist in paving the way toward organizational acceptance and compliance with the *COSO* internal control framework.

Of course, with benefits come challenges. If internal audit decides to work towards a full *COSO*-based approach to executing individual audits, they should ensure several foundational elements are soundly established within their audit protocols. These may include the following:

- *Ensure management fully comprehends aspects of COSO* 2013, *the 17 principles, and related points of focus.* Utilize the *COSO* concepts to demonstrate to management how application of the framework within individual audits can assist in overall organizational understanding, buy-in, and comprehension of the importance of internal control. As internal audit executes each individual audit on the audit plan, utilizing a *COSO* risk-based approach will serve to enhance the education process for organizational management.
- *Demonstrate how the approach can support the organization's corporate-wide attestation to the COSO framework.* Utilizing a *COSO* evaluation within individual audit areas can be beneficial in aggregating and supporting the organization's corporate-wide attestation to the *COSO* framework.
- *Explain how a COSO approach to audit evaluation will increase efficiency in identifying how an audit should progress.* Reiterate the importance of maintaining updated and relevant policies, procedures, and risk analysis for internal audit to identify the proper control activities to test within the area being audited. If internal audit has the opportunity to assess the control environment and risk assessment processes of the individual audit area, they may be able to identify gaps in the formal

procedures that require attention prior to executing control testing that may or may not be relevant.

If management is not receptive to formally including the *COSO* framework within the internal audit process, the audit department can still consider utilizing the methodology and maintain an informal tracking of their assessments based on audits performed. This information may be useful later when summarizing and evaluating information for overall control environment attestation. If this is done, internal audit should ensure they appropriately document observations and assumptions for their assessment. This would be especially important if the information is utilized for consideration in the overall control environment attestation. If there are any significant concerns that arise within individual audits regarding the *COSO* evaluation, internal audit must address the concerns with management. In the end, if the observations could have any negative implications or impact on the overall control environment assessment, the audit team should address the issue pro-actively rather than waiting until the year-end attestation.

Step 3: Understand, Identify, and Assess the Risks

As stated by the *COSO* Foundation, risk assessment is an iterative process. It should not be a one and done. Similarly, the process of assessing risks for any individual audit should not end once the risks to test have been identified. Auditors must be cognizant of ever changing business environments and how those changes may impact the need to adjust the audit process.

Procurement Scenario To illustrate the concept, let's assume that a review of the procurement area has been initiated. The risk assessment identifies the following areas to be reviewed: vendor selection, contract management, and supplier delivery. The auditors stratify the vendor database and select vendors for testing whose contracts are of the highest dollar value to the company.

During fieldwork, the auditors overhear a procurement specialist speaking about an expected price increase on a particular product. The increase is due to the increasing cost of raw materials. Vendors selected for testing do not currently supply the product in question. The product is one that is considered critical to certain operations of the company. The auditors decide they should identify which vendors actually supply the product in question.

When reviewing basic information, they identify concerns in vendor financial stability and viability especially as it relates to the particular product. The company's industry and in particular their operating jurisdictions have been dramatically impacted by recent economic events that have resulted in strained financial stability of several critical vendors. The auditors had not considered the risk of vendor viability within their initial risk assessment. The audit team is halfway through the fieldwork stage and is on a very strict timing schedule. What is the appropriate course of action?

When applying a risk-based audit approach, the audit team should ensure they are evaluating the risks that may prevent the area being audited from accomplishing its overall objectives. In the above scenario, vendor viability appears to be a valid concern.

Understanding the questions and sensitivities that may arise by the perceived change in course midway through the audit, the team should apply their due diligence to determine whether the risk of vendor viability should be included within the current review or possibly added as an extension of the audit. However, caution should be applied when simply adding the audit risk to the audit plan for review at some future date without providing management counsel and insight into the identified concern. If the audit team were to conclude their current review and write an audit report that did not include the identified risk and related concern, they have not appropriately applied their risk-based process. In addition, if the risk identified actually manifests in some type of impact that would be considered of concern to management, it is possible that the question will arise: "Why didn't the auditors find it?"

This is a fairly simplistic example of following the risk. The audit process should be adaptable enough to adjust to emerging issues that were not known at the time of initial audit planning.

Challenge 34: Understanding, Identifying, and Assessing Risk

As we have stated, to be able to effectively identify and assess risks, the internal auditor must first have a strong understanding of the organization and its business processes. Once an understanding is obtained, the appropriate level of professional judgment must be applied in order to develop the most relevant audit procedures. The risks that present the greatest potential to impact the areas objectives will be the risks where audit procedures are focused. In addition, auditors must always consider the potential risk for fraud within any process. Procedures applied to test fraud risk will vary based on the organization's identified tolerance levels.

The audit process must be adaptable to allow the audit team to adjust the scope of their review when needed. Of course, this is easier said than done. Often, management will contend "The audit scope has been set," and "If the new risk was so important, why wasn't it identified within the risk assessment?" Another argument may be, "There is no time to adjust or change the scope of the audit. Just complete the work, and we will address the new risk later." These are each questions and challenges that internal audit should have protocols in place to address.

Challenge 34 Potential Actions: Understanding, Identifying, and Assessing Risk In the event new risks emerge after the audit has begun, the audit team should have a protocol in place for determining the appropriate action to take. Considerations should include the following:

- *A formal protocol within the audit methodology that outlines the specific process that auditors will follow when new risks are identified at various points in the audit.* This protocol will assist in providing guidance to auditors when issues arise. For example, new risks identified within the planning stage can easily be incorporated into the current audit scope, whereas risks that may emerge during fieldwork or even the reporting stage will require a specific protocol for reviewing the risk, determining its significance and its impact on the current audit projects timing as well as communicating information to management.
- *Provide proper notification to both management and the audit committee.* If the identification of new risks requires a shift in the audit focus, management and the audit committee should receive timely notification. In addition, the CAE must communicate how the additional time required to evaluate the

new risk(s) will be covered within the current audit plan. For example, will the allocation of hours result in a reduction in hours allocated to future audits or possibly a removal of a project to the audit plan?

- *Ensure supporting information is available to validate the inclusion of the new risk within the audit project.* Auditors must be able to justify the significance of the risk in relationship to other risk areas under review.
- *Estimate how timing of the completion of the audit as well as required resources will be impacted.* When changing the scope of an audit, it is important both audit management and process area management have an understanding of how the expanded scope will impact timing for finalization of the audit. In addition, there should be an understanding of the need for process owner time or additional auditor time.

Step 4: Measuring the Risk Impact

Measuring and assigning risk impact to identified issues requires a strong understanding of management risk appetite and tolerance, relevant knowledge of the identified risk, and significant professional judgment. To effectively assess risks and ensure that the assignment aligns with management tolerance levels, the internal audit department must also have a strong understanding of management's attitude toward control gaps and findings. Auditors will face significant difficulties if they are unable to appropriately position or communicate the risk impact of a finding to management. Management must understand the potential exposure that a control gap may present when unremediated. Consider the following actual scenario to illustrate the difficulty in assessing control gaps and assigning relative significance.

Impact Scenario 1 ABC Company is a regional financial institution with several operating branches. Internal audit has typically provided the audit committee and management a copy of the entire written internal audit report. The reports lists all identified issues or exceptions found during testing and are often very lengthy in content. The audit committee has become concerned that they cannot identify the issues of greatest significance to the company. They feel the current internal audit process of tracking the numbers of findings and completion of remediation acts does not provide a clear understanding of the control environment of the area being audited. They have asked internal audit to develop an executive summary report of each audit. The purpose of the executive summary would be to list the overall scope and objective of the audit, a summary of the audit results, and a listing of only those issues that would provide some element of risk that would prevent the audit area from meeting its objectives. They have told internal audit they would like to see a potential rating assigned to the overall audit. At the very least, they would like the auditors to rate the impact and the control effectiveness of those risks that are considered most significant. The impact and controls assessment must be more than a scoring assignment. The auditors must explain the reason behind their assessment. No further guidance is obtained from the audit committee or management.

During the next quarterly audit committee meeting, several reports are provided to the audit committee as executive summaries. One audit completed dealt with a review of the bank teller process. Within this audit, a particular facility was found to have poor controls around the cash receipt and recording process. There are three teller collection booths that are often left unattended and unlocked. In addition, the supervisor of the area has access to accept cash, approve overrides, balance and reconcile the drawers, and prepare the final remittance to the main branch. The auditors provided the following ranking for the teller cash collection process:

- *Impact*: The inherent impact of this process is considered high due to the potential for fraud or collusion of activities.
- *Control effectiveness*: The control effectiveness of this process is considered weak due to the inadequate segregation of duties and the ineffectiveness of key controls identified in the process.

Management is very unhappy with this characterization of the process. They believe it infers there is fraud in the process.

What is your assessment of this issue and the manner in which it was characterized? Some questions that may be considered include:

- *Did the internal auditors obtain a tolerance assessment from management and the audit committee for their measurement of impact and control effectiveness?* In a financial institution, a significant concern would be to ensure the potential for fraud is appropriately managed and monitored. However, without a tolerance assessment, the internal auditors are applying their own judgment to the area.
- *Was there a discussion with management on how risk wording was developed and the meaning behind inherent impact?* The internal auditors explain to management and the audit committee their assessment is not meant to infer fraud is occurring in the process, but due to very nature of the process, the inherent potential of fraud is high when the opportunity exists for controls to malfunction. However, management may not understand the characterization of inherent impact.

In this scenario, it may have been appropriate to engage in discussion of risk wording and risk assignment prior to moving to a new reporting format. A discussion may have assisted in addressing management's concerns and allowed the audit committee to provide input regarding the areas of risk they deem most significant. Without this discussion, the internal auditors are applying their own personal judgment.

Impact Scenario 2 The audit team is reviewing system access identifications (IDs) for the company's general ledger system. The team identifies a significant number of Super User IDs (IDs that allow free and open access into the system to make changes and corrections). The auditors find the use of the IDs has not been monitored or regularly evaluated for appropriateness. They are unable to evaluate the use of the IDs because audit trail evidence is deleted on a regular basis. The audit team views this control gap as one that provides a high inherent risk of unauthorized activity as well as providing the potential opportunity for inappropriate access. They assign the risk impact significance as high. Management strongly challenges the issue and requires evidence that having excessive Super User IDs is a significant control issue. Management does not comprehend the potential risk in the identified control gap. In their mind, although the auditors identified the excessive IDs, they did not present evidence that the IDs were used inappropriately or that there were any implications on the data.

Even though the auditors explained the concern surrounding the elimination of the audit trail on usage of the IDs, management does not accept the argument that the existence of the IDs creates a threat or risk to the company. This is an actual scenario faced by a CAE. In this instance, although the finding was relevant and presents many concerning red flags, management was able to convince the board that the internal auditors did not find any misuse of the IDs during test work. The issue was presented by management as being blown out of proportion. Even the external auditors, who were well aware of the issue, did not comment on the finding. They simply increased their substantive testing for the financial statement audit.

Regardless of your opinion on the ranking assessment of this issue, as an internal auditor you most likely recognize the potential impact of this issue on the company. The inability by management to grasp the potential severity of the issue not only creates a significant control gap but also an opportunity for inappropriate usage of the IDs that could manifest in fraud. However, there may be a few lessons learned from this example:

- *The audit team may not have appropriately supported their finding.* Analysis was not provided on the number of IDs, how the IDs were assigned, and what the purpose for the related use of the IDs were. They also did not provide information on the termination or approval process for the IDs.
- *The auditors were unable to provide sufficient explanation and clarification to the audit committee on why the issue was rated as inherently high risk.* The inability to adequately relay the finding and ultimate impact rests in the hand of the internal auditors. With this in mind, even if the communication was clearly relayed, the auditors should be concerned over management's lack of focus on internal controls.
- *Management had not identified any type of tolerance threshold for these operational processes.* In their world, the auditors needed to provide evidence that the IDs were inappropriately used and

then also be able to quantify the impact the misuse resulted in. This again points to the concern that management does not consider the potential threat of control gaps.

- *Management had no concern about potential misuse or abuse that did not impact the financials or did not raise the eyebrow of the external auditors.* This is a glaring fact and should provide the internal auditors with a sense of how management focuses their level of concern.

Challenge 35: The Concept of Risk Tolerance versus Risk Appetite

If you have ever visited a hospital emergency room, you may be familiar with the frequently asked question "On a scale of 1–10, how significant is your pain?" Since we know everyone tolerates pain on a different level, you have to ask yourself how the doctors calibrate individual patient answers. If there is any prioritization of patient care based on their described level of pain, we could probably guess some patients would be smart enough to say they are at a 10 in order to get quicker attention.

Both risk appetite and risk tolerance set boundaries on the amount of risk an entity is prepared to accept. Auditors and management often have a difficult time differentiating between the two concepts.

Risk appetite is a higher-level statement that considers broadly the levels of risks that management deems acceptable. An example would be a company who declares that it does not accept risks could result in a significant loss of revenue base. This would be a description of risk appetite.

Risk tolerances are more narrowly defined. They set the acceptable level of variation around the objectives. Utilizing the example given for risk appetite, assume the same company declares it does not wish to accept risks which would cause revenue from its top five customers to decline by more than 15 percent. This would be a description of risk tolerance.

Operating within risk stated tolerances provides management greater assurance that the company remains within its risk appetite. This would in turn provide comfort the company will achieve its objectives.

Risk Appetite

When the concept of risk appetite is defined by an organization, it can be a fundamental element of the business and assist in allowing the organization to appropriately reach its goals. But again, risk appetite is difficult for management to articulate. When defining risk appetite, management must understand the following concepts:

- *Risk appetite can be complex in nature.* It may utilize various measurements of financial, operational, and compliance metrics. Risk appetite is more than just a financial number.
- *When appetite is expressed, it should be measurable in some aspect.* The organization may employ performance metrics, shareholder value measurements, or key control and risk measurements. Whichever measure is utilized, it is imperative the organization has availability to relevant and accurate data pertinent to the given measurements.
- *Risk statements should be complementary to the organization's overall control culture and operating style.* In some organizations, management has an aversion to the acceptance of risk. In other instances, if an organization is exploring expansion opportunities, risk may be more acceptable. In general, risk statements should reflect the organization's control philosophy.
- *Risk appetite is often not a single fixed concept.* This is another area that becomes difficult and complicated for management to comprehend. There can be a range of appetites for different risks. In addition, the appetites can vary over time depending on internal and external influencing factors.
- *The articulation of risk appetite should be relational to the organization's risk management capability and overall maturity.* When organizations get caught up in developing complicated risk statements, their ability to manage, monitor, and implement those statements can fail.

The utilization of the concepts of risk appetite and risk tolerance is intrinsically important to the execution of a true risk-based audit process. Auditors must embrace the concept and utilize their educational skills to assist management with the process necessary to develop risk appetite and risk tolerance statements. This will assist in assessing audit issues as identified.

Risk appetite and risk tolerance are evolutionary processes in the world of internal audit. Management may view the internal audit process as one that utilizes checklists to validate controls and processes. This is considered a black and white analysis technique. Either the control works, or it does not work. Often, audit departments list within their reports the number of transactions tested and the rate of failure identified. Leading practice for internal audit reporting guides internal auditors away from using this as reporting philosophy. Auditors must be able to assign some measurement to control gap and testing exceptions. The measurement should relate to more than a stated financial impact. It can relate to elements of operations, information technology, communication, or even regulatory impact. In essence, auditors should be prepared to answer the question "so what?" Some questions to consider include the following:

- If the control failed the test, what is the potential ramification to the company that might occur because of the gap?
- Is there any possibility that the failure or exception could reach a level that would cause a significant amount of effort to mitigate? Can you define the word significant? It may mean resources, dollars or both.
- Could the testing exception or failure reflect a gap where opportunity is created, and fraud may occur now or at some time in the future?

Most auditors understand there are various levels of control findings. However, just like controls are not created equal, control findings are not created equal. Consider an example relating to policies surrounding system access.

System Access Scenario Assume that the auditors are testing access into various systems such as the general ledger and financial consolidation model, procurement subledger, and accounts payable subledger. The results of the review identify gaps in how access IDs are assigned to specific modules. The company's procedure for assigning new accesses to each module is to establish profiles similar to those of other individuals within the department. This procedure may initially work, but what happens when an employee leaves the department? Are the accesses effectively reviewed and changed? When measuring the significance, would management have a greater concern about an individual having access into the annual financial consolidation module or inappropriate access assigned to the procurement subledger?

This is where the concept of varying levels of tolerance can be considered. Auditors must understand this tolerance measurement when relaying their findings within a report. This will help assign the appropriate control effectiveness ranking to the risk area.

Risk appetite statements can be specific to the industry, business, and organizational culture. An important concept to remember about risk appetite is that in the event that risk appetite has been breached, the issue may be one that has more of a significant impact to the organization. This is one of the important reasons why organizations must utilize the defined risk appetite to further define management risk tolerance levels.

Risk Appetite and Tolerance Scenario Years ago, I was with an organization who experienced a series of extreme operational issues which significantly threatened the ongoing viability of the company. The issues occurred during the same time frame as Sarbanes–Oxley. The board began questioning how management was assigning and assessing impact to various incidents. The questions included how internal audit was determining the classification of identified issues. With input and assistance from the board, a tolerance framework was developed and utilized by internal audit to classify audit findings.

Management utilized the framework when developing strategic plans. The matrix classification was not intended to be a fall off the edge of the world classification. It was to be used as a guideline for understanding the type of risk issue to communicate to the board. In theory, this would allow for time to initiate mitigating actions before the issue resulted in impacts that would put the company at an unacceptable level of risk. The board also understood that risk impact was more than simply dollars. Risk could be manifested through health and safety issues, reputational and shareholder issues, operational and even data issues. The tolerance guideline was used to identify the level of risk classification where the board should have timely visibility into identified issues. This would enable proper monitoring of mitigating actions.

The concept worked for this company because the personnel accepted the theory, and it was driven by the board. In the beginning, individuals were sensitive to the high-risk classification issues, but once they understood the purpose of the matrices, it served as a useful tool in managing and operating the business.

This business was sold in 2008. I continue to follow the topic of risk tolerance and risk appetite and the continual debate that surrounds the issue. Many companies resist the concept because they believe it isn't applicable to their business, or it is too hard to define. Those that have attempted to embrace the issue will often relay the sensitivities to the high risk ranking.

Risk Tolerance Scenario Are budgets a form of risk tolerance? Company personnel spend countless hours and efforts developing strategic corporate budgets to provide managers guidance on acceptable spending limits. Those limits roll up into an overall corporate threshold for spending. Now correlate this concept and consider whether there is some applicable method that can be used to provide guidance on decision making? The guidance should be more than corporate budget parameters. Absent recommending some detailed matrices and grids that define multiple scenarios that might be expected to dramatically impact the company's strategic goals, it would seem logical to think there is some value to gain by establishing some basic parameters to ensure that important decisions are all considered utilizing a similar tolerance scale.

It is relatively easy to understand why the issue is difficult to embrace and apply. Some individuals who have been part of organizations that have experienced significant turmoil can attest to the importance of the concept. They have witnessed the bad thing happen and understand how the definition and recognition of tolerance can be similar to managing a budget or any other business process. Similar to the concept of pain, if you allow the issue to reach that seemingly intolerable level, it is much more difficult to bring under control. So, by having an established tolerance guide, the organization can institute mitigating actions before things get out of control.

Challenge 35 Potential Actions: The Concept of Risk Tolerance versus Risk Appetite We've acknowledged there is a great deal of discussion and opinions on the topic of risk tolerance and risk appetite. All businesses take some level of risk every day. If they didn't, they may not thrive. Yet, it is all too frequent that we hear significant pushback from corporate managers who profess they cannot express or quantify a corporate risk tolerance for their companies. If this is true, then are we relying on the individual risk tolerances of various managers to run the business? If so, what assurances does the board have that individual risk tolerances won't collide or add up to something that may be far above what the company as a whole would find acceptable? When working to develop risk appetite and tolerance guidelines, consider the following elements:

- *The concept of risk tolerance and appetite requires buy-in from all relevant parties.* There must be no sacred cows for specific process areas. Management must accept the rating as evaluated utilizing the set risk appetite and tolerance guides. The concept is of little use if there are never any issues that reach the high ranking. There would be nothing to mitigate.
- *Risk tolerance is not meant to assert that some catastrophic event will occur.* It is purely a measurement to ensure issues are timely identified so that effective mitigating action can be taken. If management believes the high ranking correlates to a catastrophic event, then the concept of risk tolerance is not well understood.
- *Risk appetite and tolerance can be difficult concepts to define.* We have already acknowledge this fact. However, without well defined criteria, auditors are using their independent judgment regarding the significance of identified control deficiencies. This judgment can often collide with the opinion of management.
- *If the organization has not defined a risk appetite or risk tolerance guideline, internal audit can assist in vetting out the components important to establishing the guidelines.* The auditors would first want to address aspects of risk appetite. We previously discussed a few concepts about risk appetite that should be considered; the following are considerations for establishing risk tolerance thresholds:

- *Understand the organization's overall culture and attitude toward acceptance of risk.* This will provide insight into areas where management has varying levels of tolerance.
- *Consider the organization's current structure.* If the organization has distinct business segments, specific risk tolerance guidelines that address each distinct segment may be most relevant. Organizations that have complicated structures where business units provide varying contributions to overall profit margin may find it difficult to develop one overall risk tolerance measurement.
- *Ensure management understands the importance of considering aspects of financial, compliance, operational, and regulatory considerations when developing risk tolerance.* Similar to risk appetite, risk tolerance is not solely dependent on financial measurements. There may be aspects of operational or regulatory processes that should be considered:
  - Management may be averse to accepting the risk that a certain area of the operations could be inoperable for a period of time. However, they may be tolerant to work outages that may be lower than their appetite statement.
  - The organization's risk appetite may indicate they are not acceptable to federal violations of law that put the operations and health and safety of their employees and customer at risk. However from a tolerance perspective, they may be tolerant of fines or sanctions that are warnings about control concerns. These warnings would be acceptable to the extent they could be timely and efficiently remediated, and in the event of a control failure, no significant health and safety risk is presented.

Risk tolerance guidelines can also be varied depending on the process, industry, and specific controls structure. However, risk tolerance statements would typically be those internal auditors would utilize as a guideline when rating the control findings. Management must understand risk tolerance is a measurement to help manage the method in which controls deficiencies are addressed. Often, when auditors attempt to utilize tolerance concepts within their analysis, management feels that rating something at the high threshold is equivalent to the organization identifying an ICFR material weakness. This is not the case. Tolerance is the level at which the organization feels it is necessary to allocate resources to properly mitigate a control deficiency to ensure it does not reach a significant deficiency or material weakness level. Matrices for risk tolerance measurements can be more detailed and include more attributes than a simple risk appetite statement. However, the establishment of relevant risk tolerance measurements will provide the organization with an effective method for executing risk management protocols.

Internal auditors can provide management with assistance and guidance in understanding the aspects of risk tolerance as well as risk appetite. Working with management to develop templates or frameworks to categorize their risk tolerance statements can provide strategic value. Two examples of potential tolerance risk matrices are shown in Exhibits 5.4 and 5.5.

An example of a corporate-wide risk tolerance matrix is depicted in Exhibit 5.4. In this instance, the company has chosen to categorize the areas of measurement into areas of financial, compliance, and operational impacts. Within each classification, specific attributes have been listed that, if identified during the course of an audit or other review, would provide guidance on whether the issue should be reported to the audit committee. The audit committee alert column is the risk tolerance threshold. This is management's definition of the point where an identified issue should be closely followed by the audit committee to ensure remediation. The management alert column would represent issues the audit committee, management, and the board have agreed are those which may be handled at the process level area.

A second example tolerance matrix is shown in Exhibit 5.5. This example tolerance matrix represents a specific business area (e.g., environmental, health and safety). In this instance, the table depicts management tolerance threshold as the darker box. At the point an issue is identified which may reach the stated tolerance, the issue would be reported to the audit committee to ensure appropriate remediation and follow-up. In this example, management has chosen to provide detailed definitions of the thresholds at a low, moderate, and high level. However, the matrix allows for some consideration of an

Impact/outcome	Audit committee notification	Management alert
Financial Reliability of financial data including financial reporting. Includes internal and external reporting	Covenant violations or other liquidity triggers. Financial impact (increased expenditures or lost revenues) equating to $XX. Material disclosure is false, incomplete or omitted, or lacks clarity. Loss, claims, or premium impact over $XX. Assets destroyed or diverted with financial impact exceeding $XX.	N/A–refer to high-risk criteria. $XX million. N/A–refer to high-risk criteria. Loss, claims, or premium impact over $XX. Assets destroyed or diverted with earnings impact $XX.
Compliance Adherence with relevant laws, regulations, and corporatepolicies/ procedures, including defined internal control framework. Includes potential for fraud.	Potential fine or sanctions that could impact reputation or regulatory and/or customer relations. Threat of indictment, allegations, or proceedings resulting from inadequate compliance or noncompliance of relevant laws and regulations. Threat of federal investigations; outrage among customers within significant portions of the company. Material ethics violations committed by senior or executive-level management and including individuals within sensitive internal control positions. Lack of proper functioning key internal controls or existence of inadequate key internal controls in significant process related to Sarbanes–Oxley compliance. Existence of these conditions would result in either process design issues or operating effectiveness issues that could be classified as Sarbanes significant deficiencies. The following represent examples: • Inadequately defined or executed policies and procedures, inadequate segregation of duties for major control points • Ineffective establishment and execution of monitoring processes • Inadequate procedures in place to assess risk within the defined process • Inadequate procedures in place for management evaluation of control design and control operating effectiveness	N/A–refer to high-risk criteria. Threat of local headlines or reduced confidence; vocal concerns among customers or in the community. Immaterial but not isolated violations. Internal control weakness that, in isolation, may be identified as a gap for Sarbanes-Oxley. Issue is not systemic in nature. (e.g.,) Some policy and procedures, definition and execution issues that result in periodic exposure to unacceptable risk. Monitoring process established but may not be consistently executed. Risk assessment processes are informal and not consistently executed.
Operations Efficiency and effectiveness of the entity's operations including performance and profitability goals and safeguarding resources against loss.	Critical financial, operational, or information data corrupted or confidential information accessible to unauthorized individuals. Control failures viewed as having strong probability to manifest themselves in pervasive health hazards, significant injuries, or potential death to employee or customers. High turnover that is systematic throughout the organization and pervasive employee dissatisfaction. Pervasive customer dissatisfaction in major portions of the corporate territories. Inadequate IT systems, inadequate defined IT general controls, and/or appropriate IT application controls. Key strategic objectives will be significantly difficult to achieve.	Noncritical data corrupted or sensitive information accessible to unauthorized individuals. Minor injuries or temporary health hazards. Above normal turnover and localized employee dissatisfaction. Localized customer dissatisfaction. IT systems lack consistent reliability; IT general controls and/or application controls are not standardized or consistently executed. Key strategic objectives will be more challenging to achieve.

Exhibit 5.4 Organizational risk tolerance example.

Environmental and Quality Assurance Example Tolerance Matrix Management "tolerance" threshold is indicated by gray shading. This would be the point at which the issue would bereported to the audit committee and closely followed for appropriate remediation.					
	Low		Med		High
Cost impact	$xxx in expenditures (defined by the management) as a result of incident or fine.		$xxx in expenditures (defined by the management) as a result of incident or fine.		$xxx in expenditures (defined by the management) as a result of incident or fine.
Food quality–plant level	Minor findings identified during a food quality review. Findings are easily remediated with minimal cost.		Identification of an issue that impacted several plants and required additional management effort to remediate that had not been planned or budgeted.		Identification of an issue impacting a significant amount of product and requiring a plant shutdown.
Food quality–quality assurance audit	Minor findings were identified during food quality audit that were easily remediated.		Identification of an issue during a food quality audit that is reoccurring from previous findings, systemic in nature across the plant, or requires focused resources to mitigate.		Identification of an issue during a food quality audit presented evidence that there were potential health and safety concerns to the customer.
Environmental internal review	Findings during the review were minor and will be easily correctable within a 3–6 month time frame.		Environmental issues were identified that resulted in significant effort on the part of operations management to remediate. Effort exceeds budget limitations		Environmental issues were identified (e.g., waste release) that could impact the health and safety of the community or the customer.
Notice of violation (NOV)	Minimal NOVs received that resulted in financial fines totaling less than $XX20K.		NOVs received on several issues that appear to present systemic internal control concerns throughout the territory.		Numerous NOVs for the same plant that have gone unremediated.
Third-party outside audits	No findings of any significance. Audit received passing rating.		Audit revealed noncompliance issues that could manifest themselves into health and safety issues if not timely remediated.		Audit revealed noncompliance and issues on numerous areas of which one or more were considered significant and could cause major health and safety issues.

Exhibit 5.5 Example tolerance matrix: Environmental and quality assurance process area.

in between measurement. This would require some applied judgment by the auditor when evaluating the issue for assessment.

Step 5: Summarizing Results and Identifying Risk Mitigating Actions

Years ago, the report writing process for internal audit was one where the internal auditors reported their control findings, and management provided a response to the identification of issues. In many ways, this process sets both the internal auditors and management in a position of defense. If management did not agree with the auditor's findings, there would be a lengthy management response. The internal audit group would be in the position of addressing the responses. Today's internal audit processes have transitioned to working with management to develop agreed upon solutions to identified risk gaps or control issues.

Challenge 36: Summarizing Results and Identifying Risk Mitigating Actions

In today's business environment, many audit groups work toward coming to agreement with management on the identified issues, their significance ranking, and the development of risk-mitigation actions. This process provides a customer-oriented approach. However, it can also lengthen the time frame for completion of the internal audit. This may occur when management resists the observations, ratings, and potential solutions. It is important for the internal audit methodology and process to include procedures to employ when working through identified issues and potential mitigating actions.

Challenge 36 Potential Actions: Summarizing Results and Identifying Risk-Mitigating Actions An underestimated portion of many audits is the wrap-up and reporting phase. From management's viewpoint, the audit work is completed. The auditors should be able to quickly summarize the issues and findings and provide relevant suggestions for mitigating actions. In reality, this can be one of the most controversial phases of an audit depending on many factors including the following:

- How verbal or written communication of identified issues occurred during the audit process (this includes informal e-mails).

- How involved management was in determining the impact of the findings.
- Whether there were tolerance measurements applied to the findings and the organization protocol for escalating issues. This process can be both time consuming and politically sensitive.

In order to facilitate the most effective reporting and wrap-up process, following are some specific considerations that may be beyond those typically used in reporting methodologies:

- *Don't underestimate the time required for summarization of results, report writing, and management agreement.* Audit functions often utilize a generalized approach to allocating audit hours to each phase of the audit. As an example, the total project hours may be allocated similar to the following: 20 percent planning, 60 percent fieldwork, 20 percent reporting. The utilization of this approach as a general application to all audits can prove difficult. Audits that are new to the organization may require a larger percentage of planning time. Alternatively, if an audit is performed in an area where there are typically difficult control issues or management has strong opinions and perceptions, the audit reporting phase may take more time than anticipated. It is important for internal audit management to appropriately consider the various dynamics involved in each audit to ensure sufficient time is allocated for all phases, including reporting.
- *Timeliness and transparency on identification of audit issues is critical.* Many internal auditors have been given the direction that issues should be fully documented and evaluated prior to any communication to management. However, there is also the concept of no management surprises. The ability to balance these two philosophies will contribute to the success or challenge of any audit reporting process.
- *Report writing is an art.* Make sure you understand the protocols of your organization. Organizations have varying requirements and expectations for the manner in which issues are stated and even the manner in which the report template are outlined. Some organizations write detailed audit

reports, whereas others utilize a summarized PowerPoint. Presentation format is often as important as the words relayed within the report.

A CAE relayed his experience when management rejected the internal audit report because it was written in landscape memo format. Management did not like the presentation format because they were accustomed to portrait mode. In another instance, management continued to reject the audit report because they felt the issues included too much detail. When the auditor reworked the report in an attempt to be more concise, management again rejected the report because they felt the wording was too curt and didn't provide proper representation of the issues. In that instance, the auditor indicated they rewrote the report more than twenty times prior to management agreeing to the manner in which it was presented. Needless to say, the time and effort expended on the continual revisions was significant and resulted in a significant impact to the audit hours for the project.

From an internal audit *Standards* perspective, this may appear to be characterized as undue influence on the reporting process. Depending on the circumstances involved, it is certainly a possibility management was exerting undue influence on the process. The internal auditor has the right and obligation to take any reporting concerns to the audit committee. In the scenario relayed, the auditors spoke to the audit committee. The response was that the committee expected any audit reports to be first agreed to and approved by management to ensure the issues were properly represented. Unfortunately, the audit committee may not have been aligned with the concept of maintaining an environment where management could not place undue influence on the reporting process.

- *Internal audit's fiduciary duty is to the board and shareholders.* If the auditors feel they were being unduly influenced by management, they have the responsibility to inform the audit committee. As described in the scenario above, this action may not always present the auditors with the outcome they expect. However, if an auditor feels their report process is hampered by management pressure, it may be important to revisit the *Standards* with both management and the audit committee.

The concept of risk-based auditing employs many components which extend from audit plan identification to individual audit area risks, concepts of risk appetite and tolerance, and risk-based reporting protocols. The internal audit team must have full agreement and understanding with management on how the risk-based auditing will be employed within their organization.

Section 2: Internal Audit's Role in Corporate Governance

Introduction

The role of internal audit as it pertains to governance activities is another topic that receives a great deal of debate. In the past, internal audit's role was relegated primarily to participation in the audit committee meeting. However, with the onset of the Sarbanes–Oxley, internal audit became known as one of the basic pillars within a company's governance structure refer to Chapter 1. Although governance is included within the definition of internal audit, the role the function plays may be dependent on how management has previously structured their governance processes. Let's consider a few scenarios.

Governance Scenario 1 At one point in my career, a very senior leader of the organization delicately informed me to use caution when communicating information to the audit committee prior to informing the CEO. This advice was given at a time in the organization's history that involved significant change. The company was experiencing major business issues. It was also in the initial years of Sarbanes–Oxley, and the external auditors were digging deep into organizational control issues. As the CAE, I was tasked with balancing the needs of the shareholders, the desires of the board, the expectations of the external auditors, and the concerns of management. Internal audit's involvement in governance processes had not been well established at the time. The majority of board related processes were managed by the company's legal function. With the impending expectations of control environment and entity level controls evaluations for Sarbanes–Oxley, our organization felt we should apply a more detailed evaluation to the control environment than the approach of checklists being proposed by the external audit firms.

The internal audit group had experience in the utilization of the maturity model approach for evaluating various operational processes. The deployment of the approach proved to be a successful tactic. The audit team felt the process could be utilized to assist in a deeper evaluation of entity-level controls and the company's control environment. As such maturity matrices were developed that outlined various entity level controls. Once the approach was developed. The audit group proposed facilitated sessions to execute the evaluation. A presentation was made to the senior leadership team (SLT). With some apprehension, they agreed the approach would provide insight into various cultural aspects which the organization was attempting to address during its restructure effort. The SLT also felt it was an important aspect of attesting to the company's control environment culture and tone at the top.

Initially, sessions were conducted with the extended leadership team (ELT). The ELT was comprised of individuals who reported directly to a member of the SLT. Although we had obtained buy-in from the SLT, execution of the sessions proved to be a greater challenge than originally anticipated. Members of the ELT expressed concern that individual comments or voting would be relayed back to their direct supervisors. We received questions from individuals such as "Are these sessions being tape recorded?" or "Will comments made in the session be communicated as coming from specific individuals?" Session participants were obviously concerned about the manner in which any comments would be taken.

Sessions were conducted with the ELT through facilitated events that lasted approximately 6 hours. During the sessions, the participants discussion provided a great deal of insight into the tone of the organization as perceived by professionals. The sessions worked toward consensus voting on the maturity stages. The session information and voting was summarized in graphical format for later reporting to the SLT.

Prior to reporting the results of the SLT sessions, the same voting exercise was conducted with the ELT. Keep in mind that the attributes being analyzed were soft components of the control environment.

They included attributes such as management ethical values and ethical behavior, tone at the top, board composition and board reporting, audit committee competence and execution, authority, reporting lines, organizational structure, whistle-blower hotline, code of conduct, conflict of interest, management philosophy and operating style, staffing, commitment to competence, training, human resource policies, and many other attributes that could be interpreted as politically sensitive.

During the SLT session, voting was consistently higher than that of the ELT. When the session concluded, a graphical depiction of the variation in the voting between the two groups was displayed. The SLT was surprised their direct reports had consistently assessed the elements a full stage or more lower than what the SLT team assessed. Some SLT members felt the lower assessment was simply due to the perception of their direct reports and not a reflection of the true stage of the attributes. After a great deal of discussion, the CEO spoke up and commented that perception is often reality. If their direct reports felt these attributes were being managed at a lower maturity than the SLT assessed, there must be some disconnection within the process. It was incumbent upon the SLT to evaluate variances and determine gaps that needed to be addressed. There was a dedicated sense of ensuring that the company could positively attest to a strong control environment.

This approach and evaluation method provided the internal audit group a step forward for involvement in governance processes. However, there was still a strong aversion to allowing internal audit access to board level procedures. The internal audit group proposed audit reviews related to the board appointment process, board and committee charters, the company's code of conduct, and conflict of interest process. While there was some level of success with certain review proposals, other projects received rejection from management.

This experience may be similar to those faced by other internal audit groups. To gain an understanding behind the reason for the reluctance to allow internal audit to evaluate board level governance processes, it is important to understand how the concept of board level processes has evolved in corporate America.

Governance Scenario 2 There is no question that any review of a company's governance process can have political implications. As a CAE, I have personally experienced those difficulties.

In one of my roles, the internal audit group was evaluating the company's code of conduct and conflict of interest policy. The review had been approved by the audit committee, chief legal officer (CLO), and CEO. Internal audit was in the midst of the review when a regularly scheduled audit committee meeting arose. I had not received the audit committee materials until the beginning of the meeting. As I was glancing through the materials during the session, I noticed the current code of conduct and conflict of interest policies were included in the board materials for annual approval by the audit committee. I was surprised, and thoughts raced through my mind on how I would handle the topic when the item came up on the agenda. The approval was scheduled to occur before the internal audit report. I would not have the opportunity to remind the committee members, the CLO, and the CEO about the current internal audit review before my segment of the meeting began.

When the topic came up during the meeting, I asked for consideration that the policies be tabled until after the internal audit review was completed. Unfortunately, this did not go over well with management. The audit committee was receptive and agreed that since the internal audit review was still in progress, the policies should not have been included within the material for approval. However, the accountability for these policies had always remained with the legal functions.

They were the group who had included the materials for update. To this day, I still question the series of events that transpired. The legal team was aware that internal audit was reviewing the policies; we had even interviewed several members of the legal team regarding the process. However, for whatever reason, I had not been informed the policies would be included in the current quarter's audit committee materials for approval. Should I have known about the approval timing? Should I have brought the issue up during the meeting or just allowed the policies to be approved and, if adjustments were needed, ask for them in the next meeting? At the time, I felt it was not appropriate to approve the policies when I had knowledge internal audit would have recommendations for changes. However, the action became one of extreme political sensitivity and created a difficult atmosphere in the meeting as well as in the succeeding months. In the end, the policies were tabled until the next quarterly meeting when certain recommendations were incorporated in the updates. However, the instance required a great deal of effort to remedy feelings and perceptual territorial boundaries. Although the situation was difficult on both sides, we came to a better understanding of the roles and responsibilities of both groups and were able to engage in a closer working relationship.

Challenge 37: Evaluating the Board of Directors

Traditionally, being appointed to a company's board of directors has been considered an indicator of reaching a level of professional expertise and recognition. Especially in the pre-Sarbanes–Oxley years, presence on a corporate board was considered a great resume attribute. Post the Enron incident and the passing of the Sarbanes–Oxley legislation, the responsibilities and liabilities of individuals who served as members of corporate boards dramatically rose. Legislation now holds directors strongly accountable to their fiduciary duties. Stakeholders and shareholders support this stance. To serve on a corporate board in today's business, an individual must be ready to spend considerable time understanding and executing on their fiduciary responsibilities to the organization. It is no longer acceptable to appear at the quarterly meetings, provide input, and collect director fees. Now, directors are expected to be well prepared and ready to take a step above and beyond traditional duties of quarterly board meetings.

Accountability in any corporate role is much stronger in today's business world. It is only reasonable to ensure that corporate directors are following the same trends. Most organizations have done a good job of ensuring their boards have updated charters to align with regulatory and compliance requirements. They have also followed the recommendations and mandates around ensuring a certain level of financial expertise exists on their audit committees. These are all positive advancements in moving into the new arena of responsibility. However, there is so much more that should be focused on. This is where internal audit groups can assist in further evaluation and recommendations.

CAEs should work with management and the board to understand and evaluate aspects of the company's governance process. The level at which internal audit is involved may depend on the CAE's relationship with the audit committee and the board, as well as the company's overall view of internal audit's role in governance. Regardless, the CAE should attempt to understand various aspects of the governance process to gain a sense of assurance regarding the overall control environment.

Challenge 37 Potential Actions: Evaluating the Board of Directors Having an understanding of the organization's procedures and process for selecting board members is a strong start in gaining an understanding of the governance process. Consider some of the following questions that may assist in evaluating the composition and performance of your board.

- *How were board members selected?* In years past, board seats were assigned by the CEO or executive team through personal appointments or recommendations for placement that were included in the company's proxy. Often, these recommendations came from long-term relationships and ties to the company or members of the executive team. CEOs would surround themselves with individuals whose philosophy was much like their own. Thus, the concept of fiduciary duty and independent thinking was hard to execute. In today's world, companies are encouraged to develop a robust process when selecting directors. Directors should be able to appropriately challenge management and ask the tough questions on issues such as strategy budget, risk management, and internal controls. This requires directors to have a strong knowledge of the company's business model as well as a level of independence that will allow them to maintain an arm's-length relationship with the CEO and other senior executives.
- *Do directors have a full understanding of all relevant governance requirements?* When was the last time your board underwent a comprehensive training session executed by a third party or independent trainer? Does the board understand all governance requirements they should abide with? Do they take their role of risk oversight seriously? Do they properly communicate with the internal audit function and take a strategic interest in compliance and enterprise risk processes? Are they aware of the *Standards* internal audit must abide by? If the answer to

any of these questions is no or unsure, then consider evaluating the need for independent training for board members. If the board members are to be held accountable for responsibilities, it is only appropriate to ensure they receive relevant, timely, and independent training on all areas of their fiduciary duty.

- *Have you evaluated the composition and charters of each board committee in light of the exchange listing requirements as well as legal requirements?* Legal requirements and potential personal liability are a strong concern for professionals who hold board seats. It is important that organizations, as well as directors, ensure individuals serving on committees are sufficiently qualified to discharge the expanded responsibilities.
- *Companies must find ways to adequately evaluate the number of board members who are truly independent.* Independence can be hampered by more than just the obvious conflict of interest. Long-term relationships or external interests can complicate board efficiency and effectiveness. If an independent director has served on a board for an extended period of time, companies should question whether that director's independence is impacted when they are attempting to execute their responsibilities. They may have personal ties or alliances to the CEO or other members of management that can inhibit their fulfillment of responsibilities. Long-term relationships are often difficult to severe; however, in the best interest of both the company and the director, the severance of those relationships will create a more independent culture. Consider an instance where a board member has served on a board for 10 or more years. Obviously the knowledge the person has gained is valuable to the organization. But consider how the long tenure has impacted his/her ability to objectively question management on difficult issues. The long-term association has most likely come with the development of close relationships with the senior leadership team. This may unintentionally create apprehension for questioning certain actions of management.
- *What is the acceptable practice of board communication with individuals outside of senior management?* How often do members of your board communicate with employees and/or management who hold positions outside of the executive committee?

Is this type of communication and interaction encouraged, discouraged, or ignored? There may be no right or wrong answer. It could very well depend on the organization as well as the director's time commitment. If the decision for limited communication is something that is championed by management, companies should evaluate the reasoning. Truly independent directors should be able to communicate with whoever they believe necessary to understand the inner workings of the company. This should not be limited to the executive team or individuals approved by management. If this occurs, management must also evaluate whether they are sending unintended messages regarding the access of the board to employees. In addition, frequent and open communication should be encouraged between board members and the internal auditors, compliance professionals, and legal professionals. If communication is limited to quarterly meetings, board members should be reaching out to these positions often to gain clarity on issues.

- *Does the board have input into corporate strategy?* The Enron, World Com, and Tyco scandals all support the reasons why it is important for the board to be actively engaged in the company's corporate strategy. Pre-Sarbanes–Oxley, boards were often the yes men to management and were only included in corporate strategy discussions after strategies were approved. By this time, management had developed the company line on the strategy direction. Boards were told what management felt they needed to hear to approve the strategy of the company. New risk management procedures strongly suggest that boards should be integrally involved in strategy discussions and decisions. If the board has not been sufficiently exposed to strategy discussions and alternatives, they may not have the information needed to make informed decisions that are best for shareholders.
- *What is the board's role in understanding fraud investigations, whistle-blower issues, and corporate misconduct?* One of my favorite phrases is "Sarbanes–Oxley was not put in place because someone forgot to document accounts payable from beginning to end." Sounds simple, but we sometimes forget the importance of the concept of tone at the top, culture, code

of conduct, conflict of interest, segregation of duties, and internal controls.

Management can often get caught up in the tactics of conforming to Sarbanes–Oxley requirements. When this occurs, the forest gets lost in the trees! If you don't agree, ask yourself, "What information is the board given on fraud investigations, whistle-blower issues, or conflict of interest issues?" Management will be quick to indicate that "We report to our board on these issues quarterly!" But is the reporting focused on quantitative concepts only? Does it lack the quality reporting that allows the board to appropriately evaluate the issues and ask probing questions? Many companies report to board members the number of calls coming through the whistleblower hotline. But, how often does the board hear the true details behind those numbers? Are the true details known? Have the complaints been adequately investigated by the appropriate independent parties? Also, if corporate misconduct has been identified within the organization, are assessments made as to what, when, and how the board will be informed? If so, does this make sense? Of course you don't want to overload the board with insignificant issues, but who is making the determination of what is/isn't significant? If the concept of corporate tolerance has not been fully vetted, ask yourself and your organization why.

- *Does the board have input to performance appraisals of the CEO, CFO, CAO, and CAE officer?* Can you ask this question of your management, or is it considered a political question that is only relevant to a few insiders? This may sound harsh, but part of tone at the top encompasses having the board assist in establishment of corporate culture. What better way to have an impact than to have a direct say into the performance evaluation of individuals within the organization who hold roles that have specific fiduciary duties to the company and to shareholders.

  A CAE relayed an instance where he recommended to his management that the audit committee should have input into his personal performance appraisal. The recommendation became a political career killer for the audit executive. Management took his recommendation as inappropriate and outside of the audit executive's realm of authority. The CAE indicated the recommendation came subsequent to a quality assurance review conducted in line with the *Standards*. The review was sanctioned by the audit committee and management. Of the handful of recommendations made, the vast majority had to do with internal audit's lack of independence and connection to the board and audit committee. Unfortunately, none of the recommendations were accepted by management or the audit committee.

The CAE left the company within the succeeding months. Regardless of whether these actions were connected, the fact that the recommendations of the quality assurance review were ignored, and a long-term employee of the company (the CAE) left within months of the review, may infer the internal audit function experienced some independence issues within the organization.

- *Are there roles within the organization that, by charter, have responsibilities requiring direct access to the board?* If so, does the board have input to the performance of individuals within these roles? Performance appraisals should be considered as a proper governance step. This is not an attempt to exert management's authority over personnel evaluations; it is an important consideration of the true independence and reporting relationship of individuals tasked with board reporting responsibility.
- *How is the evaluation of the board of directors conducted?* This exercise can take on multiple scenarios. The most important aspect of the exercise will be tied to the intent of the evaluation. If the evaluation is to comply with Securities and Exchange Commission regulations or other charter requirements, the process employed may not always be the most effective.

Board evaluation processes can be tricky. There is the need to evaluate the performance of the board and respective members performance while appropriately balancing legal issues that could ultimately surface. Board evaluation processes are as varied as boards themselves. Consider the variance in the following methods:

Board Evaluation Scenario 1 ABC Company is conducting a board evaluation process. A high-level survey is provided separately to each board member. The survey is a set of standard questions related to fiduciary requirements. The form uses a simple yes or no check the box response. What are the benefits of this scenario?

- A high level board survey will provide some insight into the overall evaluation of the performance of fiduciary duties.
- If the survey is completed independently, each director will have the opportunity to answer the questions without any immediate pressure from management members.
- From a legal viewpoint, this method may be less controversial than open-ended questions.

What are the challenges of this scenario?

As with any survey process, individuals may interpret questions in different ways. This factor can make standard survey forms difficult to evaluate for accuracy and effectiveness. Consider the following challenges:

- Lack of a consistent delivery method for the survey may result in inconsistencies of questions interpretations by various directors. This in turn may result in an inconsistent responses.
- A simple yes or no response does not provide a transparent evaluation of how effectively responsibilities were executed.
- A survey that is only provided to the board may not allow for a full 360-degree assessment of their performance.

Board Evaluation Scenario 2 ABC Company has enlisted the assistance of an independent third party to perform an independent review of board performance. The review will include individual interviews, facilitated board discussion, review of charters and board minutes, and a complete independent assessment of effectiveness. What are some of the potential benefits of this scenario?

- A review executed by an independent third party may provide the best insight into the company's governance process.
- An outside party assessing governance elements would not be encumbered by political ties or other relationships that could make evaluation techniques and questions difficult to pose.
- Separate independent interviews of board members and management utilizing open ended questions may provide the best insight to process effectiveness.
- Facilitation of an interactive discussion with the board can provide valuable insight to how board duties are being executed.

What are some of the challenges with this scenario?

- If proper due diligence is not performed when selecting the independent third party assessor, the organization may experience various challenges in execution of the assessment. These challenges can be both positive and negative.
- If an assessment body is selected that utilizes very strict standard evaluation attributes that are not in line with the objectives and processes of the organization, the evaluation assessment may not be reflective of the needs of the organization.
- If the assessment group selected has some connection to the company either through past engagements or individual relationships, the assessment may not be as independent as expected.

The effective execution of a completely independent assessment, interview process, and facilitated session can bring with it many organizational and political challenges. This can often be a limiting factor in effective execution of an assessment.

Board Evaluation Scenario 3 JHK company is conducting an internal board evaluation review. The review will be conducted by someone within the legal, compliance, or the internal audit function. The review will include individual interviews, review of charters, discussion with management, and an overall assessment of effectiveness. What are some of the benefits of this scenario?

- An internal evaluator may understand certain intricacies and aspects of how the board operates and is managed. This may provide unique insights into board effectiveness or challenges.
- Utilizing an internal resource may be more cost effective for the organization.

What are some of the challenges of this scenario?

- This method may present the largest political challenge and implications related to assessment accuracy. An internal resource may have unintended pressures and expectations for the manner in which they execute the assessment as well as report the overall results.

Which alternative would you view as providing the best assessment for your organization? The answer may depend on your organization culture, regulatory requirements, or overall reason for performing the assessment. Whatever method is selected, the organization should understand both the benefits and the challenges of the assessment process.

Board and Internal Control

How does the board respond to the identification of internal control issues? Management may sometimes feels the board has more important responsibilities than to listen to control gap issues identified by internal audit, compliance, or the external auditors. However, part of the board's fiduciary duty is oversight of the audit process as well as Sarbanes–Oxley compliance. As hard as it is to listen to what may be deemed as internal control issues that management should address, the board must set the right tone and ensure they focus on those issues brought to their attention. It would be helpful if the board provided some guidance to internal control functions on risk tolerance and/or risk appetite. Ultimately, everyone wants to utilize the board's time wisely. This would assist in insuring issues reported to the board are at the level of concern which they feel they should be made aware of. The board must remember that all groups who provide board reporting services have their own fiduciary duty. Sometimes, judgment and personal assessment drive the need to further discuss an issue with board members. If the board isn't willing to accept those occasional inputs, they may be sending a message to the organization that they don't fully trust the personal judgment of those hired to assess various issues. That can be a troubling situation.

Summary

Accurately assessing board performance and effectiveness is a crucial aspect in today's corporate governance world. The board and management must all understand their individual responsibilities related to execution of board duties as well as the challenges related to effectively assessing the execution of those responsibilities. Ultimately, if it was an easy process, there probably wouldn't be so many alternatives and debates surrounding the manner in which it should be executed.

Section 3: Internal Audit's Role in Fraud Processes

Introduction

Auditors typically find the subject of fraud an interesting topic. Yet, with all of the educational material and information available, internal auditors may find when they stumble onto a situation that presents red flag behavior, there are many difficulties encountered when addressing the issue with management. Why would this occur? Is it due to the inherent instinct by organization personnel to protect their own? Is it because of fears that other individuals will assume management has not performed their job properly? Is it because of personal implications to the individual? Regardless of the reason, working on projects that present fraud red flag behavior can be a significant challenge for auditors from many viewpoints.

Over the course of my career in internal audit, I've seen many situations that presented red flag behavior. In the vast majority of incidents, when findings were brought to the attention of management, the issue was removed from internal audit's responsibility. In addition, the incidents were addressed by management and never reached the level of fraud investigation or prosecution. In some respects, this reaction may have been one to protect our own. In other instances, it may have been the most relevant and cost-beneficial approach. As I look back on some of the scenarios, although there are some that I still question, I have a better understanding of why management may have reacted in the manner that they did.

Fraud is a topic that raises concerns at all levels of the organization and is one that is more openly discussed than it was 10 years ago. However, taking a step back and evaluating the various positions that may be represented when red flag behavior is identified may help the auditor understand whether additional efforts are needed when bringing the issue to the attention of senior management or the board.

Before visiting our stated challenges, let's review a few typical scenarios that have been submitted by various CAEs as instances encountered that appear to represent red flag behavior. The scenarios are categorized as those that occurred pre- and post-Sarbanes–Oxley.

Pre-Sarbanes–Oxley Issues

Scenario 1: Fleet Cost During an audit of the company's fleet vehicle process, internal audit identified certain corporate vehicles with an unusually high number of tire change outs. The vehicles in question were primarily utilized by two separate operational managers. In many cases, a full set of tires would be changed out within a 1 month period. This was considered four times more than the typical vehicle used for the same purpose. When the issue was brought to the attention of management, the auditors were asked to provide their findings and were told management would determine the next steps. The issue was not reported to the audit committee or brought to the attention of the executive team. In this circumstance, internal audit did not have the organizational authority to bring the issue to the attention of the executives. The organization had taken an approach to the internal audit function as a pure compliance area and did not recognize the audit committee reporting line.

Was this fraud? On the surface, many red flags were identified. This issue occurred in an environment prior to utilization of fleet credit cards or having access to data analytics for monitoring of maintenance. Management deemed the financial impact of the issue as small. It was not considered an issue that should be reported to the audit committee. In today's business environment, this issue may have a very different outcome. Recognizing this issue occurred prior to Sarbanes–Oxley, what actions might the internal audit group have taken to further address the issue? Consider the following:

- *Ensure detailed documentation is maintained in the internal audit files.* Because this issue occurred prior to Sarbanes–Oxley, many internal audit groups may have not been intricately familiar with the *International Professional Practices Framework* and their responsibility for reporting issues such as potential fraud. Even though the auditors had been informed they could not report the issue to senior management or the audit committee, they should have ensured the issue was documented within the audit work papers. Documentation should have included the auditor's evaluation of any potential financial, reputational, or compliance impact. This may not seem a sufficient answer in today's business world, but it may have been one of the only remedies the internal audit group had at the time. Documentation would be important to potential future follow-up of the issue.
- *Ensure that the issue was communicated through internal audit's organizational reporting line.* In this instance, internal audit reported to a vice-president of compliance who reported to the chief operating officer (COO). Although the internal auditors had informed their CAE, they had not informed the vice-president of compliance due to pressure from management. However, the audit team should have, at a minimum, ensured that the vice-president of compliance was aware of the issue.
- *Include a follow-up review on the audit plan.* Since the auditors were blocked in their efforts to report the issue to the audit committee, they should ensure that a follow-up review was included within the audit plan.
- *Consider the need for other relevant communications.* Recognizing that this issue occurred prior to Sarbanes–Oxley, the company in question was a publicly traded organization. The internal auditors had a fiduciary responsibility to report their concerns. The auditors should have ensured, once they fully documented the issue and potential impact,

that the issues were communicated to not just the vice-president of compliance but also the audit committee and the external auditors. The issue presented all of the red flags of potential fraud.

Scenario 2: Lottery Tickets An internal auditor received a call from an operational jurisdiction located in a small town within their business area. An administrative assistant was summarizing receipts and completing an expense report associated with a credit card assigned to an operations manager who had left for vacation. The assistant noted the regular occurrence of miscellaneous charges for amounts from $5 to $30 each time the card was utilized at a specific quick-stop retailer. The charges listed a code of miscellaneous. The administrative assistant called the internal audit manager whom she had a close working relationship with. The internal audit manager called the quick stop and was informed the code was for the purchase of lottery tickets. Further review indicated in the previous 3 months, the operations manager had purchased approximately $4000 in lottery tickets. The internal audit manager informed legal counsel who took ownership of the issue.

When the operations manager returned from vacation, he admitted to using the card to purchase lottery tickets. The company terminated the operations manager. He was not asked for reimbursement of the $4000, and no inquiries were made as to whether the tickets had any winning numbers. The legal counsel made the determination that the time and effort that would be expended in trying to prosecute the operations manager for the action would not be cost beneficial to the company. The issue was not reported to the audit committee. Should it have been? From management's perspective, they took care of the issue and terminated the employee. In addition, in relationship to the company's size, the amounts were minimal. From an internal audit viewpoint, the department found that in the succeeding months, other individuals liberally used their cards for personal purposes. The issue resulted in some difficult internal control concerns. But again, the expenditures were small and below management tolerance levels. This situation may be viewed differently in today's business environment and the access to more data-centric information. What are some of the alternative actions the audit group could have taken?

- *Consider relevant communication considerations.* This issue was identified outside of the normal course of an internal audit, and the auditors chose to inform legal counsel who then took ownership of the issue. The audit committee was not informed because of the perceived immateriality of the issue. Although we do not know the full extent of other communications, in this scenario, the internal auditors should have ensured their departmental management was aware of the issue and that it had been handed over to legal.
- *Consider extended internal control considerations.* The employee was terminated; however, the company did not ask for recovery of the funds. When other operations personnel learned of the issue, it resulted in ongoing control issues. Field personnel realized that the company did not have a strong process to identify these issues. As a result, other abuses followed. At a minimum, the internal auditors may have wanted to add an audit to the current plan to review the process for utilization of the specific credit cards.

Scenario 3: Company Assets Used for Personal Purposes Senior executives were regularly utilizing company assets for personal purposes. This included utilization of company aircraft, vehicles, and company funds to entertain family as well as lavish expenditures on business meals and personal trips. These issues were openly known by many professionals within the company, but since the personnel taking advantage of the issue were senior leaders, it was assumed acceptable. This is an issue that gained national attention and entailed more than 12 years of significant litigation. The issue became public post the Enron downfall. In this instance, there were many legal proceedings that discussed the appropriateness or impropriety of the actions. Even the courts took varying opinions. The issue points to the culture of corporate America during this time period and the lack of transparency and accountability for utilization of company funds. What actions may have been appropriate for internal audit to take?

- *Communicate the noncompliance with the company code of conduct.* Information about the relevant use of company property for personal purposes was included in the code of conduct. In this instance, since the activity of the executives was well known, internal audit had a fiduciary obligation to inform the audit committee of the issue. Unfortunately, the executive at question was the CEO. He held a very close reign on what was reported to the audit committee. As the issue went through the courts system, members of the internal audit group were subpoenaed to testify regarding their knowledge of the incident. The fact that the auditors had to testify under oath that they did not feel they could report the issue may have been a factor in how some of the legal proceedings evolved. Understanding that this was a time prior to Sarbanes–Oxley, this is a stark example of how CAEs need to understand their professional obligation for communication to the audit committee especially when it involves inappropriate activity.

Scenario 4: Personal Expense Reimbursement Internal audit was engaged to perform an audit of expenditures for a professional society in their industry. This audit was an annual review that was rotated between the internal audit groups of the companies who were members of the association. During evaluation of expenditures for the director of the association, the internal auditors identified expenditures being reimbursed without proper documentation. Many of these expenditures were excessive in nature including undocumented tips to convention personnel and personal travel costs.

When the issues were first identified, the internal auditors attempted to determine how long the process had been occurring. From records, they could identify the trend in submitting expenditures had occurred over the past 3 to 5 years. The auditors contacted the internal audit groups of the other companies who were association members and who had been engaged in previous years to perform the audit. The auditors acknowledged they had similar observations. However, the association director had explained his rationale for the expenses. The auditors had reported their findings to their internal management. The issues were not deemed significant.

The current auditors were uncomfortable with the level at which the expenditures had escalated. The decision was made to present the information to the association board. The internal auditors presented the information with the association director present. Although the board did not request the repayment of the excessive expenditures, they made the decision that the association was no longer of benefit to the members. The association was disbanded.

Should there have been other ramifications? All association members were eventually notified. None reimbursement of funds from the director. In addition the members requested no one asked for further prosecution of the issue. What other considerations should have been given in this situation?

- *Full disclosure and communication with other members of the association*. This scenario stated that past auditors from companies who were part of the association had recognized the issue of excessive expenditures. Although they informed their management, the other corporate members of the association were not informed.

  In looking at this issue in the rearview mirror, previous auditors should have reported their observations to the other association members. Instead, they made their individual determination that the issue was not significant. Because the issue involved inappropriate expenditures, it would have been advisable to report the issue to all association members.

Post-Sarbanes–Oxley

Scenario 1: Funds Missing During a year-end reconciliation of a company brokerage account, the treasury accountant identified that funds within a stagnant corporate account were missing. The account had maintained a balance just under $100,000 for the past 5 years. The account had been in existence for more than 10 years. It was established at a time the company was engaged in various business initiatives. Although the account was no longer used, it had not been closed out. The account was reconciled on a monthly basis. In January, the treasury accountant identified that the funds had disappeared. Internal audit was notified. The CAE worked with the treasurer to evaluate the issue. It was determined that through a series of missteps, the funds within the account were transferred out of the company account to a separate personal account of an employee.

Several control errors had occurred in the process that could be attributed to both the firm and the brokerage company. When the funds were located, they were repaid by the individual whose account they had been transferred to. The account was a special brokerage account which had specific requirements when opened. The account had not been properly closed due to miscommunications between the company and the brokerage firm.

Although this issue seems to present several red flags, the circumstances involved many control issues that occurred both on the company's part and the brokerage firm side. No intent could be proved. Since the funds were returned, no prosecution was pursued. In this instance, the audit committee was informed. Were there any additional efforts that internal audit should have pursued in this instance?

- *Further process of investigation and evaluation.* In this instance, the issue was not turned over to an external forensic investigator. Due to the dollar value involved and the red flags identified, it may have been appropriate to suggest to executive management and legal counsel that the issue be evaluated independently by an outside party. Acknowledging that the funds were repaid, the transfer of the funds from a company account to a personal account points to significant red flags. A forensic investigator may have been able to effectively evaluate and obtain evidentiary evidence that would provide the full view of the issue.

Scenario 2: Invoice Splitting During an internal audit review of a large project initiative, it was noted that a particular vendor was submitting numerous invoices on the same day of the month for slightly less than $10,000. In some months, the vendor submitted more than twenty invoices all under $10,000. The individual amounts were within the authorization approval level of the area supervisor responsible for the project. The issue appeared to be a classic example of invoice splitting.

When the information was presented to management, the explanation given was that the supervisor approving the invoices had appropriate authority to do so. The person had been given responsibility for the administration of a multi-million dollar project. The bills associated with that project regularly exceed the supervisor's authorization limit. The supervisor assumed that since he had been assigned administrative authority over the project, he had appropriate authority for approval of all expenditures. The supervisor viewed the process of asking for an adjustment in his documented authority level as an imposition on management. He instructed the vendors to submit invoices for an amount that was within his authority level to approve.

When the issue was identified by internal audit, management was informed along with the legal counsel. In the end, the supervisor's authority limit was increased to allow him to approve invoices that were in line with the project. Although the issue appeared to be invoice splitting, other circumstances made it difficult to determine whether there was intent to deceive involved. The audit committee was informed, and processes where changed.

Was this fraud? Should there have been other implications? This is certainly possible, but again, there were many control issues surrounding this scenario. The observation was taken to the appropriate level of management, and the audit committee was alerted. Ultimately, there were other changes made to the administration of the project, and the supervisor was provided training on the process relating to invoice approval. What could have been done differently in this situation?

- *Initiate a formal process of investigation and evaluation*. Because this issue involved a large sum of money, it may have been advisable for the company to turn the evaluation into a formal investigation. In this instance, senior management supported the supervisor and felt what had occurred was not representative of any type of intent or fraud. However, the issue represented numerous red flags. Internal audit was unable to obtain certain information related to the vendor's business. They did not have legal authority to subpoena this type of information. It may have been advisable to suggest to the audit committee that a formal investigation be initiated by an outside party.
- *Recommendation for reassignment of the operational project*. Although management provided the supervisor with additional administrative training related to invoice approval, it may have been advisable to consider a recommendation of

additional oversight for the project outside of the specific supervisor. Based on the information provided, the supervisor did not have experience with this size of a project and may not have been appropriately trained in aspects of managing the expenditures of the project.

Scenario 3: Conflict of Interest During a review of the procurement area, internal audit identified procurement mangers were regularly accepting gifts from vendors. This was a regular practice that had not been questioned in the past. The gifts were typically small in dollar amount and would periodically include tickets to suites or large sporting events.

During the course of the audit, a review indicated that the occurrence had escalated when specific managers had been promoted. The internal auditors brought the issue to the attention of management and the legal function. The company's code of conduct did not specifically address the acceptance of gifts. Management and legal counsel indicated the trips and gifts were known and approved and the issue was not deemed improper. The internal auditors were told by legal and senior management they should not include the observations in the report. The company adjusted their code of conduct policy for gifts. Within 1 year, the procurement managers in question left the company.

Was this fraud? Were the actions of the procurement managers improper? Should internal audit have taken additional steps? Although the issue occurred post-Sarbanes–Oxley, the internal auditors were informed by executive management the value of the items accepted were not significant. They felt including the finding in the audit report would characterize the issue as more concerning than it was.

In the end, the internal audit group did not include the findings within the audit report. However, during a private session with the audit committee, the CAE informed the committee of the findings. The audit committee questioned management who validated the issue but indicated it was not significant and they felt the internal auditors were inappropriately characterizing the significance of the issue. The audit committee chose not to take further action. The resulting political implications to the CAE were very difficult because management felt he had inappropriately communicated a finding. In the end, the

CAE left the company within six months. What other considerations might have been applicable in this scenario?

- *Enhanced process of issue communication.* The fact management informed the internal auditors not to include the issue within the internal audit report would be considered a red flag. The auditors had a fiduciary duty to include the information within the report. If they feared repercussions by management, the issue should have been reported to the audit committee prior to the formal meeting.
- *Educate management on the fraud triangle and implications of this type of activity on the company's control environment.* Take the personalization out of the issue. If management was resisting efforts to report the issue, the internal auditors may have wanted to approach management with information and statistics about these types of issues and the risk that could be manifested into. By relaying to management information on similar issues that have occurred in other companies, they may have been able to properly communicate the relevance of taking additional action or reporting the issue to the audit committee.

Scenario 4: Merger Activities The company was expanding its service line into another area. They were in the process of purchasing small retail who dealt within their business target. During a due diligence review of a proposed buyer, the internal auditors identified the owners of the retail group had run through an excessive amount of personal charges the month prior to the closing of the deal. These personal charges included purchasing expensive sporting tickets, prepaying for certain business trips, large entertainment costs, and certain expenditures for other personal purposes.

The internal auditors alerted executive management who then alerted the legal department. In this instance, the legal department took steps to further examine the issue, and internal audit was involved in the interviews and evaluation. Ultimately, the issue was included within the internal audit report that went to the audit committee. The acquisition was completed; however, senior management chose to replace the management of the company that was being purchased. In this example, it appears internal audit took the relevant steps to ensure management and the audit committee were aware of the issue.

Scenario 5: Petty Cash Fund The internal audit team was performing a review of a subsidiary operation in an overseas location. The location ranked high on the corruption percentage index (CPI). During the review, the team was informed by the operations manager that the location maintained two petty cash funds. Fund A was the "white fund," and Fund B was the "black fund." Both funds held balances larger than most typical petty cash funds. Each fund was approximately $100,000.

The auditors evaluate the two funds and realized the black fund lacked supporting documentation on more than 60 percent of expenditures as well as fund replenishments. The white fund was well documented. Management provided an open and transparent response on the issue. They indicated the black fund was utilized for expenditures where the operations group needed ready access to cash. This typically occurred to be able to facilitate a payment which related to a permit, fee, or other administrative expenditures the location was required to pay. These expenditures were considered administratively burdensome or red tape due to the jurisdiction. To eliminate the need to complete an abundance of regulatory paperwork, the managers found local officials would accept cash payments and provide the proper paperwork to move forward.

The internal auditors informed management this process was not acceptable. They instructed management to close the black fund, account for all cash since inception, and complete the necessary paperwork.

In this company, the internal audit department administratively reported to the legal group. During the review, they timely informed legal counsel of the issue. Upon return from the assignment they were instructed that legal counsel would follow through on the issue. Internal audit was informed they did not need to take additional action.

Approximately 1 month later during a routine follow-up on the issues, the audit team found the black fund had not been closed. It was still being actively utilized. They also found that no action had been taken to resolve the identified issues. The auditors again approached the legal team and were told that it would be handled. During a scheduled audit committee meeting, the CAE informed the audit committee of the incident. Within a few weeks, the CAE as well as two members of the audit team were terminated.

Does this scenario raise any red flags? Should the auditors have done anything differently, or did they handle the issue appropriately? The details outlined in this example were provided by individuals involved in the internal audit process. They were inquiring what they could have done differently and whether they had indeed exacerbated the significance of the issue. Further discussion of the issue identified a few considerations the audit team may have wanted to make:

- *The auditors could have alerted management earlier in the process.* They had attempted to gather appropriate information while onsite. They then presented the information in a phone call with the legal group. However, during the call, they did not raise the level of concern that was later raised when they returned from the assignment.
- *When informed by legal counsel not to follow up, the auditors should have clarified their individual fiduciary duty.* At the very least, internal audit needed to understand the timing with which the issue would be resolved and how or if it would be communicated to the audit committee.
- *The audit team indicated they informed the external auditors about the incident prior to informing the audit committee.* It may have been advisable to work with the legal counsel to coordinate those communications.
- *The head of internal audit spoke to the audit committee in a private session because he feared management repercussions.* It is uncertain how the information was relayed to the audit committee and whether the head of internal audit had pre-informed senior management of his intent to update the committee. If this had not been done, there could have been a misunderstanding in the communication process. This was an instance where the head of internal audit felt they were appropriately executing their fiduciary authority. Management had a different view.

Challenge 38: Internal Audit's Role in Fraud Awareness

How does your organization define the role for internal audit in fraud-related work? Do they deem internal audit as an area that can provide fraud awareness training or educational information about the aspects of fraud? Is internal audit considered qualified to perform a fraud risk assessment for the company? What about performing a fraud investigation? The answer to these specific challenge questions will vary based on the organization, the composition of the internal audit group, and the related skills maintained in the function.

The *Standards* state internal audit's obligation for evaluation of potential fraud:

> Internal auditors must consider the probability of significant errors, fraud, noncompliance, and other exposures when developing the engagement objectives.
>
> **Institute of Internal Auditors Standard 2210 A2**

As we have discussed, management does not always understand the *Standards* or the relative guidance provided to the profession. Often, when issues arise that may present as fraud red flags, management may choose to turn the issue over to the legal professionals or even an outside investigator. In many instances, this may be the right approach. Just because the *Standards* indicate internal auditors must consider the probability of fraud does not mean they have the requisite expertise to execute a fraud evaluation. Contrast this thought to an individual who is a lawyer. The fact that the person has passed the bar exam and obtained his/her license to practice does not mean the lawyer can execute on all aspects of the law. Lawyers have specialties just like other professions. A contract lawyer would not litigate a criminal case in a court of law.

Internal auditors must establish the appropriate parameters and expectations for how, when, where, and why they become involved in fraud related procedures. Those parameters will be based on the expectations of the organization along with the experience and credentials of the individuals within the internal audit function.

Challenge 38 Potential Actions: Internal Audit's Role in Fraud Awareness The importance of fraud awareness in today's business has exponentially increased. With the ever evolving technology in everyday business, companies must understand aspects of fraud, why it occurs, how it could occur, and the potential risk that exists if control gaps are not addressed. These important attributes all point to the criticality of establishing a proper fraud awareness programs. With that understood, some organizations have an aversion to allowing internal audit to be involved in fraud awareness processes. They may not want their internal auditors talking about fraud to process owners. However, it is important for management to understand that one of the best prevention techniques for fraud is fraud awareness. Allowing the internal auditors to take a role in fraud awareness processes can add strategic value to the organization's overall control environment. There are a multitude of roles internal audit can effectively execute when considering a company's fraud awareness program.

- *The role of educator and facilitator when executed appropriately can provide significant value to the organization.* As indicated by the *Standards*, internal auditors are not expected to have the requisite expertise of a forensic investigator; however, they should be qualified to evaluate the aspects of fraud and understand fraud red flags. This quality puts internal auditors in a unique position to assist the organization in fraud awareness education and communication. Tactics employed can range from providing fraud educational information for business leaders to executing individual training sessions for high-risk fraud processes. In some instances, internal audit groups have worked to create educational fraud awareness training course modules or internal websites for employees to access as a resource. These methods are within the realm of providing specialty or consulting advice.

  In one of my roles as a CAE, our department worked on a fraud awareness training and informational site for the organization. The module was embraced by the organization and the audit committee. The external auditors considered it a strong attribute to the company's antifraud program.
- *Although auditors can play a strategic role in fraud awareness, they should not be placed in a position of creating a "policy."* The creation of individual policies is a responsibility of management.

- *Update management on the Standards for internal auditors and fraud responsibilities.* Internal audit management who experience challenge from the organization about the role of internal audit in fraud awareness should consider providing information to management related to the *Standards* and the expectations of the profession. Providing this information along with relaying the particular control and risk skills maintained by the internal audit staff can help management understand the ultimate value that can be created through involvement in fraud awareness programs.

Challenge 39: Internal Audit's Role in Fraud Risk Assessment

Depending on the processes executed within the company, a fraud risk assessment may be a task that is facilitated and managed by a separate risk process area. Fraud risk assessments can vary from high-level enterprise-wide assessments to more detailed fraud scenario assessments for specific business units. These assessments can be very different than individual fraud assessments conducted by internal audit for the annual audit plan. As indicated by the *Standards*, internal audit must consider the risk of fraud to the achievement of objectives. Regardless of the level of the fraud assessment, internal auditors can provide strategic value through involvement in the assessment and evaluation.

Challenge 39 Potential Actions: Internal Audit's Role in Fraud Risk Assessment To provide strategic value to the organization in relationship to fraud risk assessments, internal auditors must ensure they have an understanding of the varying levels of assessments that may be conducted. This understanding should extend to the following concepts:

- *Fraud risk assessments are executed in different ways and at different levels of the organization.* It is important for internal auditors to understand the variance in the types of assessments that may be executed within the organization. This understanding can assist in ensuring the process effectively meets organizational goals and identifies information relevant to the organization. Often, organizations are unsure as to the proper level of evaluation to undertake when assessing for fraud.

Understanding the type of assessment required will allow the internal auditor to contribute their knowledge about the overall risks of the company as well as the individual risks in business unit or process areas.

- *Auditors can be a valuable resource in brainstorming processes related to assessing the risk for fraud.* Regardless of formal fraud risk assessment processes undertaken by the organization, it is not uncommon for business areas to perform their own scenario analysis when setting goals and objectives. The process area may not even realize they are brainstorming fraud risks. Often, this analysis is performed during strategic planning sessions. The business area assesses its individual strengths and weaknesses. During the assessment they brainstorm risks that could impact objectives. Internal auditors who have the opportunity to be involved in these sessions can assist management with the brainstorming process.
- *Auditors can execute brainstorming of fraud scenarios during the initial audit planning processes.* Audit groups who utilize a risk-based audit approach should consider the risk for fraud within the individual process area. Utilizing a group brainstorming approach within the planning meeting either with process owners or within the internal audit group can assist in identifying potential fraud scenarios that may be important to evaluate.
- *Internal audit management must have appropriate personnel with the requisite skill set assigned to fraud risk assessments.* To be able to identify fraud you must be able to conceive of the event. Young auditors may not have the relevant businesses expertise to conceive of potential fraudulent acts. Audit management must provide staff with the proper knowledge and support when assessing the risk for fraud. This is critical to ensure that the organization obtains ultimate value from the process.

Challenge 40: Internal Audit's Role in Fraud Investigation

Fraud evaluations are very different from fraud investigations. An evaluation would be an initial examination of a process to determine the potential for fraud. An investigation is considered the next step in the fraud protocol. An investigation would infer there is some probability an actual fraud has incurred. An investigation will typically involve more formal protocols related to procedures performed, documentation maintained, and reports issues. Internal auditors can take a role in both evaluations and investigations. However, it is important internal audit understand the distinction between the evaluation process and investigation process.

Challenge 40 Potential Actions: Internal Audit's Role in Fraud Investigation Following are some considerations when determining internal audit's role in fraud investigation:

- *Ensure internal audit has the appropriate expertise to perform the investigation.* This speaks to more than just having certified fraud examiners within the department. Having a specific credential does not always mean the person is experienced enough to effectively execute the process. The CAE must ensure individuals assigned to the fraud investigation possess the requisite background, skills, knowledge, and respect to effectively execute an investigation. If the expertise does not exist within the department, auditors should critically evaluate their role and whether it is appropriate to involve an outside investigator or expert.
- *Determine if there is a need to obtain legal advice for the investigation.* Internal auditors should be aware of the need to obtain legal consultation on specific investigations or issues. If there is any possibility the issue could go to litigation, the audit team will want to ensure they have maintained the appropriate chain of evidence within the review.
- *Identify responsibilities outlined in the audit department charter related to fraud investigations.* This ties to one of our lessons learned about ensuring that the audit department charter is fact and not fiction. Typically, if the expectation is for internal audit to be involved in fraud investigations, the responsibility will be outlined in the department charter.
- *Ensure internal audit has the dedicated time to execute upon the review.* Fraud investigations can take a significant amount of time. If internal audit does not have sufficient allocation of time within their audit plan, decisions will need to be made

as to whether the fraud investigation will replace something that is currently on the plan.

- *Ensure approval of the audit committee.* When fraud investigations are conducted within the company, it is advisable to ensure the audit committee is aware of the issue, time, and resources allocated to the project.

Summary

The topic of fraud and potential role for internal audit may take on has many considerations. The CAE must balance the requirements for internal audit to be involved in these reviews with requirements for other projects listed on the audit plan. There are many additional considerations outside of those listed within this narrative. It is advisable for the CAE to establish a comprehensive protocol for the department's involvement in any fraud process work.

Section 4: Performing Consulting Engagements

Introduction

The definition of internal audit includes the concept that internal auditors can provide consulting service to their companies. In fact, the concept is mentioned within the first sentence of the definition:

> Internal auditing is an independent, objective assurance and consulting activity designed to add value and improve an organizations operations.
>
> **Institute of Internal Auditors—Definition of Internal Audit**

Internal auditors often face many challenges when executing the role of consultant. There can be an inherent concern on the part of management related to the impairment of independence if auditors were to perform controls consulting that may later have a need for an assurance review. We examined within Chapter 2 the variances between consulting and assurance activities. In essence, the primary difference between assurance and consulting is that a consulting service is subject to agreement with a client, and there is no third-party attestation or assurance given.

Today's business world is dynamic and ever changing. Controls, processes, procedures, technology, and personnel are always adjusting to new and emerging issues or circumstances. Internal audit can play a valuable role to their organization by taking a proactive part in new initiatives, systems, and processes and assisting in consultation on control issues that may impact the business.

Still, management will periodically contend that auditors cannot fulfill this role because of the need to maintain independence from the process. As recognized by the *Standards*, internal auditors possess skills of objectivity and skepticism, which should mitigate the concern related to independence issues. In addition, when performing consulting activities, the internal auditor should not engage in management decision making or policy setting. Before we review our challenge for this area, let's consider a simple scenario.

Consulting Scenario ABC Company has just implemented a six sigma process improvement function. The process is administered by the operations area of the company and includes many cross functional professionals. Training for the project has been significant, and certain professionals have earned the six sigma black belt certification. Several process improvement and efficiency projects are identified, and the black belts are looking for professionals to source on their team.

One of the processes imbedded in the six sigma procedure is to have a formal validation, post the completion of each project. This is done to verify the calculations of projected savings to actual savings. The operations COO asked the CFO to provide an internal auditor to perform each of these validations. Recently, internal audit took over the responsibility for Sarbanes–Oxley work. The CFO had disbanded the finance department's internal control function which had previously managed the administration and testing. Although internal audit absorbed the Sarbanes–Oxley work, they were not provided any additional resources. They were informed the audit plan must remain intact.

The CAE has significant concerns about now allocating auditors to validation of six sigma savings. He explains to the CFO his concern about the staffing and resourcing as well as his evaluation of the level of importance of the project risk in relationship to areas currently on the audit plan. The CFO indicated he promised the COO that an internal auditor would perform each validation. What should the CAE do? Following are some considerations:

- *Provide the CFO with an analysis of internal audit's current time obligations for audits and Sarbanes–Oxley work.* Analyze any variance in resource issues that would be created by this additional request. Indicate the need to address those issues with the audit committee.
- *Discuss with the CFO alternatives to having internal audit perform the validation.* This is a process which many finance or accounting professionals could adequately perform. The risk significance of the project may not justify the time spent by internal audit.
- *Compare this request with other requests internal audit has typically worked on.* Is the request reasonable? Can you justify the extra time and effort the project would require?
- *Is there any danger of inability to complete the audit plan?* If so, this is an issue that should be brought to the attention of the audit committee.

The CAE must ensure any work on consulting engagements is within the relative expertise of personnel, the department has adequate time and resourcing to handle the request, and the request holds a similar risk threshold as other risk areas included on the annual audit plan.

Challenge 41: Internal Auditors as Consultants

Many of the challenges that come with performing consulting activities are those associated with the particular process, the relationship of the individual auditor to the process, or the particular role the auditor takes on the project. Auditors who attempt to take an active involvement in the actual interworkings of a project policy or decision making could indeed impair future independence if the need arises for an assurance review.

Consider the instance of a company that is implementing a multimillion dollar enterprise resource planning system. The organization has obviously identified this initiative as critical to the overall future success and strategy of the company. In fact, the implementation of the system will have significant impact on the various financial, operational, and compliance processes of the organization. It would seem feasible to have an internal auditor consulting and advising on control procedures up front rather than waiting 6 months after the project is completed to come in and test whether the controls are adequate.

When an internal auditor serves as a consultant on a project, management must maintain responsibility for decision making and final implementation of any recommendations or controls. In fact, although an auditor may recommend a control or procedure at one point in time does not mean that 6 months down the road, processes should remain exactly the same. It is management's responsibility to ensure the controls implemented are effective and are relevant to the business. If the auditors receive challenge from management on their involvement on a new initiative, typically, the concepts of independence and objectivity are the concerns raised. However, these issues can easily be addressed if approached in the right manner by internal audit management.

Challenge 41 Potential Actions: Internal Auditors as Consultants When internal auditors serve as consultants, there are several key concepts that should be managed and handled directly and transparently:

- *Management must understand the auditors are giving control advice at a point in time.* Auditors cannot see the future, and controls should evolve along with systems and processes. Management must take ownership and make the final decision regarding any control recommendations that may be presented. Management should not rely on the old saying of "The auditors told us to do it that way."
- *The assignment of a consulting auditor must be carefully considered by internal audit management.* The person should have adequate knowledge of the business area in order to add value to the project. Periodically, when these initiatives arise, the CAE may look to a subject matter expert within the department who has a strong understanding of the operations surrounding the initiative. This may be an appropriate method. But the CAE must keep in mind how they may source future assurance engagements in the area. The auditor assigned to a

consulting project should not be the auditor assigned to later review the project.

- *Internal audit management should use caution when assigning individuals to a project as a learning experience.* Consulting projects are often those which may be of significant importance to the process area. Individuals assigned must have the requisite knowledge and expertise to execute on the engagement.
- *Auditors assigned to consulting projects must understand their role is for controls consulting.* They should not be involved in any elements of management decision or policy writing.
- *Internal audit management must ensure they understand the requisite time required for the consulting project.* Typically, internal audit groups put aside time for special projects during the year. However, the time allocated must be commensurate with the need. If the time required for an auditor will put other portions of the audit plan at risk for not being completed, the CAE must ensure he/she has a plan to adequately cover those audits.
- *The CAE must carefully evaluate the consulting request to determine its priority in relation to other projects on the audit plan.* If the request is one that represents an administrative check and balance of a budgeting activity or a small project, it may not present the same level of need which a large systems or new initiative would require.
- *In the event the request is for an extended period (assume a systems implementation project that will last 18 months), the CAE should ensure they have the support of the audit committee and management.* Ensure clarification of the role of the auditor on the project, and maintain adequate contact with that auditor to ensure the role is being executed in line with expectations. Consulting projects can become a deep dark hole with no bottom. If the project is large, process owners are always looking for extra legs and arms. They must understand the time requirements of the auditor and know the level of support that can and cannot be provided.
- *Consider what the departmental requirements will be for any type of internal documentation by the consulting auditor.* Although the assignment is one that will be agreed to with the process

owner or client, if it pertains to a large system initiative or other project, some level of documentation for internal audit purposes may be appropriate and helpful for future assurance reviews. Remember, a consulting review does not provide any assurance to a third party. So, if the process area expects a memo of sign-off by the auditors, this would cross the line of a consulting activity.

There are many variations of projects that internal audit may be asked to be involved with. If the department plans to engage in these activities, they must ensure they have the relevant expertise, the obligation is appropriately outlined in the department charter, management and the audit committee understand the variance between consulting and assurance engagements, and the project assignment represents an issue that is equivalent or higher than those on the current audit plan.

6

Internal Audit Reporting and Communication

Introduction

Formal reporting by internal audit can be a difficult, time-consuming, and politically charged issue. The acceptance of internal audit reports by management will depend on the organization's expectation for how issues should be communicated as well as how the internal audit group defines, phrases, and outlines the reports. The concept can even extend to the visual manner in which the report template is outlined. We previously discussed some reporting challenges related to presenting risk-based auditing. Whether reporting is represented through PowerPoint, detailed memos, or detailed reports which outline each exception, and management agreed to actions or reports which outline issue observations, formal reporting is a sensitive issue. Words, no matter how carefully crafted, can be interpreted in various ways depending on the perception of the reviewer.

Within this chapter, we will cover the following challenges:

- Challenge 42: Internal Audit Reporting Format
- Challenge 43: Internal Audit Report Writing
- Challenge 44: Management Action Plans versus Management Response
- Challenge 45: Providing an Overall Internal Audit Opinion
- Challenge 46: Management Representation at the Audit Committee Meeting
- Challenge 47: Reporting to the CFO or CLO
- Challenge 48: Reporting to the CEO
- Challenge 49: Reporting to the Audit Committee
- Challenge 50: Understand Legal Privelege
- Challenge 51: Management and the Audit Committee's View of Internal Audit is Different from the *Standards*

Section 1: Internal Audit Reporting Methods

Introduction

Individuals who have spent several years within internal audit and who have had exposure to various companies understand the variations in presentations and report writing. Internal audit reports pre-Sarbanes–Oxley were often very lengthy and comprises of many pages. The procedure utilized during this time was to allow for management responses to identified findings. The difficulty came once draft findings were released to management, and internal audit later received the responses. Many process owners expected their management responses to be stated word for word within the internal audit report. Responses could be contradictory to the finding and periodically would be contentious in their wording indicating that management did not agree to the exception or control gaps identified. This created a difficult situation. Internal audit would have to re-validate the control gap before the report could be released. By the time auditors were able to retest the control, management may have made changes or corrected the error. This would put the auditors in a new predicament of determining how to phrase or report the issue. This back and forth of issues created significant delays in the release of audit reports.

In years post-Sarbanes–Oxley, internal audit reports have migrated to obtaining management agreed upon solutions. This facilitates the ability to work through the control issues with management to obtain a proper balance between how the issue is described and how management prioritizes the issue for mitigation. Even in these cases, the length of time between the close of the audit and gaining management action buy in could be detailed and result in a lengthy process.

In other instances, internal audit groups would attempt to assign a rating to either the audit overall report or to individual audit findings. Our challenges outlined in earlier chapters covered some of these issues. We will now take a more detailed approach. *Standard 2450* addresses the concept of providing audit report rankings:

> When an overall opinion is issued, it must take into account the expectations of senior management, the board, and other stakeholders and must be supported by sufficient, reliable, relevant, and useful information.
>
> **Institute of Internal Auditors Standard 2450**

The interpretation of this *Standard* outlines the expected information required when an overall audit opinion is issued. This includes the following:

- The scope, including the time period to which the opinion pertains
- Scope limitations audit project
- Consideration of all related projects including reliance on other assurance providers
- The risk or control framework or other criteria used as a basis for the overall opinion
- The overall opinion, judgment, or conclusion reached
- The reasons for an unfavorable overall opinion must be stated

The challenge of providing an overall opinion in internal audit reports is that management may correlate the process to how it is used by the external auditors Any indication of an unacceptable review would be tantamount to receiving a qualified opinion from the external auditors. This opinion would often result in strong opposition and debate from management. Some audit groups have moved away from providing a "pass" or "fail" assessment and attempt to use words such as "acceptable," "needs improvement," "immediate action needed," or "unacceptable." This still creates concerns because management would be resistant to any reports that were something other than "acceptable" or "needs improvement."

This may all sound as if the auditors are in a no win position. In reality, that position was often dictated by how management and the audit committee viewed the internal audit function, their value, and their skills as well as the CAE's personal relationship with the audit committee. In addition, a great deal hinged on how reports were worded or phrased and presented to management and later to the audit committee.

These difficulties resulted in some internal audit groups separating the detailed audit report from management's executive summary report. The intent was to provide the process owners with some level of comfort that lower level exceptions or findings would not be exacerbated with the audit committee or senior management. In these instances, internal audit would write a summary level report that would be provided to senior management and the audit committee for review. This assisted in eliminating the potential that the audit committee would become bogged down in report detail. The committee would be able to focus on the higher level assessments and the outcome of the audit.

Although this sounds like a great compromise, periodically, this tactic would become difficult to employ. Initially, it would be embraced by process owners. They were relieved that every individual finding was not presented in a lengthy report to senior management. The procedure alleviated some of their concerns about the perception of the overall review. However, after a period of time, process owners would forget the procedure where audit committees received the detailed report. They had become accustomed to the concise summaries. As expected, their focus switched to being concerned about how many issues were stated in the executive summary. The preference would be that the summary simply list the scope of the review, the audit objective statement, the background of the audit area, and then an overall summary indicating no issues were identified that were considered significant enough to bring to the attention of the audit committee. As you can see, there are many implications involved with report writing. So the question becomes, what is an auditor to do? Let's further examine some of the individual challenges of report writing.

Challenge 42: Internal Audit Reporting Format

Initially, you may think the manner in which an internal audit report template is developed would not be a significant concern of management. However, all organizations have their idiosyncrasies when it comes to presentation format. Many organizations go to great lengths to develop standard company headers for organizational memos and PowerPoint presentations along with standard guidelines regarding fonts, layout, and other seemingly minor issues of report presentation. The concept of how internal audit presents their audit report may fall into these parameters.

Scenario: Report Writing Format One CAE relayed an experience he faced with a new organization on how the internal audit reports were visually outlined. The CAE was new to the company but had been a CAE for a separate company for many years. Upon arrival at the new company, he was informed that his initial assignment was to clean up the internal audit report writing process. The CAE observed that internal audit used a memo style format for reporting. The reports would be lengthy and were difficult for the process owners and management to identify issues of greatest significance. The CAE attempted to present a new format to senior management. One of the visual changes was the inclusion of a risk matrix on the front of the report along with developing an executive summary separate from the detailed report. The format was presented in landscape mode rather than the organization's past practice of having audit reports presented in portrait mode. When the proposed template was presented to the CFO and CEO, the biggest contention was the utilization of landscape mode. Although the majority of reporting provided to the audit committee by finance and other areas of the company were completed in landscape mode, the CEO had a strong aversion to changing the audit reports to adjust to this style. In the end, the CAE was required to re-template the reports back into portrait mode.

Although this scenario may sound menial, it resulted in a significant amount of lost time. When determining the most relevant format for your internal audit reports, CAEs may want to consider some of the following concepts.

Challenge 42 Potential Actions: Internal Audit Reporting Format

- *Understand the company's preference for internal written communications.* As indicated earlier, many companies have standard memo headers and PowerPoint requirements. In the event you are considering an adjustment to the internal audit reporting style, ensure you understand the company's expectation regarding internal communications.
- *Be cautious when changing report style format without proper pre-communication with management.* Management and the audit committee become accustomed to a particular format, and even the slightest change may cause confusion on their part. When considering a new or improved reporting template, it is advisable to mock up a report and allow senior management and the audit committee to provide input on the style and expected content.

- *Consider a formal review or education session with management and the audit committee on the new reporting method.* Be cautious when changing reporting templates without first alerting management. It may result in management focusing more on the template changes than the report itself. This can even extend to concepts such as the style and type of font to graphics that may be presented within the audit report. It is advisable to spend some educational time with management to ensure they have a sufficient understanding of the report format utilized.
- *Be conscious of preferences of the organization for the specific media used for the presentation.* When considering a change in your reporting media (e.g., PowerPoint, memo presentation, etc.), it is important to ensure that management understands the reasons and benefits of this approach. Again, any style changes can result in mis-focused attention by management and the audit committee.

Overall, it is important to utilize a format and method of communicating audit reports that are acceptable and well understood by the organization. Don't underestimate the impact of the visual report.

Challenge 43: Internal Audit Report Writing

Report writing courses and protocols have significantly changed in concept and style over the years. Pre-Sarbanes–Oxley, internal audit groups included significant detail in their reports including the population size for each individual test performed, the number of exceptions identified, and the number of control gap failures. The difficulty with this approach was that it didn't provide management with an understanding of why the finding was important or what particular impact it may have on the company.

Today's style of report writing encourages auditors to focus on the control gap and the root cause of the issue rather than the number of exceptions identified. In the end, risk-based auditing is focused on evaluating those processes that could have the greatest impact to the organization's goals and objectives. Providing numbers and statistics on control exceptions may not be as beneficial as pointing to the actual control gap and explaining the potential impact the gap may have on the process.

In addition, the selection of wording within reports can often be a source of contention. Consider the following scenario relayed by a CAE regarding report writing.

Scenario: Report Writing The internal audit group had completed reviews of a very sensitive topic—executive expenditures. The CAE was required by management to rewrite the audit report multiple times. The CAE worked with members of finance management to attempt to write the reports in a manner that would be clear and acceptable. This entailed altering the format of the reports. Management disagreed with the risk wording; they felt that the issues were described in too much length, or the description of the issues exacerbated the true control break. After multiple attempts, the CAE was unable to write the report in a manner that that was acceptable to management. Management was concerned about characterizing any type of potential misappropriate use of executive expenditures to the audit committee. As audit committee time approached, the CAE continued to stress the importance of issuing the reports which had been in process for over 8 months. The CAE did not have ability to issue the reports independently. He was required to obtain approval from the CFO. A week before the audit committee, the CFO allowed the reports to be issued. However, the CAE was unaware that the CFO called the audit committee chairman to present his version of the his perception of the nonsignificance of the reports and related issues. Although the audit team had reviewed the reports with management and gained acceptance on the content, at the audit committee meeting, the CAE was reprimanded for the manner in which the reports were written.

This appeared to be a no win situation. So, what are some considerations the internal auditors should be aware of when writing reports?

Challenge 43 Potential Actions: Internal Audit Report Writing The art of report writing is as varied as the individual professional or internal audit group delivering the report. Wording, phrasing, format, and presentation can dramatically impact the effectiveness of a report. Each internal audit group must determine the most effective method for their companies. With this in mind, there are some general considerations that may be applicable:

- *Understand the company's communication style requirements.* This recommendation includes understanding your organization's preference for a full description of the issue identified or utilization of more concise bullet points to summarize the issue. Each organization has their preferences in how much detail they feel is appropriate within a formal report. Internal auditors can still provide detailed memos for their working files, but when issuing formal reports, understand the expectations of management on how the issues should be presented.
- *Be cautious of utilization of risk wording that management is not familiar with.* As auditors, we understand risk wording. We also understand the variance between standard and inherent risk. However, this understanding does not always extend to management's vocabulary. They may view risk wording in a different light and may assume that the wording is trying to reflect a lack of adequate control around their individual process.
- *Ensure that management understands the meaning of "inherent" risk.* Some audit departments organize their reports individual risk areas. Standard risk wording is utilized to define the risk being evaluated. For example, assume that the audit team is evaluating fraud risk within a process area. The "inherent" risk may be defined as follows within the report:
    - *Fraud risk: The risk that some intentional act of misappropriation of funds, diversion of assets, or concealment of information will go undetected and unreported.*

When management reads this "inherent risk" at the beginning of an audit report, if they do not understand risk language, they may perceive the auditor is inferring that there is fraud in their process. Auditors may want to consider defining the risk in a manner that does not give the perception that the risk is already occurring within the audit area.

- *Focus on the control gap and not the individual exception.* An unstated cardinal rule of report writing is to not utilize employee names within the context of an audit finding. In today's world of information privacy and defamation of character lawsuits, auditors are better advised to utilize position titles or process area names rather than focus on individuals that the control gap may have been associated with. It is much more valuable to highlight the actual control gap, the root cause of the gap and its potential ramification to the company rather than single out a particular individual. Consider the following example.

Scenario: Control Gap Assume that internal audit is reviewing the credit application process in a mortgage loan company. During testing, a control gap is identified where the manager of credit has several responsibilities that result in a segregation of duty concern. Ultimately, this control gap could result in the organization issuing loans to individuals who are not credit worthy. The audit report should focus on the control gap of segregation of duties and the impact the issue has to the organization rather than focusing on the individual manager where the issue was discovered. Unless fraudulent intent can be proved, auditors should focus on the control issue and not on an individual person. Roles change over time, and individuals move in and out of job classifications. However, a control gap, gone unremediated, may be one that is unintentionally passed along to the new management.

- *Be conscious of the level of detail provided within the report.* This is linked to the style of audit report written but extends a bit further. The CAE must have a strong understanding of the organization's desire for the level of detail to be included in audit reports. This understanding will drive the need to utilize detailed reports provided to line area management or higher-level summaries presented to senior management and the audit committee. The key is to determine how much information is necessary within the written report to ensure that the process owners understand the control gap and the importance of mitigation.
- *Be conscious of the level of detail included in reports sent to the audit committee.* Audit committees have significant responsibility for overall controls and governance. If committees receive lengthy detailed reports with wording that is difficult

to understand, it complicates the task of measuring the overall significance of the various control issues. This may lead to the perception that internal auditors are picking on the small things. CAEs must have a strong understanding of the level of detail the audit committee requires versus senior management. This is why utilizing an organization risk tolerance guideline is of strategic benefit.

- *If the concept of utilizing a separate detail report and executive summary is employed, ensure that management understands the reason.* In addition, if a different method is utilized for presentation of the audit issues to the audit committee, ensure that any issues reported are in line with those represented in senior management's executive summary.

Challenge 44: Management Action Plans versus Management Response

As we have discussed, many internal audit groups have moved in the direction of agreed upon management action plans. Although this approach presents some strong benefits, it also comes with its own set of challenges. The approach of management response within audit reports is a less utilized concept; however, it is still practiced. Regardless of which method your department utilizes, there are a few considerations that are important to keep in mind.

Challenge 44 Potential Actions: Management Action Plans versus Management Response

- *Ensure that the approach is understood and accepted by management and the audit committee.* Ensure both management and the audit committee understand the actual procedures and both the challenges and benefits of each of the varying approaches. The audit committee should recognize that when presented with management action plans, in essence, management has fully agreed to the issue as stated and has willingly arrived at a mitigation action. When utilizing management responses, auditors should apply stronger diligence to ensure the audit reports do not become a source of contention on minor issues that management may take exception to.

- *Ensure a management action plan approach is properly established.* The concept of management action plans will incorporate working with management to arrive at acceptable responses and actions to the issues identified within the audit report. This approach is best managed during the audit fieldwork process. As issues are identified, the auditor and management should be aware of the specific issue, the potential control gap, and discuss relevant alternatives for action. If the auditor waits until the closing meeting to present management with the findings, they are likely delaying and complicating the process of issue resolution and mitigation. It can be more time efficient to work with management as issues are identified. This allows the auditor to ensure that management understands how the issue will be represented or characterized in the report and begin discussions of appropriate mitigating actions. In some instances, management may be able to initiate action prior to the audit report being issued. The auditor can then represent within the report that the issue was identified, and management has established immediate mitigating actions to close the gap.

  When action plans are utilized, ensure there is an assignment of responsibility for mitigating action identified along with the expected completion date.
- *If utilizing a management response approach, ensure that guidelines exist for obtaining the responses and resolving any conflicts that may arise.* It is important that management feel the report is accurately representing the issues. This will assist in ensuring the responses focus on addressing the control issue and not defending a specific stance on the process.
- *When utilizing management response, ensure the expectations are clear regarding the tone and requirement for the response.* If management disagrees with a finding, internal audit should evaluate whether the observation is correct before issuing a report which shows management disagreement with the issue.
- *Establish a timeline for obtaining responses from management.* In either scenario of management agreed to solutions or management response, it is important to establish a standard timeline requirement for closing the issue. It is a good practice to address the timing expectations in the opening conference.

By setting the stage with management regarding expectations, the audit team is more likely to obtain timely feedback. In addition, consider including a working session in the closing meeting that talks through either agreed upon solutions or management response requirements.

Challenge 45: Providing an Overall Internal Audit Opinion

The utilization of overall audit opinions within reports is extremely varied. Some groups provide an overall rating to the area being audited. Other groups assign individual inherent risk rankings as well as control efficiency assessments to specific risk areas. Other audit groups establish pass/fail assessments to individual audits. *Standard 2450* outlines the expectations regarding internal audit opinions. The standard interpretation also specifically addresses the basis for how an opinion should be presented. Specifically, an internal audit opinion should include the following:

- The risk or control framework or other criteria used as a basis for the overall opinion
- The overall opinion, judgment, or conclusion reached
- The reasons for an unfavorable overall opinion must be stated

We have discussed the various adjectives internal audit groups may use to rate reports or provide overall opinions. The caution in this area is to ensure the rating's definition is appropriately outlined to allow for definitive evaluation by management and the audit committee. For example, one CAE indicated their company utilized a report rating process similar to the following:

Rating 1—Insignificant issue: No internal audit follow-up required. Management follow-up will be verified the next time the business area is reviewed by internal audit.

Rating 2—Minor issue: The responsible manager provides written verification to internal audit that findings have been corrected within the agreed upon time frame.

Rating 3—Moderate issue: Internal audit verifies the findings have been corrected within the agreed upon time frame through follow-up visit and/or sample re-auditing of the impacted area.

Rating 4—Major/catastrophic issue: Requires mandatory presentation to the CFO, the CEO, and the audit committee by the responsible manager and division head to present the proposed plan or actions already taken to comply with the findings. Internal audit verifies the findings have been corrected within the agreed upon time frame through follow-up visit and/or sample re-auditing of impacted area.

When utilizing this process, the CAE found the internal audit team was consistently rating audit reports as either a two or three rating. The definitions assigned to Ratings 1 and 4 events were so unlikely and extreme and in reality were never utilized. The general theory was, if the auditors rated the area as a Rating 1, why was the area even included on the audit plan? In contrast, if the area was given a Rating 4, the issues would be so substantial that the audit committee would ask why the area had not been audited sooner.

As you will notice, the Rating 4 criteria included the word "catastrophic." In reality, internal audit should identify an issue before it reaches the catastrophic stage. The CAE found that the rating system was not providing a true representation of the audit results. He concluded that if audits were never assigned the Rating 1 or Rating 4, then the rating scale should be re-evaluated. When he approached the theory with management and the audit committee, he came upon significant resistance to the concept. Management had become comfortable and complacent in the rating process and was concerned about upsetting the apple cart by adjusting the rating scales. In the end, the CAE was able to adjust the rating process to a scale that included three rankings. But the CAE found in the succeeding months there was significant pressure from management regarding rating any audit below the two rating.

Challenge 45 Potential Actions: Providing an Overall Audit Opinion When utilizing an approach that applies an overall rating to individual audit reports, CAEs should consider the following concepts to determine the best approach for their company:

- *Ensure that you have a representative rating scale that both management and the audit committee understand.* The perception should not be that audits will never reach the highest rating scale. Management must understand that a high rating simply means that the issue is one in which mitigating actions should be promptly established.

- *The scale definition should consider that internal audit is a line of defense to assist in identifying control issues before they become significant to the organization.* As such, a high rating does not necessarily equate to "catastrophic." It simply means that immediate action should be taken to mitigate the issue identified.

Challenge 46: Management Representation at the Audit Committee Meeting

Some companies utilize a process of having management of the area being audited as a representative at the audit committee. The intent is to allow management to address the actions or issues identified in the report. This process can cause significant conflict for both process area management and the internal audit team. A request to appear in front of the audit committee to address report findings can be likened to being called to the principal's office in grade school. It immediately puts management in a posture of defense. Regardless of the intent of the process, management, the internal auditors, and even the audit committee may feel uneasy when this process is employed.

Scenario: Management Response at the Audit Committee Meeting A CAE relayed his experience with this process. The internal audit group had just completed a difficult audit. They worked diligently with management to understand the issues and posture them correctly within the audit report. Management and the internal auditors agreed on the issues within the report and the specific actions to mitigate the issues. However, when called in front of the audit committee, process area management became defensive due to the line of questions posed by the audit committee and CEO. They retracted their agreement of the audit issues and indicated to the audit committee that they had been pressured into the actions by the internal auditors. This statement resulted in significant debate and discussion during the audit committee meeting as well as criticism of the internal auditors about the process utilized. The audit committee in this instance sided with management. Later, the CAE found out the issue had been discussed with the audit committee outside of internal audit's knowledge. The CAE felt that in this instance, his group had been purposely set up for failure.

Challenge 46 Potential Actions: Management Representation at the Audit Committee Meeting Organizations that utilize a process where representative from the process area present to the audit committee may want to consider several concepts:

- *It is difficult to predict how presentations and questions will occur during a live discussion.* Just like in a court of law, it is difficult to predict what questions the prosecutor will ask and correspondingly how the witness will answer. It is advisable to have a pre-meeting with management to understand how they will communicate their position to the audit committee.
- *Obtain a copy of any materials that process area management plans to provide to the audit committee.* In the event that management prepares materials for the audit committee based on the audit report, the internal auditors should obtain a copy of the information prior to the meeting.
- *Re-examine the process of having members of management present their thoughts on a formal audit report.* The process may be one that was established at a different time when the internal audit process worked differently. The audit committee should be able to rely on the internal audit group and their reporting methods. The act of requiring management appearance at the audit committee meeting sets a stage of contention and may not be the most beneficial for the company. Revisit with the audit committee chairman the purpose for the process and the reasons it is in place.

Section 2: Functional and Administrative Reporting Lines

Introduction

Reporting lines for internal audit are an important topic and one that is often underrated by organizations. As indicated in previous chapters, the predominance of CAEs continue to report to the CFO. This is a fallback from the pre-Sarbanes–Oxley days. *Standards* suggest the administrative reporting line of the CAE be to an individual with a sufficient level of organizational authority. Some interpretations suggest that this reporting line be directly to the CEO. Functional reporting should be to the audit committee. However, there are still very few functions that have this relationship.

The merits and challenges of these concepts can be debated, but since it continues to be an active practice, let's focus on the challenges and actions with various reporting lines. In reality, it can be very difficult for CAEs to gain a true independent reporting relationship to the audit committee. However, it is a concept that has a strong potential. CAEs must be cognizant of the various reporting relationships and what obstacles or advantages they may provide. The following challenges will evaluate various reporting line challenges and advantages.

Challenge 47: Reporting to the CFO or CLO

Studies continue to show that the majority of CAEs administratively report to the CFO. In addition, there is an increasing prevalence of reporting lines to the CLO. Sarbanes–Oxley had some impact on the reporting line issue. Audit committee's began to exercise their oversight authority more closely. When evaluating the potential challenges you may face when your administrative reporting line is directed through the office of the CFO or CLO, consider the following questions:

- *Does the CFO/CLO utilize their authority to influence parts of the audit process?* In some instances, CAEs have concern when performing audits under the area of responsibility of their administrative reporting line. When the CAE's reporting line is directed to the CFO or CLO, those individuals must maintain an independent and non-invasive presence in reviews. It is important that the CFO or CLO balance the findings identified during the audit with their desire to defend their areas of responsibility.
- *Are open communications between the CAE and the audit committee allowed?* Executive management including the CFO and CLO are in positions that typically have established a close relationship with the audit committee. CAEs may indicate they are not provided the opportunity to speak with the audit committee before the scheduled meeting. In these

circumstances, the CFO or CLO are the individuals who establish the agenda with the audit committee, and internal audit must abide by those mandates. This is a situation that can result in many political issues.

- *Is independent release of the reports allowed?* Does the CFO or CLO allow independent audit reporting and issuance? Do they require the audit group to ensure all reports be reviewed in detail by the CFO or CLO before being released to the audit committee? How much "word smiting" occurs when the reports are reviewed prior to release of the report? Do the changes impact the intent of the finding?
- *What is the political protocol for speaking to members of the senior management team?* CAEs may find that although they have a direct reporting line to the audit committee, in reality, independent communication may not be an appropriate action prior to clearing the discussion with senior management. This can be perceived as a form of intimidation.
- *If the CFO/CLO disagrees on a project or issues, how is it resolved?* Does the audit committee listen to both sides of the argument equally? Often, the CFO/ CLO's relationship with the audit committee is one of long standing and deep trust. Those positions are truly viewed as part of the executive leadership team. When reports are written that may have contentious issues, periodically, the senior leaders will quietly speak to the audit committee without the knowledge of the CAE.
- *What areas of the CFO or CLO have been audited in the past?* Can you ensure that audits under the CFO or CLO are treated similar to audits of other areas? Whenever the internal audit department administratively reports to an organization area outside the office of the CEO, there will always remain inherent pressure on the auditor when reviews are performed within those areas. The CAE must walk the political line when executing these reviews to ensure they are representative and in line with the organization's audit methodology.
- *How is the internal audit budget managed?* Does the CAE have control over their departmental budget, or is it dictated by the CFO/CLO? In cases where the internal audit function is small, the budget may be managed at the higher organizational

level. This puts the CAE at a strategic disadvantage. Without direct responsibility for the department's budget, it is difficult to monitor the expenditures throughout the year and appropriately align projects to budget parameters. In addition, when management works through typical budget cutting exercises, often, internal audit's voice is not heard.

Challenge 47 Potential Actions: Reporting to the CFO or CLO In the event the CAE's administrative reporting line is to a business area other than the CEO or directly to the audit committee, consider the following concepts:

- *Revisit the Standards with you administrative management and the audit committee.* Ensure they understand the importance of the reporting relationship for internal audit. Reporting to the CFO or CLO can be workable as long as true independence and objectivity are maintained with no threat of influence.
- *Ensure there is true independence in releasing audit reports.* The CAE should be allowed to determine the timing and release date of the audit report without specific approval of the CFO or CLO. As long as they have followed their protocol for vetting issues with management and gaining agreement on the issues and action plans, the report should be released independently. Some CAEs find that when they report administratively to the CFO or CLO, there are significant difficulties in releasing reports.
- *Establish an open communication line with the audit committee outside management interaction.* Regardless of reporting line, the CAE must work to establish an open and transparent relationship with the audit committee. This may mean periodic phone calls, video conferences, e-mails, or off-site meetings. Inability to establish this relationship will create difficulties for internal audit when executing any level of administrative reporting.

In the end, the prevalence of reporting lines extending to the CFO or CLO still remains a dominant practice. The relationship can work well; however, management must embrace the role of internal audit and allow appropriate communication with the audit committee.

Challenge 48: Reporting to the CEO

Standards suggest the reporting line of the internal audit function to be at a sufficient level of authority within the organization. This is often interpreted as the need to report to the CEO. Many organizations are not ready to take this step for several reasons. As an audit manager and CAE I have had the opportunity to report through various areas within a company, one which included reporting to the CEO. That experience gave me the ability to have a true seat at the table and listen and learn on strategy meetings. It provided significant benefit to the internal audit group. However, this is not always possible especially in very large organizations. The challenge with reporting to the CEO is having the ability to truly gain sufficient time to utilize his knowledge to benefit the internal audit organization. In many cases, the CEO is focused on business strategy and, as such, may not have a great deal of time to spend with the CAE. If the current reporting line for internal audit is to the CEO, consider the following questions to ensure it is efficient:

- Is the CAE included in strategy setting meetings with other members of the leadership team?
- Is the CAE able to periodically meet with the CEO privately to gain an understanding of the perception of the internal audit function?
- Does the CEO fully understand and embrace the *Standards*?
- Does the CEO allow independent issuance of audit reports to the audit committee?
- Does the CEO allow for regular private sessions with the audit committee?
- Is there any semblance of counseling by the CEO prior to entering audit committee meetings to caution the CAE on what to and not to communicate?

While there may be other elements of consideration when reporting to the CEO, it is important to understand the elements of the organizational culture, the availability of the CEO to allocate time to the internal audit function, as well as the overall responsibilities incumbent on the CEO.

Challenge 48 Potential Actions: Reporting to the CEO In reality, the CEO's role in the organization includes many requirements. The CEO must understand and embrace the value internal audit can bring to their senior management team. If the CAE reports to the CEO, they should be viewed as a true leadership team member and be included within the senior leadership team meetings. For organizations that currently have a reporting line to the CEO, or for organizations considering this step, following are some potential actions to ensure the reporting line works as effectively as possible:

- *The CAE should have a true seat at the table within the senior leadership team meetings.* The ability to have a presence at senior leadership team meetings will provide the CAE strategic insight into the organization's goals, strategies, and risks.
- *Establish a regular protocol for meeting with the CEO in order to build appropriate relationships and ensure he/she understands the direction and objectives of internal audit.* Reporting to the CEO should include more than a simple administrative line. The CAE should work to establish an open and trusting relationship with the CEO. Work to schedule regular meetings with the CEO to address the internal audit function's goals, objectives, and challenges. Enlist the CEO's recommendations regarding audit projects, reporting, and process owner relationships.
- *Provide the CEO information regarding the Standards to ensure he/she understands the obligations of the profession.* Providing the CEO information regarding the *Standards* and their purpose may assist in gaining the CEO's support on various initiatives.
- *The CAE should work with the CEO to ensure there is a clear and transparent relationship with the audit committee.* If the CAE administratively reports to the CEO, they may still experience political challenges when attempting to independently speak to the audit committee. The CEO must understand the importance of this concept and the overall value to the organization. Enlist the CEO's support to allow the CAE to establish regular, independent communications with the audit committee. Ultimately, the CEO will have the most direct relationship with the board and committees. Obtaining his/

her agreement and buy-in regarding the importance of the CAE's relationship with the audit committee will provide significant advantages in facilitating a strong relationship.

Challenge 49: Reporting to the Audit Committee

Standards suggest the CAE have a functional reporting line to the audit committee. In today's business world, this practice is common at least in theory. Many organizations indicate the CAE has a direct reporting line to the audit committee, but the true test of that relationship is the manner in which the CAE is able to access and speak to the committee. In some cases, CAEs have an administrative reporting line as well as a functional reporting line to the audit committee. There can be benefits and challenges to each of these relationships.

Consider the following concepts when examining whether both a functional and administrative reporting line to the audit committee is appropriate for your company:

- *When the CAE reports administratively to a member of senior management, they will typically be included in staff and strategic meetings of the area.* Without some internal administrative reporting line, the CAE may miss the opportunity to have insight into strategic information that is communicated through internal meetings.
- *When the CAE's reporting line is directly to the audit committee, this may create a difficult internal atmosphere when dealing with management.* Management may feel they have little to no input into the internal audit process.
- *Although the audit committee is responsible for governance oversight, their understanding of organizational processes and issues comes through communication from management.* They are not part of the day-to-day business and may not always have certain strategic insight into risk areas that would be beneficial for the internal auditor to be aware of.

Whether both a functional and administrative reporting line to the audit committee is effective for your organization can depend on many factors including the expertise of the audit committee, their understanding of the company background and industry, their relationship with management, and their accessibility to the internal auditors. Acknowledging these challenges, there are some considerations that may assist in facilitating an effective reporting line structure to the audit committee.

Challenge 49 Potential Actions: Reporting to the Audit Committee When reporting both administratively and functionally to the audit committee, the internal audit team must ensure they work to instill proper relationships with management to gain the appropriate insight into strategic initiatives and management issues. The CAE should speak to the audit committee about having some type of seat at the table within the CEO leadership team or the CFO leadership team. The ability to be involved in regular staff meetings will provide the internal audit team valuable insight into the risk areas of the company.

- *Ensure the ability to regularly meet or speak with the audit committee chairman.* When reporting lines are directly to the audit committee, it is not sufficient to wait until the quarterly board meetings to speak with the audit committee chairman. In addition, be cautious of e-mail communication. This method is not considered confidential.
- *Work with management to ensure they trust your relationship with the audit committee.* If management feels threatened by the reporting line, the ability to effectively execute upon audits may be compromised.
- *Work with the audit committee to facilitate an effective relationship with management.* The audit committee must understand that communications from the CAE must be kept confidential. If the CAE has concerns regarding information being relayed to management that may be misinterpreted, the reporting relationship will be difficult to manage.

The CAE must critically evaluate the pros and cons of this type of reporting relationship and ensure it is the most effective for the organization.

Section 3: Legal, Regulatory, and Discovery Concepts

Introduction

The internal audit process can be used to verify compliance with applicable laws, regulations, and internal policies. It is important for companies to remember that results of internal audits can be discoverable by regulatory authorities and in court proceedings. Protecting the results of internal audits from disclosure is a difficult concept and important for legal counsel to determine the extent of applicable privileges and protections.

In general, opposing litigants cannot discover information that is deemed privileged within a court proceeding. Failure to protect privileged information from disclosure can result in the waiver of applicable privilege.

Protection against discovery of internal audit reports may be available under a common law self evaluative privilege or critical analysis privilege. Protection may also be available under attorney–client privilege, but the attorney work product doctrine generally does not protect such reports. We will cover a high level overview of the application of these privilege doctrines to internal audit reports. Concepts related to obtaining privileged information include self evaluative privilege, attorney–client privilege, and attorney–client work doctrine. Specific requirements are attached to each of these concepts, and the internal auditor should discuss the aspects with their individual legal counsel prior to attempting to attach any type of privilege to audit reports.

Challenge 50: Understand Legal Privelege

Courts recognize each category of privilege in varying ways. In addition, certain aspects are attached to privilege that must be in existence. Some specific criteria for each element of privilege are as follows.

Self Evaluative Privilege

- Information must come from an analysis that is completed by the party seeking protection.
- The public must have a strong interest in preserving the free flow of the type of information.

- The information must be of the type that would be curtailed if the discovery was allowed.

Some courts have required the following two additional elements:

- The preparer and user of the material both had an expectation of confidentiality.
- Steps were taken to protect the confidentiality of the information.

Attorney–Client Privilege This prohibits the disclosure of communications between an attorney and his client related to legal advice within the scope of the attorney–client relationship. The privilege only protects against the disclosure of communications of confidential information. It does not protect against the disclosure of the underlying facts of the communication. It only applies to internal audits in situations where an attorney carries out the review and only for purposes that predominately concern legal issues. Conditions that apply include the following:

- The person asserting the privilege must demonstrate there was a communication made between privileged persons in confidence for the purpose of obtaining legal assistance.
- In order to receive protection under the attorney–client privilege, internal audit reports prepared by attorneys should clearly state the report constitutes legal analysis and advice rather than general business consulting.

Attorney–Client Work Doctrine This doctrine protects from disclosure of confidential work product prepared in anticipation of litigation. The doctrine does not generally apply to internal audit reports conducted in the ordinary course of business rather than in anticipation of litigation. Even if the purpose of the internal audit is to identify circumstances that may eventually lead to litigation, many courts do not consider such a review to be in "anticipation of litigation." As such, privilege is not extended to the internal audit report.

Challenge 50 Potential Actions: Understand Legal Privilege The topic of privilege is best left to the legal professionals. If any audit review is one that management or the audit committee request that privilege be attached, the internal audit team should consult with the legal team to determine whether the request can be fulfilled.

Section 4: When Management and Audit Committee Support Is Lacking

Professionals who are considering a role in internal audit may examine the *Standards* and feel comfortable they will receive sufficient and adequate support from both management and the audit committee. As we have examined throughout this book, many challenges exist when performing the role of internal audit. Those challenges may be due to a lack of understanding by management of the true role of internal auditors and the existence of the *Standards*. Other challenges may come from how management and the audit committee view the internal audit function versus the manner in which the CAE views the function. Throughout this book, we have examined many challenges faced by internal audit along with potential actions. Those challenges have included everything from reporting relationships to report writing. Let's briefly discuss conceptual and relationship challenges that can be created.

Challenge 51: Management and the Audit Committee's View of Internal Audit is Different from the Standards

When this challenge exists, CAEs may question the direction to take the internal audit group. As reviewed, management often has their expectations for the function, and often, those expectations can have a narrow focus that relegates the function to purely compliance or even Sarbanes–Oxley work. Although the *Standards* outline the varying roles that internal audit can provide, management and the audit committee are the ultimate authority when it comes to defining the role of the internal audit function. When a CAE's view of internal audit is significantly varied from that of management and/or the audit committee, what are the potential actions that the CAE can take?

Challenge 51 Potential Actions: Management and the Audit Committee's View of Internal Audit is Different from the Standards Whether entering a CAE role with a new company or assuming the role within an existing company or even attempting to evolve the role currently held, CAEs should ensure that they are fulfilling their fiduciary duty related to internal audit. Ultimately, the CAE may be required to accept the decision on the role of internal audit as that which management and the audit committee define. However, prior to blindly accepting that decision, the CAE can provide some critical information to those involved to ensure they understand the implications.

- *Educate those involved as to why the Standards were developed and the benefits of having a function that is in compliance with the Standards.* Ensure that both management and the audit committee understand the true role of internal auditors as defined by the *Standards.* Include within that information the risks or challenges that the company may face if the internal audit function is narrowly defined.
- *Provide case examples to management.* Demonstrate examples where the lack of a robust and diligent internal audit function has existed and may have contributed to inability of organizations to adequately manage internal controls and risk management issues.
- *Revisit concepts of COSO* 2013, *the PCAOB reports, and Sarbanes–Oxley legislation.* These are all critical guidelines to support the need for a robust internal audit function.
- *Enlist the assistance of the external auditors.* When speaking to management and the audit committee about the needs and requirements of internal audit, the support of the external auditors can be extremely valuable.
- *Consider whether the variance in opinions has some relationship to personalities.* Even if there are distinct personalities, individuals involved in each of these roles should be professional enough to understand factual and non-emotional information.
- *Consider speaking to management about having a quality assurance review of the internal audit function performed by an outside provider.* Sometimes, observations provided by outside parties may gain a stronger level of attention from management.

In the end, if management and the audit committee have a strategically different perspective of internal audit from that of the CAE, and all actions taken do not assist in altering that perception, the CAE must make personal determinations as to whether the role is one that they can personally fulfill and provide value in.

7

FINAL WORD

Introduction

Throughout this book, we have reviewed various lessons learned for internal audit along with over 50 challenges that auditors may find themselves in when executing their role. We began the book with lessons learned of a CAE. Let's take a similar approach and conclude with considering ten "potential" commandments for internal auditors.

Ten "Potential" Commandments for Auditors

1. *Thou Shall Serve the Audit Committee* This is the primary responsibility of internal audit. Serve the audit committee with honesty, integrity, openness, and trust. They are the governing body tasked with oversight of the function. The auditor's responsibility is to ensure the committee has the relevant information needed to perform their overall responsibilities.

2. *Thou Shall Abide by the Institute of Internal Auditor Standards* The only way internal audit will advance as a profession is to ensure all internal auditors and CAEs abide by the professional *Standards*. When CAEs deviate from the *Standards* without addressing the concern with management, they in essence are allowing the profession to take a step back.

3. *Thou Shall Maintain Ethical Standards and Honest and Transparent Communications* A foundation of internal audit is the ability to maintain ethical conduct and honest and transparent communications even in the most difficult situations.

4. *Thou Shall Not Allow Undue Pressure and Influence from Management* Internal auditors will always face challenges when working through audit findings and issues. Sometimes, the line of demarcation is not always clearly black or white. However, when there is ongoing and or clear influence from management that alters the intent or message of audit communications, the CAE has the responsibility to bring this issue to the attention of the audit committee.

5. *Thou Shall Not Lie or Cheat or Steal or Defame* I packed a lot into this one because it seems the very foundations of corporate business could use a strong overhaul. What would a workplace be like if people were always honest and truthful, and there was no such thing as corporate fraud? Internal auditors are considered one of the pillars of a strong corporate governance structure. Their ability to proactively inform management of risks that may exist within the organization is one of the very attributes that make the function a critical endeavor. Auditors must abide by their professional code of conduct and ensure their communications with the management and the audit committee are upfront, transparent, and timely.

6. *Honor Not Just Thy Superiors but Also Thy Peers and Subordinates* We recognize as internal auditors there is a pecking order in the business world. However, it is critical for auditors to establish strong and effective relationships. This requires professionals to show respect not just for superiors but also for process owners. Remember the example of assisting team members in building their own confidence levels. This is an aspect of honor thy subordinates and helping them on the learning curve of the organization.

7. *Thou Shall Listen to the Explanations and Recommendations of Others* Business owners understand their processes better than the auditor might. Just because a gap is identified does not mean that there is only one reason the gap occurred. Listen to the explanations and recommendations of management. Then, consider all relevant facts before coming to a final conclusion.

8. *Thou Shall Mentor and Train Other Auditors in the IIA Standards* CAEs should not assume just because their staff has a college degree or

passed the CIA certification, they fully comprehend and understand the various aspects of the *Standards*. Periodic review of the *Standards* and requirements with all staff is an integral part of maintaining a quality function.

9. *Thou Shall Know When You Have Personally Stepped Over the Black Line* Sometimes, it is very difficult to "do the right thing." Recently, I had a CAE tell me that all of the best CAEs they have known have been fired from at least one position in their career. This is because the CAE believed in his/her responsibilities and executed them to the full extent of the *Standards*. Unfortunately, management did not see eye to eye with the CAE, and ways were parted. However, fear of retribution or concern over a potential job loss will not advance the profession. CAEs must uphold the *Standards* by which they are guided by.

10. *If You Cannot Uphold the Standards, Thou Shall Step Down* This goes hand in hand with commandment eight. Ultimately, if the CAE does not feel they are in a position which will allow them to properly execute their responsibilities in line with the *Standards*, they must adequately inform the audit committee of their concern. If the issue isn't resolved, the CAE will have to make a personal decision regarding his/her ability to stay in the position knowing it is not one which embraces the *Standards* of auditors.

There could certainly be a host of other commandments to consider when executing the role of internal audit management. In the end, the inability to uphold the *Standards* in form, execution, and intent results in an ineffective audit function.

Index

S